Disorder and Progress

DISORDER AND PROGRESS

*Bandits, Police, and
Mexican Development*

Paul J. Vanderwood

UNIVERSITY OF NEBRASKA PRESS
Lincoln and London

Copyright © 1981 by the University of Nebraska Press
All rights reserved
Manufactured in the United States of America

Library of Congress Cataloging in Publication Data

Vanderwood, Paul J.
  Disorder and progress.

  Bibliography: p.
  Includes index.
  1. Police, Rural—Mexico—History—19th century. 2. Brigands and robbers—
Mexico—History—19th century. 3. Outlaws—Mexico—History—19th century.
4. Mexico—Rural conditions. I. Title.
HV8161.A2V36   363.2′0972   80-22345
ISBN 0-8032-4651-X
ISBN 0-8032-9600-2 (pbk.)

To Mom and Dad and other good friends

Contents

Maps and Illustrations

Preface

This book is about order and disorder in society, their constant presence, overlap, and blend. When times seem peaceful, a substantial amount of active unrest perdures—more than is thought. The opposite is also true; order is rarely as pervasive as it seems. Order and disorder are created by humans to serve their needs and ambitions. Order serves one group and disorder another. As peace does not often equal progress for everyone, some employ disorder to advance. Order can encroach on liberty, so it is resisted. People also use order or disorder, or both, to protect their interests. Some who induce disorder may eventually join the order they sought to disrupt, which is where they wanted to be all along. Others, such as successful revolutionaries, may establish a new system of their own, but it will always have its challengers. In this persistently unsettled environment, individuals can shift from compliance to dissent and return to order with unsuspected ease. Why they do it, and when, is linked to the galaxy of individual motivations and historical circumstances that make generalizations elusive, if not useless. Yet it is fascinating to watch the maneuvers take place, especially among such highly visible members of society as bandits, proponents of disorder, and policemen, agents of the state. Thus this book also concerns brigands and lawmen as double agents of order and disorder.

The setting is Mexico—the provincial cities, traditional villages, haciendas, and country towns, mainly in the nineteenth century when capitalism took root. And although there is deliberate emphasis on bandits and police as highly motivated opportunists, they are viewed within the political and economic circumstances that shaped their possibilities and direction. The

bandits, such as the "Plateados" ("Silvered men"), Heraclio
Bernal, and Santanón, are *puros mexicanos* (truly Mexicans), and
the policemen are Mexico's Rurales, famed among the world's best
constabularies. Both groups are colorful, deadly, and interchangeable. Both groups created and contributed to order and disorder, and they exchanged their roles with ease, often by official
invitation. Because they frequently worked both sides of the
equation without separating its components, they earn the term
bandits-Rurales.

Threads of the narrative run from the relative calm of rural
colonial Mexico to the brutally destructive centralist-federalist
competition of early Independence. Then they join the campaign
for domestic order launched by the classical Liberal modernizers
and crisscross the turmoil of the supposed Porfirian peace. Finally, the warp and woof of the historical cloth ripped apart in
the Revolution of 1910. Periodization, however, is little more than
a handy organizational device. The continuing presence of order
and disorder naturally blurs distinctions of time, and changes in its
form and substance do not deny its existence within any time
frame. The advent of so-called modernization, for instance, undoubtedly altered the appearance of order and disorder, but Adam
Smith's "invisible hand" of development did not create stability
and disruption. It merely changed their nature.

Although this study concentrates on Mexico, wider implications may be drawn. The practice of turning criminals into
policemen is by no means unique to Mexico or to the nineteenth
century. Nor is the citizen's paradoxical perception of the police, or
the tendency to brand dissenters as outlaws, or the failure to read
the social message in banditry. Order and disorder exist
everywhere, all of the time. Perhaps most people are not much
concerned with compliance and dissent, but they are involved in it
just the same. Several direct comparisons are made here with
events, conditions, and institutions in other countries. With further
research, other analogies are possible. Mexico's Rurales must bring
to mind the Royal Canadian Mounted Police, the Texas Rangers,
Spain's Guardia Civil, the French gendarmerie, and Italy's carabinieri.

I have drawn on Eric Hobsbawm's stirring assertions about banditry along with David Bayley's provocative analysis of the political foundations of modern police forces. They are both hardy pioneers toiling in difficult and unworked terrain, and their tentative markers substantially assisted my own trailblazing. The specialist will recognize some controversial ideas, such as my perception of the loose nature and limitations of Porfirian rule, and the important contribution of brigands to political federalism. I also believe that the capacity of modern development to lure converts from traditional cultural modes has generally been underestimated. Plenty of imaginative but stultified country people welcomed and embraced railroads and a money economy, which is not to say they at once became modern. Capitalistic development arrives in uneven waves. And in rebellion I see much more individual opportunism than ideological fervor at play.

I have attempted not to moralize about order-disorder and bandits-Rurales. Instead, I want to say, Here they are, and to tell why. Order and disorder are an integral part of the historical process, and bandits and Rurales are people caught up in it. They are human beings trying to direct conditions to their advantage, but at the same time they are overwhelmed and swept along by them. I recognize that I interchange the usual definitions of order—that I use order to mean both public peace and an arrangement of society. But I do so deliberately, as I do with bandits and Rurales, to underline the vital relationship between the elements.

My study of Mexico's Rural Police Force began in a University of Texas graduate seminar in history with that demanding but thoroughly supportive professor, Nettie Lee Benson, who is deservedly much honored for her knowledge of Mexican historiography. Dissertation research followed in Mexico's National Archive, where the administrative records of the corps lay disorganized, pigeon-fouled, but bundled, tied, and preserved much as they had been left after 1914, when the organization dissolved in the midst of civil war. How those bureaucrats loved to push paper! Trimonthly reports from the field, targets used in rifle practice, complaints against corpsmen, and their responses; budgets, rosters, official orders, operating procedures; bills for rents and forage; certificates of vigilance; intra-office memos—a mountain of rich historical documentation is contained in some two thousand un-labeled bundles. When the bits were pieced together, some surprises emerged: the revered Benito Juárez, not the dictator Díaz, had founded the Rurales. Juárez had much more deliberately recruited bandits than had Díaz. The corpsmen were frequently in conflict with local authorities and elites, rather than being their handmaidens. Rurales could be authoritative, even brutal, but they were not often oppressive in policing common Mexicans. Desertions, insubordination, and drunkenness permeated the organization and became even more prevalent in the final decade of the Porfiriato. Contrary to legend, the Rurales in pursuit of criminals seldom got their man. Yet they were a heralded symbol of Mexican nationalism and acclaimed abroad, even if they received credit for many things they were not, along with blame for much they did not do. Without a doubt their image, enhanced by those handsome *charro* outfits, far outshone their performance. Typical police, these Rurales, in that regard.

Thousands of personnel reports on individual policemen naturally lent themselves to computer analysis—thirty-four pieces of information on each man in a sample of two thousand—and a fascinating institutional picture developed, in part statistical, that rather thoroughly contradicted what had previously been believed about the corps. For instance, most guards were artisans and campesinos from central Mexico with few qualifications for police work. Perhaps it did not matter, because so many ended up in routine, stationary assignments. Finally, the disintegration of the dictatorship in those last ten years is clearly mirrored in the overwhelming administrative and behavioral problems that beset the corps.

Research reveals that the Rurales were throughly representative of the social conditions in the Mexico in which they worked. Although they seemed to be everywhere, there were relatively few of them, only some two thousand at any one time, and most were concentrated around the capital. The word "rurales," then as now, meant almost any policemen: federal, state, municipal, private, and even those in specially authorized units, such as that commanded by the "Mad Russian," Emilio

Kosterlitsky, along the United States-Sonoran border. This study, however, focuses on the federal rural policemen, although the task of separating them from myriad others may not always have been successful.

How and in what ways police influence or are influenced by their environment remains an important but difficult issue. But in composition, assignments, procedures, and performance, Mexico's Rural Police Force certainly changed over the years. The shift of governmental policy from emphasis on rural pacification as a prelude to modernization to emphasis on control of those unionized and increasingly angry proletarians fundamentally affected the corps. So did the growth of central political power financed by foreign investments. Juárez's Rurales were one thing, those of Díaz quite different, and the Revolution spawned its own breed. Today's vision of the corps has been crafted by the necessity of the nation's power brokers to help legitimize their position in the name of the Revolution.

Bandits, in my research, proved much more difficult to locate and to reduce to statistics and prose. They left few written records, although many of the leaders were literate. The search for the brigands has therefore been concentrated in newspapers, the archives of organizations dedicated to catching them, personal remembrances of those affected (one way or another), folklore, and some studies of banditry. By bandits I mean mainly self-interested individuals and their followers who found themselves excluded from the possibilities and opportunities, not to mention the benefits, of society at large, and who promoted disorder as a lever to enter a system reserved for a few. The bandits tended not to be revolutionaries or even serious reformers, although they sometimes paraded as such. Some contend that outlaws (which means persons outside of the laws set by those in power) like Manuel Lozada and Miguel Negrete were more revolutionaries than bandits, that they wanted to change the system, and that they are close cases worthy of more research and discussion. But most of the brigands encountered in this study simply wanted proceeds from the system already established.

The bandit leaders were not normally reacting to extreme deprivation, but less is known of their followers. The majority did not seek justice for others but opportunity for themselves. They were not petty cattle thieves or small-time smugglers, although the availability of substantial profits in such work at times erased the distinctions. Mexican brigands were often types of social climbers. They made deals with power brokers to get going, and in some periods and places the brigands themselves became strong enough to set the business terms with their contacts. They were pragmatic, cunning, determined, and difficult to separate from their myth. They still are.

But bandits are people of flesh and blood, with their human highs and lows. Only a few, like Joaquín Murieta in California, were largely invented by an imaginative writer in search of revenue. Even Murieta existed, if only as a minor cattle rustler around Los Angeles. The outlaws knew love, some of it tender and much of it frustrated. They also possessed a substantial fear of death. Robbing trains, hiding out in mountains, and evading pursuit fueled by reward do not make the good life. Bandits caught and hurled back the hot lead of lawmen only in legend. Many more died in squalor and a bloodbath than in comfort and in a bed.

Brigands, however, are not only people but also symbols, and the fact that they are more remembered in fantasy than in reality only sustains and enhances their power to stir feelings. It is no coincidence that the movie *Bonnie and Clyde* achieved immense popularity at a time in the 1960s when college students were bombing the Bank of America, or that the film *Viva Zapata!*, which had been buried in Cold War McCarthyism, was resurrected by the hopes and disorder of the '60s.

Precisely what these persistent and reconstituted brigands symbolize is open to interpretation. Hobsbawm found the nineteenth-century variety representative of a constant peasant yearning for freedom and justice. They were, in the main, for him, prepolitical rebels who drew their inspiration and sustenance from the peasantry. In more modern terms, he might see them as poor people reacting to urban frustration and injustice. But the attraction that the bourgeoisie feels for bandits, then and now, should not be overlooked or underestimated. Middle-class Mexicans acclaim the same brigands as do campesinos. Well-off Americans in the 1960s made heroes of the celluloid Butch Cassidy and the Sundance Kid along with Bonnie and Clyde. If, as Hobsbawm believes, bandits symbolize equality for peasants, they also personify energetic enterprise and capitalistic venture for more prosperous and socially mobile people. These groups obviously define social justice differently, but they prove the ways bandits can be molded to serve distinctly different interests. In the real lives of brigands, similar variations can be noted.

Bandits in myth and reality certainly excite the imagination. They may induce a romanticized yearning for escape from drudgery, but they seldom move large groups of people to militant action, at least not with revolutionary intentions. In fact, they do just the opposite. They absorb in dreams energies that might have been directed toward effecting social change. Like so much popular culture, they are both distractive and narcotic. They are in this sense government agents. Emiliano Zapata is now the hero of Mexico's thoroughly institutionalized revolution. The government deliberately polishes his image and fawns over his agrarian aspirations while it pursues its own quite different agricultural program. Pancho Villa has only recently been enlisted for social control, although the shape of his myth is still uncertain. No one seems quite sure if he would work better as a carefree Robin Hood or a dedicated reformer. But the official image will be worked out on television.

With bandits, as with the Rurales, it was and is the image that really matters. Their daring exploits leave them both feared and admired. Travelers in nineteenth-century Mexico bragged and gossiped about their encounters with brigands, but they had one thing in common: they seemed disappointed if they traveled from Veracruz to Mexico City without encountering bandits at least once. Bandit stories still abound in today's Mexico. And many itinerants would still welcome a chance meeting with a nonviolent highwayman, especially if their belongings were insured. But agitated emotions lead to polemics and to problems with historical evidence. In analyzing accounts about outlaws I have retained an appreciation of the exaggerations and inventions while attempting to arrive at the truth. The references documented in this work tend to synthesize the reports of hundreds who encountered bandits on the road, in the villages, or perhaps in their fantasies. Even toned down, these bandit stories can still raise one's hair.

Mexican brigandage went through transitions just as did the country's rural police. An aura of legality that stemmed from the king and his institutions, plus a lack of potential booty, limited brigandage in the colonial era, but the Independence wars unleashed aggressive brigands who claimed some stake in the new society. They worked with regional strongmen to fend off centralist encroachment, and as civil war and the French Intervention at mid-century engulfed the country, the major combatants sought the services of the bandits as guerrillas. Military service for political causes gave the bandit gangs enormous political clout; it was the high tide of Mexican banditry. When peace came, the huge bands demanded patronage, or else. The victors—and no matter who might have won, it could not have been different—made their bargains with the outlaws. Juárez had to do so. Banditry persisted during the Díaz dictatorship, and assumed a new style that is frequently labeled social banditry, a term that still defies adequate definition. These so-called brigands were loners and small bands, subsequently lionized in the public consciousness as free-spirited rebels against a repressive government, local, state, or national. What these outlaws really wanted for themselves or their society is a facet of their complex reality that needs further examination. There is, however, no doubting their strength as a symbol. Nicole Giron has recently discovered the Sinaloan brigand, Heraclio Bernal, heroized in some thirty different *corridos*, those nationally loved Mexican folk ballads, composed both during and long after his lifetime. Finally, the Mexican Revolution produced a new generation of bandit-patriots, and this book ends with their struggle for a stake in their nation's future—whatever that future might be.

The historical study of rural Mexico, in comparison, say, with rural France or Germany, is still in its infancy. Much of what has been written views the countryside from the perspective of the capital, the rulers, and the rich. A heightened social consciousness has more recently driven scholars to see the towns and villages from below, and the immense diversity of findings and opinions that has emerged has reconstructed perceptions and revised generalizations about the campesino, the hacienda, regional government, and cultural clash. Where it was once thought that order prevailed, much disorder has been uncovered. The peace of the Porfiriato has been found laden with strife. Easy generalizations about domestic security and internal peace no longer fit. This book offers further revisionist evidence and ideas.

The focus of this study, then, is from the bottom up. The emphasis is on ordinary Mexicans, because the bandits and Rurales came from their ranks and because common people to a large extent determine the blend between order and disorder. Brigands and Rurales are mentioned in almost every treatment of Mexican history, and they still thrive in the minds of the people, reinforced and reinterpreted by television and movies. Yet they remain only an appendage to national affairs, when they belong in the mainstream—as do the bandits and police of most other countries. To my taste, order and disorder have also been locked too firmly into political regimes and time periods, with insufficient attention accorded the continuing presence of each and the changing mix of the two. I intend to free the historical bandits and police, to reassert order and disorder as a blend and balance—in sum, to emphasize important dimensions of reality that have been largely ignored.

Since Professor Benson first interested me in Mexico's Rurales, I have discussed and debated the themes of this book with many colleagues and acquaintances on both sides of the border. Their knowledge, insights, and enthusiasm greatly stimulated my own thoughts and encouraged me to put them on paper. Grants from the American Philosophical Society and the San Diego State Foundation funded further research. Professor Rosalie Schwartz helped me to rethink and reorganize the initial draft. Professors David H. Bayley, John M. Hart, Thomas F. McGann, Michael C. Meyer, and William B. Taylor clarified my direction in revisions. To you all, and to so many others who assisted me along the way, my sincere gratitude. And special thanks to close friends who boosted me over some of the highest hurdles.

PART I

THE BALANCE OF ORDER AND DISORDER

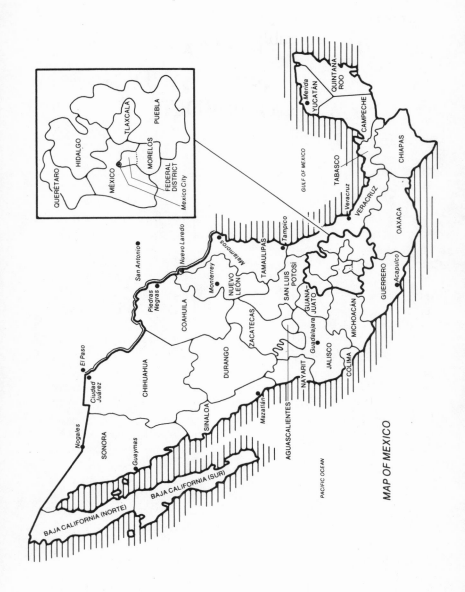

MAP OF MEXICO

Chapter 1
Ambitious Bandits: Disorder Equals Progress

The rather prissy and decidedly pompous French Minister to Mexico surveyed national conditions at mid-nineteenth century and concluded that banditry had become institutionalized. In fact, asserted Dubois de Saliguey, "It is the only institution that can be taken seriously and functions with perfect regularity."[1] The minister was not exaggerating. Brigands had indeed earned social status as one of the best-organized special interest groups in the country. The robbers not only had to be dealt with—they set the terms of the deal. Mexican banditry was in its heyday, so when a *New York Times* correspondent boarded the stagecoach for the capital he prepared himself to be robbed.[2]

The journalist had hung around the Mexican Gulf port of Veracruz for a few extra days, hoping to find traveling companions willing to give the brigands a fight for their money. But experienced travelers knew better. Battling brigands was more romantic than wise. Besides, riding in those jostling coaches with loaded pistols at the ready-wait could be even more dangerous to passengers than the bandits were. So the reporter stuffed a few everyday items into his small carpetbag, rolled up a change of clothes, deposited his gun and luggage in safekeeping at his hotel, and made sure that he had several silver dollars handy to be paid the robbers on demand. On Sunday morning, June 12, 1860, he joined seven other unarmed passengers for the five-day endurance adventure. The driver pelted the eight husky mules up front with rocks and cussed them into action, and the hulking Troy coach got rolling along the 290 wrenching miles toward Mexico City.[3]

A full coach suited the newsman. It meant that the travelers were wedged in and could brace themselves against the challenge of roads gutted by rain squalls and strewn with goodsized loose rocks—roads ripped up by revolutionaries, who used the stones for their fortifications along the routes. Carry-on bundles were appropriately placed to pad ribs, knees, and heads against the bone-rattling bumps and lurches. The passengers resembled jars in a packing case ready for shipping. They still anticipated their share of bruises and cuts from the plunging, pitching stage, and hoped for nothing worse. These lumbering giants were prone to break down or roll over, because Mexico's unpredictable weather—the sudden wetness, then searing heat—constantly assaulted the wooden wheels, even those protected by an iron rim. Bandits, no doubt, were the main attraction, but the trip itself was high drama. One foreigner noted that you started travel in Mexico by writing your will.[4]

As they groaned along at six to eight miles an hour through the countryside, the effects of the nation's incessant domestic turmoil, at this point a raging civil war, became evident to them in burned and battered buildings, unattended farms, and abandoned villages. In its search for direction, Mexico was pulling itself apart. Conservative, Liberal; bandit, patriot; royalist, republican; nationalist, imperialist—people cut labels to fit their disposition and opportunities. Bandits carried political proclamations under their shirts so that, if captured, they would not be shot as common criminals. Printed political decrees became a kind of lifesaver. If one was arrested by those who had issued the manifesto, no problem. If taken by an adversary, one simply changed sides. Civil war creates a seller's market for soldiers, and brigands were in demand as guerrillas. In this atmosphere the stagecoach from Veracruz pulled up the steep grade that led onto the central plateau of Mexico at the formidable old castle of Perote.[5]

The castle, actually a fortress, had been built by the Spaniards soon after the Conquest to provide a nightly stopover point along the crucial Mexico City-Veracruz roadway. It had later housed a garrison of soldiers needed to clear the route of bandits. During the civil war it changed hands several times, but now it was inhabited by a Conservative general, José María Cobos, whom the journalist dubbed a robber in the services of Holy Mother Church. Cobos was feared for his cruelties as a former bandit chief, and in these uncertain times anything went, so it was a nervous, if not terrified, group of passengers that debarked at the general's insistence. But Cobos could not decide what to do with the travelers, nor could his lieutenants. After several hours of disjointed debate among their captors, the passengers were freed to pursue their journey toward Puebla through well-known bandit country. The writer dressed in his second-best outfit and declared himself "in a condition to go through the operation of being robbed." He did not have long to wait.[6] Soon the coach driver whistled a warning to his fares. Seven horsemen, masked and well armed with muskets and pistols, approached the stage. The travelers planned no resistance; they debarked as ordered and were promptly robbed of their valuables. The newsman lost his silver dollars, as anticipated. But not all—the brigands let him keep one for his breakfast.[7] Such courtesy was common among bandits. Many were outright gentlemen and apologized for the need (as they put it) to rob. If a priest appeared among the victims, the thieves might beg his absolution and kiss his ring before riding off with his funds and religious jewelry. Bandits stole the silver dishes being shipped by one woman, but returned a plate so that she would have a pattern with which to order a replacement set. Another traveler admitted her prejudice against being looted, but advised that, if it had to happen, "let it be by a Mexican robber, by all means." Bandits, of course, can afford to be suave when they are in control of highway travel, but with success less certain they are much less patronizing toward their prey.[8]

The robbery ritual continued. Face down in the dirt of the road went the passengers, warned not to peek while the brigands ransacked the coach, pulled apart the linen side-panels, and dug under cushions for hidden valuables. Their mission accomplished, the bandits departed for the security of nearby mountains, while the journeyers dusted off and prepared to travel on toward Puebla. The brigands had at least spared them their clothing; others had not been as fortunate. The reporter must have glowed as he scribbled his account: "This is being robbed in Mexico after the usual and most approved fashion." Routine, this one, but the chances were that other bandits waited further down the road. "This is travelling in Mexico," he concluded, "and thus it has been, to a greater or less extent, since the country had a history."[9]

Mexico had indeed experienced an epidemic of banditry since its wars for independence had sputtered to success in the second decade of the century. But it was not until the outbreak of civil war in 1857 that the brigands began to command regional control. When in the 1860s the war culminated in a foreign intervention, the brigands in an important way helped to decide the winner. The victors then had to meet their post-war demands or suffer the consequences. As a result, the order and disorder of previous years developed a new mix, with bandits as the arbiters.

Reformers loosely grouped as Liberals took control of national affairs in 1854, with plans to reorder society. They curtailed the traditional privileges of the army, the Catholic Church, and the Indian communities in their determination to build a nation and a political constituency. At the same time they overlaid the new structure with strands of republicanism and capitalism that were meant to modernize Mexico along the lines of the United States and Western Europe. Disruption of the former order naturally created new disorder. But even as the Liberals triumphed in civil war, foreign interlopers, sponsored by French imperialists and encouraged by Mexican dissidents, disrupted the country's leadership, and civil strife became entangled with national sovereignty. Nothing cultivates banditry like ineffective central government mired in a war for survival. Distinctions between soldier, brigand, patriot, and avenger simply disappeared.

Bandits were for sale—but at their own price. And they did not hesitate to change sides when better remuneration bid them elsewhere or when battlefield results advised new allegiances. The brigands did not scout, or gather intelligence, or maintain communications between disparate military units, for pay in the usual sense. They were instead allowed to plunder as they went. Pillage sustained and rewarded them. However much the participants lamented the necessity of employing known bandits as combatants, they did it just the same, especially the beleaguered Liberals under President Benito Juárez.[10] They were hanging on by their fingernails, but the bandits saw them through. First the brigands raised so much havoc in the countryside that the Conservatives who held the capital could not finance the pacification necessary to consolidate their regime. Bandits bled the Conservative treasury dry. Then, when French army regulars threatened to snuff out the final republican resistance, bandit guerrillas rampaged behind their front, denying the foe victory until the end of civil war in the United States and the threat of Prussian aggression against France persuaded Napoleon III to recall his troops from Mexico.

How these plundering adversaries fought! Antonio Rojas and his Galeanos in Jalisco were hunted by the likes of the French army captain, Berthelin, and his French counter-guerrillas. Rojas was a cutthroat of the worst order. He burned down entire towns that were not warmly hospitable to his band and murdered Mexicans who declined to furnish him with comfortable lodging and tasty meals. He was undoubtedly an embarrassment to the Liberals, but he maintained their cause in much of central-western Mexico in the critical year of 1864. Still, the republicans were somewhat relieved when French regulars shot down Rojas in January 1866 near Tecolotlán, Jalisco.[11]

Berthelin was, if possible, worse than Rojas. The Frenchman was a blood-thirsty racist, a tiger in victory. He was distinguished by his effeminate attire and was adorned with jewelry, flamboyant rings, cosmetics, and perfume. He killed perhaps five hundred Mexicans in Colima and Jalisco. Some days he murdered every Mexican he came across, regardless of their political disposition, just to prove the superiority of French civilization. Mexican militiamen finally caught up with Berthelin in November 1866 near Coalcomán in Michoacán. They killed him and took a large chunk of his scalp to Coalcomán so that the citizenry could sniff the greasy pomade in the hair.[12] Nothing about all this bloody business is, of course, only Mexican or all French. The United States Confederates at just this same time commissioned the known horse thief and murderer, William Clarke Quantrill, who promptly raided Lawrence, Kansas, with his irregulars and wantonly murdered a hundred and fifty men, women, and children for the Southern cause. Nor was Berthelin the only brigand to spruce up for the pillage. Brazil's *cangaceiros* (backland bandits) did the same, with brilliantine in their hair and plenty of perfume splashed on their unbathed bodies, so that their distinctive odor became one of their trademarks. Perhaps they only intended to imitate the rich.[13]

Mexico's decade of continuous turmoil, from 1857 to 1867, produced all kinds of banditry, from full-scale combatants like Rojas and Berthelin to any number of small gangs and soloists, like "La Carambada." Dressed in men's clothing, she accosted travelers around Querétaro. After robbing one victim, she waved her pistol in one hand and bared a breast with the other. "Look who has looted you," she crowed, which in itself was quite an attack on machismo.[14] Supply trains fell victim to brigands less often than did passenger stagecoaches, because the convoys were well-guarded, sometimes by hired bandits. The stages also had their security guards, but they were notoriously undependable and often in league with brigands down the road. Or the guards would charge the travelers a fee and then disappear.[15] In fact, a kind of toll system developed. It was not as well-organized as in Spain, where journeyers could buy travel insurance, called a *viaje compuesto*, against being robbed, or pay less for their ticket and take their chances with a *viaje sencillo*.[16] In Mexico, however, safe conduct could be purchased in Veracruz. It was also possible at times to purchase safe passage for the remainder of the trip from the first robber encountered. Otherwise, a voyager stood the possibility of suffering a succession of despoliations en route to a destination. There often was not much left for the last robber in line, so he usually took all the clothing of the itinerants. More than a few arrived at their Mexico City hotels wrapped in newspapers. Their dash from the coach to the hotel raised quite a stir among onlookers.[17]

Passengers, such as the *Times* correspondent, tried to protect themselves by carrying as few valuables as possible, but nothing angered a bandit more than an empty booty bag. One posted a message in the capital warning that any traveler he stopped who lacked at least twelve pesos would be beaten or otherwise manhandled. Bandits near Río Frío, dissatisfied with their take, once kept a passenger shivering in only his shorts while they debated whether or not to hang him. The coach driver warned them that the murder would cause the stage line to cease operations. Then they would have no one else to rob, so the brigands released their captive.[18]

The best-known bandits of the period were the Plateados of

Morelos, who like most bandits were both feared for their raw power and admired for their haughty dash. Above all, they were generally respected as a Mexican national type: the *charros*, best of all cowboys, possessed of a carefree, masculine arrogance that emphasizes their qualities as horsemen and lovers. No bronc escapes their lasso nor any victim their shot. But they tend to have much less luck with women. Still, they are dandies, dressed in those high-crowned and wide-brimmed sombreros, suede leather bolero jackets, and tight-fitting trousers, all trimmed with silver sewn into swirling designs. The Plateados earned their title with their especially ornate outfits, including their silver spurs and their saddles loaded with silver patterns. These men did not consider themselves outlaws. They were like the Chinese bandits who left their leggings open to expose an expensive inner lining to prove that they were no common robbers. The Plateados had class, and they dressed the part. They were, however, neither gentlemen nor Robin Hoods. Their social cause was their own enrichment. They were crass competitors in a system that still lacked well-developed institutions for exchange and legitimate means to profit.[19]

The Plateados emerged because of the inability of ranking Liberal generals like Jesús González Ortega to reward their volunteer troops with much more than thanks after they had taken Mexico City in 1860 from their Conservative opponents. Compensation during the campaign had been in the form of plunder, but now the capital had been declared out of bounds to looters. After sampling returns in the field, these veterans were in no mood to go home and subsist. So they kept the weapons and equipment they had been issued and turned to brigandage. Jesse James followed much the same route in the northern neighbor.[20]

These Plateados were not just one huge gang but a social phenomenon that occurred elsewhere in Mexico. Counterparts, also called Plateados, sprang up in Veracruz, Puebla, and Guerrero. The brigand bands were large, up to a thousand men, and they ran business in the areas where they worked. Their hideouts were well known to people: Monte de las Cruces on the Toluca road, Río Frío from the capital en route to Puebla, Cuesta China over toward Querétaro, and Tlaltizapán in Morelos. Hacendados gave them horses, money, lodging, and even banquets, under the threat of losing much more, pehraps everything. The rich had to come to terms with the brigands. To whom could the propertied appeal for protection? No effective federal police force existed in the country, and to denounce a bandit invited revenge. When bandits kidnapped the mayordomo of an hacienda, they reinforced their ransom demands with promises to destroy a recalcitrant hacendado's crops, cattle, and home. So deals had to be made. Hacendados furnished goods, arms, and safety to bandits. More than one traveler complained of being robbed in sight of an hacienda or being refused an hacendado's help after being looted.[21] Brazil's cangaceiros even made contracts with politicans and landlords to provide mutually beneficial services.[22] But the cangacieros and the Plateados were not hired retainers. They remained their own bosses. Bandits in this golden age did not often reciprocate an hacendado's favors. One of the more clever of the Plateados, Felipe "El Zarco" ("Blue Eyes"), is said to have worked his way into the highest social circles in Cuernavaca. After he won the confidence of the wealthy, he suggested certain outings in the countryside and promptly misguided his highly placed acquaintances into a nest of robbers.[23]

The most infamous Plateado was Salomé Placencia, who won a kind of fame as a Liberal guerrilla for his somewhat crazed assault on an entrenched and numerically superior enemy in June 1860 at Cuautla. Once the battle had ended, Placencia established business connections with Cuautla merchants, and he and his followers soon dominated commerce in the region. The economic competition was ruthless. One businessman faked being kidnapped and then released by Placencia to gain the confidence of other propertied residents. Then he tipped off the bandit about Cuautla's cargo shipments and security arrangements. Entrepreneurial brigands frequently formed such partnerships and used a respected merchant to set up the target and to fence their take. Bandits, in short, know the economy of the region they work.[24]

By late 1861 the Plateados could paralyze commerce in large areas of Morelos. Goods moved at their will, and they demanded heavy duty for the right to roll the wagons. Authorities, some undoubtedly in league with the robbers, declined to prosecute them, and, when they did, understanding judges, perhaps fearful of revenge, set them free. Collusion based on fear and profit sustained the operation. The victims discovered that efforts to defend themselves against the bandit monopoly were subverted by political manipulation. Residents of Jojutla, for example, complained to their governor in early 1862 that they regularly contributed to a rural police force raised in their territory, but that the district political chief who controlled it normally used the outfit to serve his personal interests and those of his wealthy friends around the village of Tetacala. They hinted that the authority had connections with the Plateados. Jojutlans saw the police only when the constabulary came to collect its monthly security fee. They pointed out that Liberalism promised equality and that many of them had fought for it. But when would it arrive? Jojutlans asked for a redistricting that would free them from Tetacala. Once that happened, they vowed they would make short shrift of the Plateados.[25]

Similar complaints bombarded the Juárez administration in that most difficult year of 1861. The Mexico City daily *Independencia* termed it "a scandal the way bandits infest the roads. What the government is thinking about, we do not know. But the bandits rampage with impunity." As proof, the stagecoach from Mexico City to Puebla had just been robbed three times in the same day.[26] Francisco Zarco, Minister of Internal Affairs, answered that the brigandage was the logical result of prolonged civil strife and that the weakness of the national treasury prevented a prompt solution. He noted that the government was developing means to cope with the Plateados and their likes, but the French landing at Veracruz ended any such plans.[27] Once in the capital, the invaders wanted peace, whereas the republicans needed to keep the interior seething. Domestic order had flipped sides. Juárez amnestied the Plateados and enlisted most of them as republican guerrillas. Most, but not all. Ever the pragmatists, a good many of the bandits sided with the French for higher pay and what they expected would be a more fruitful future. When the tide turned against the interventionists, the imperial bandits changed sides.[28]

But who turns to banditry and why? No precise pattern appears. Social and economic crisis, geography, misery, tradition, and opportunity all play a part. A Peruvian judge, Enrique López

Albújar, who analyzed brigandage in his country during the first quarter of this century, found little banditry in districts where property was well distributed among peasants. Unproductive haciendas, however, spawned bandits among their landless peons. On the other hand, commercial farming districts experienced limited brigandage because the capitalistic entrepreneurs had the will, means, and police to control it. Banditry flourished in areas where village feuds were traditional and also along active trade routes with access to mountain hideouts for the robbers. Brazil's most famous brigands emerged not in the south, where industrialization and commercial agriculture wed regional strongmen to centralist government, but in the northeast, where agrarian decay weakened old power blocks and stimulated social competition.[29]

Although the social composition of brigand units is difficult to determine, their ranks undoubtedly included army deserters, disgruntled peons, simply bored lads, opportunists, adventurers, escaped prisoners and their women. A full spectrum of personal reasons caused them to join. Some Brazilians got into trouble with their families and became cangaceiros. A thirteen-year-old boy believed that Lampião treated him better than did his own father. Others became bandits simply because they had relatives in the bands.

When bandits raided towns, they emptied the jails for reinforcements. Indians in flight from the military draft joined up. Brigands used their plunder to lure others into their ranks. The seasonal nature of Mexico's rural economy also made its contributions, as did the instability of employment in mines and other enterprises subject to market fluctuations and the mobility within the country's social stratification.[30]

Mexican society may have had only two major tiers, the few extremely rich and the masses of poor, with some rancheros and professionals in between, but there were layers within those tiers. For example, villagers who rented hacienda lands to farm did not consider themselves to be lower class. They thought they were doing better than the ranch hands and peons tied to the big estates. The life of these villagers was not one of permanent misery but rather of persistent insecurity. The slightest change of fortune, like a drought or the whim of a boss, could tumble them down the social ladder and into banditry.[31] In Brazil, the cangaceiros were often such social losers in the bitter family battles that character-ized the nation's northeast. Some infamous Mexican brigands, like Maldonado, had been tradesmen before turning robbers. Morales of Michoacán had been a shepherd. Bernal lost in a Sinaloan political struggle and turned to banditry as a temporary ex-pedient.[32] Those great pick-up armies that crisscrossed Mexico during the central-regional fight, on the way to Alamo in 1836, in defense of the republic against United States invaders at Buenavista, in the Liberal-Conservative strife, and during the struggle to dislodge Maximilian and his French support, supplied many Mexicans with a mobility that they had never thought possible. It widened their world view and encouraged the search for self-betterment. Short wars are that kind of stimulant. Banditry was an outgrowth of the process. People were on the move and determined to get ahead, and, for some, disorder best served their purposes.

Despite the odds in their favor, the brigands of this epoch rarely roamed scot-free. A variety of police forces were designed by both government and private interests to deal with them. Oc-casionally, but not often, the police got their man, and it was common practice to dangle the body of a noted thief from a tree near the scene of his last robbery, or to nail his head to a post at the site. Of course, the grisly reminders hardly deterred other bandits from their missions, but they certainly bemused travelers. Some bandits became famous through their skulls. The wife of the Spanish ambassador to Mexico encountered the head of a celebrated robber, Maldonado, nailed to a pine tree at Monte de las Cruces. That set her to thinking: "That grinning skull was once the head of a man, and an ugly one too, they say; but stranger still it is to think that that man was once a baby, and sat on his mother's knee, and that his mother may have been pleased to see him cut his first tooth. If she could see his teeth now!" Moreover, as if to show their contempt for the law, bandits had recently relieved other travelers of their luggage almost beneath Maldonado's blackened skull.[33]

Travelers seemed disappointed if they did not encounter

bandits at least once on a trip, or a reminder, like Maldonado's head. Brigands were the talk of the day, and the exaggerations of itinerants helped to construct the romance and myth that surrounded the outlaws. Yet one characteristic about them seems clear: the business of Mexican bandits was business. These were not the justice-seeking, precapitalist peasant bandits whom Eric Hobsbawm describes. The only thing the Mexican brigands seemed to protest was their exclusion from rewarding sectors of the social system. They wanted profit, position, and power, not to overturn society, and many later made good as bandits-turned-Rurales. Peter Singelmann notes the same qualities in the cangaceiros. They extorted money, true, but for themselves, not the poor. And if the cangaceiros ever thought of social injustice, "it was not to change the social order, but to find a place in it." The most infamous and admired cangaceiro was Lampião, "The Lantern," so nicknamed because he supposedly fired his guns so rapidly that the succession of powder flashes lit up is features. His biographer notes that Lampião did not object to the social system of his region but was irate because he found no place in it. The bandit admired the conservative class and yearned to be a rancher or businessman.[34] In sum, a good many bandits may have been peasants, but they seem to have been peasants who had broken with their old world, and they did not intend to look back.

Mexican outlaws hardly had the kind of empathy with the campesinos that Hobsbawm mentions. At least, not in the mid-nineteenth century. They terrorized poor country people just as they did the hacendados. Of course, they did not get as much from a campesino, only his chickens, goats, some clothing, and an occasional weapon, which were to a peon all he owned. You do not make friends with a campesino by stealing his horse; it is his only transportation. Cangaceiros treated impoverished Brazilians just as cruelly as they handled rich fazendeiros. Robin Hoods are hard to come by, although robbers sometimes pose as noble. Schinderhannes, a Rhineland bandit chief of the 1790s, was certainly not generous, although it served his purpose to proclaim that he killed only Jews.[35]

Peasant complicity with bandit activities was mandatory if Hobsbawm's bandits were to function. On the other hand, Mexican campesinos frequently turned against the outlaws who operated in their vicinity. They were more determined and vigorous than federal soldiers in tracking down rebels at Acayucan. Yaqui silver miners pledged to fight against fellow Yaquis who were disrupting commerce in Sonora. Campesinos who knew the territory helped to bring Heraclio Bernal to grief. The famed bandit Morales, who marauded around Lake Pátzcuaro, killed his wife and sought refuge among natives of the area, but they trussed him up along with a companion and carried them to the authorities, where the brigands were instantly tried and condemned to be shot. Lampião tortured, mutilated, and murdered backlanders who either informed on him or did not meet his demands. If peasants cooperated with bandits, they frequently did so out of fear, or because the police promised them no better.[36]

Hobsbawm found his peasant bandits to be the victims of exploitation and oppression, dreaming of "a world of equality, brotherhood of freedom, a totally new world without evil." The Mexicans, and many others, were much more practical about their possibilities. Hobsbawm's bandits fought to restore and protect old ways.[37] Mexico's brigands seemed to say, "I want my share of the new ways."

As double agents of order and disorder, bandits assume new forms and take on different roles as society changes under the impact of historical development. Brigands may have a major stake in order, as occurred when the French had been expelled from Mexico and the Liberals got on with their intention of making the country appear safe for capitalistic development. Or they may work for disorder, as in the nation's civil wars. Sometimes they create disorder to preserve a kind of order, which is what happened in the early nineteenth century after Independence. Or brigandage may be dormant (but never absent) because the stimulus for its presence is not sufficient or the domestic conditions for its appearance are not propitious, which was the situation in colonial Mexico. But these dips and surges over time, though not always easy to document and even more difficult to explain adequately, are certainly evident. Hence, a brief examination of New Spain is necessary before moving on to analyze order and disorder in dictatorship and then revolution in Mexico.

Chapter 2
The Aura of the King

Banditry did not flourish in colonial Mexico as it did after Independence. Forces that induce brigandage, such as internal wars and ineffective central government, were not prevalent. Nor was the sentiment to dispute royal authority very strong. Considerable discontent existed, even occasional armed protest, but also a generalized compliance with the king's will. A system of protection and appeal promised relief, even if it did not always produce satisfaction. Order definitely held sway over disorder.

Post-Independence Mexican historians like Lucas Alamán speak of endemic banditry in colonial New Spain, but later study of the epoch has, to date, produced comparatively few brigands. Those who were caught usually received special notoriety and harsh sentences, as the judges sought to make examples of them. Most death penalties were assessed against highway robbers. But even muleteers, almost constantly on the road, evidently did not worry much about robbers. They could have carried muskets or shotguns but instead had only a knife or short sword for defense. Thomas Gage, the vitriolic English Dominican friar, traveled unarmed from Veracruz to the capital and then to Oaxaca and Guatemala. He mentions no bandits. A good deal of cattle rustling occurred, and pulque in transit was fair game for thieves. Travelers got robbed and churches pillaged, but banditry as a facet of the social system was limited. What brigandage occurred was hit-and-run, and bandits did not normally set the terms of trade as they did after Independence.[1]

Relative domestic peace in the colony should not be confused with overall stasis or inertia. Considerable economic activity went on, much of it regionalized and a fair portion of it criminal, because of pirates and smugglers. Commercial enterprise and social mobility, curtailed to be sure by legal and cultural restrictions, characterized much of New Spain's nearly three centuries under Spanish rule. Many colonizers were profit-minded from the start, and some of the colonized eagerly joined in. Regional variations could be found, but with such innovations as money for exchange and a mule-drawn cart for transport, the colony's economy began to develop despite official monopolies and controls. Commerce grew because it meant personal gain, and the largely subsistence economy of the sixteenth century evolved as a capitalistic one during the next one hundred years, with the church and merchants as money lenders. A genuine business boom occurred in the eighteenth century, boosted by fiscal and marketing reforms. All this economic activity stimulated social movement both vertically and horizontally and whetted the appetite of those others excluded by caste and politics from enjoying the proceeds. The outsiders became candidates for banditry, but it took the disorder of the Independence wars to turn them loose.[2]

New Spain conducted its major business along a poorly maintained trunkline called the Camino Real, down which silver intermittently flowed through the capital on its way to the galleons at Veracruz. Even more tortuous roads, often mere Indian trails, loosely tied the provinces to the capital, which is why regional markets developed their own vigor and peculiarities. They were isolated but not out of touch. Perhaps once a year the outlanders received supplies from the capital, morale boosters in the form of fine Spanish linens and decent Spanish wines and farming tools and household goods. Goods and gossip were also exchanged at spirited regional fairs that attracted customers from a wide area. This long-distance commerce, with Mexico City as the political capital, helped in a significant way to maintain the territorial integrity of the colony.[3]

As in prehistoric days, human backs remained the main means of transport, but for long hauls the Spaniards introduced husky pack mules and then heavy wooden carts pulled by up to eighteen animals, which with luck traveled twenty miles a day. The advent of draft animals not only improved transportation—each wagon could carry four thousand pounds as compared to only two hundred pounds per mule—but produced a new skilled and well-paid job, that of the muleteer, who learned to measure his business potential with both merchants and bandits. He worked for the man who paid him the most. But wagon-train robberies did not become a serious problem for shippers until the golden age of Mexican banditry.[4]

The region through which the Camino Real stretched, north of Zacatecas, was called the "Land of War" because the fierce nomadic Indians who inhabited the area craved the clothing, weapons, wine, and food that moved along the trail. They also ate the mules they took, but evidently found no use for those 65-pound bars of silver. Indian raids forced the Spaniards to convert from mule to wagon transport. The natives could shoot an arrow right through a big mule, and rather easily cut a few of the heavily laden beasts from a long pack train, but the huge, two-wheeled carts of heavy planking protected the goods they carried and proved to be hard to budge even when separated from a convoy. So the wagons cost the Indians an important tactical advantage. Furthermore, in the 1690s the Spaniards organized convoys of carts, thirty to eighty at a time, set specific schedules, and guarded the train with some two dozen or more professional soldiers, all at the expense of the shippers, who passed the costs on to the consumers. It took a very expensive three to four months to negotiate the fifteen hundred miles from Mexico City to the mining camps at Parral in southern Chihuahua.[5]

The convoy system was reinforced by a series of forts built at the points along the road that were most vulnerable to Indian assaults. The defense worked. The Chichimecas could delay convoys, but they rarely looted them. That pleasure belonged to those wondrous bandits of the sea, some of them officially sanctioned privateers like the Dutchman Piet Heyn, who in 1628 took the entire Spanish treasure fleet—silver, indigo, sugar, logwood, and all—at the Cuban port of Matanzas. These corsairs had more than casual political and business contacts in their respective homelands. They had, in fact, official license to plunder. But these foreigners, so anxious to despoil and discredit the Spaniards, apparently made no deals with the Chichimecas to raid the land-bound silver convoys, perhaps because the Indians took slaves from their prisoners and did not distinguish between nationalities. Smuggling in less dangerous districts was, however, rampant.[6]

Smugglers are not bandits, although bandits sometimes smuggle as part of their overall strategy to work their way into society. Smugglers are secretive; bandits are open. Smugglers do not pillage, they merchandise. They simply help one entrepreneur to avoid legal marketing procedures in delivering goods to another entrepreneur. Smuggling was widespread in colonial Mexico, especially in the eighteenth century, when the crown wove an intricate web of trade restrictions to protect its long-neglected interests and those of its friends. Smuggling therefore became big business. People smuggled gold and silver to avoid the government's 20-percent tax on precious metals. Foreign products entered illegally because trade with other countries was prohibited. A variety of paper forms and transport taxes invited evasion, and monopolies such as tobacco could be cracked only by contraband.[7] Trade reforms in the late eighteenth century opened commerce but also increased official surveillance, so smugglers especially welcomed the loosening effects of the Independence wars, which rendered trade restrictions useless.

Whereas smugglers sneaked around taxes, duties, and the like, the natives of rural Mexico, collected in villages for Christianization and control, frequently resisted the levies. In his investigation of native response to Spanish rule, William B. Taylor has discovered hundreds of these mini-rebellions in central and southern Mexico. An official might try to increase tribute payments, or a priest would announce additional fees, and the villagers would riot, driving the authorities for cover with their rocks, sticks, machetes, powdered chili peppers, and anger, until militiamen or the regular army restored order.

Natives disturbed the peace for other reasons: to avoid labor drafts, to free an imprisoned comrade, to defend such customary freedoms as the right to speak their native tongue, and to settle and then resettle long-standing disputes with their neighbors. Food riots occurred periodically in major cities, and the government's expulsion of the Jesuit Order from New Spain in 1767 caused an uprising in Guanajuato, the site of six previous upheavals over tax-related grievances. Thousands of militiamen ringed Guanajuato

for more than three months after the religious outburst, which had
powerful political implications.[8]

The government, despite such shows of force against it,
normally tried to negotiate settlements. Colonial authorities hoped
to compromise with their critics. When disorder occurred, a
suspected ringleader might be singled out for exemplary punishment, and some demands of the rebels would usually be met.
Violence paid off for the Indians. It won them relief from a crown
mainly interested in retaining its colony to exploit its riches. But
occasional upheaval, together with the unsettling effects of continuing economic and population growth, generated some banditry. The mix was right. Population pressure on land and food
supplies, plus unemployment, blended with new opportunities
offered by development to create an opportunity for banditry
precipitated by sporadic unrest. These disturbances revealed to the
crown the limits of its control, and not just over the masses. The
government feared that efforts to subvert royal authority existed at
all levels. Partially on that claim, justified or not, the Jesuits were
expelled. Priests instigated some of the rural riots. Merchants
organized smuggling. Indian miners frequently stole the richest ore
at the mines where they worked and sold it at a ridiculously low
price to a local shopkeeper, who then made a nice profit passing it
on to the mineowner who had all along owned the silver.[9] And the
monarch discovered that at the highest levels his policy of divide
and rule could cost him his colony.

Some bonafide bandits thrived, like Pedro Razo in Zacatecas
and the notorious brigands of Celaya, who raided in the Bajío,
those populous central farming states of Guanajuato and
Michoacán bordered by Querétaro and Jalisco. They plied the
supply routes that fed the mining communities in the north. When
general commerce picked up in the late eighteenth century, a gang
of two hundred men under Antonio Espejo worked the major
roadway that crossed the Puebla plains. Rich merchants complained of losing their property to brigands, and treasury funds
were robbed, but the bandits, as usual, were not selective about
their victims. Modest farmers, even campesinos, at times lost their
limited belongings to bandits. Residents of Ixtepeji in Oaxaca
specialized in banditry along the trade route that crossed their

town, and the economic upswing of the late eighteenth century undoubtedly produced additional brigandage. But if more banditry cases were recorded during that period, it was partially because of the crown's preoccupation with rebuilding its authority.[10]

Initial attempts at political recentralization took place early in the eighteenth century with the establishment of the Acordada, a special police force controlled by the viceroy, the highest colonial authority and personal representative of the king. Origins of the force are found in medieval Spain, where cities organized mounted *hermandades*, or horse troops, to curb criminality on their outskirts. Queen Isabella centralized the disparate units in Castile in order to counterbalance the strength of her opposition, the aristocracy, and the institution passed in diluted form to New Spain. The extermination of banditry around Querétaro by an *hermandad* led to the formal creation of the Acordada. As a kind of roving court accountable only to the viceroy, the Acordada was empowered to catch, try, and sentence criminals in an unlimited territorial jurisdiction. Most crown officials were in some way held accountable for their performance, but not the judge of the Acordada; he possessed virtually carte blanche authority, which often was also his invitation to abuse. Protests against the excesses of the organization arose immediately, some from the falsely convicted but more often from other authorities who recognized the subversion of their accustomed powers. Their complaints, though politically inspired, were probably justified and largely ignored by the lawmen. The judge of the Acordada normally sat in the capital. His lieutenants were volunteers—hacendados and merchants—who in turn selected volunteer agents to enforce their will in the guise of the law. After fulfilling their mission, the officers and men could resign. The institution turned from two thousand to twenty-five hundred agents loose on the countryside. They must have enjoyed their unquestioned authority, because the Acordada provided unrestricted opportunity to extort and to settle grudges. It gave hacendados the armed right to expand their holdings and power. Merchants could use it to harass competitors. In 1756 the organization's jurisdiction spread to the cities, where paid service might have somewhat reduced abuses. But few policemen are ever paid enough to eliminate corruption. Mounting complaints against the lawmen led to gradual restrictions on their authority. Judicial decisions, for example, became subject to review, and by the time of the 1810 Independence movement the Acordada had lost much of its original power. So had the crown.[11]

As for criminal prosecutions, a scholar who has searched the unit's records found judgments to be "remarkably low" in number in relation to the colony's population. He concluded that the major function of the Acordada was to make central authority more obvious.[12] It reminded common rural Mexicans who was boss, and by granting rural elites the means to enforce their will, the crown hoped to ensure a loyal constituency in the countryside. Such measures, of course, can achieve the opposite result and encourage regional autonomy. The outcome depends on the disposition of the hacendado and what promises him more, allegiance or freedom.

The crown in other ways aimed to reduce the disorder that weakened its authority outside the capital. Small garrisons were posted along the commercial route to Veracruz to make certain that royal appointees and other dignitaries traveled safely to and from the capital. Such travelers were quite vulnerable riding along in carriages or those incredible coffin-like litters suspended between mules. With their leather awning and cotton curtains, these spectacles of travel were magnets to robbers, so the travelers had to have armed escorts. Although king, the king still had to prove his will and ability to govern and protect.[13]

As hardship pushed and opportunity pulled increasing numbers of natives from their customary settlements, the government erected free villages for the Indians within the boundaries of haciendas, where the natives could provide farm labor and be more easily controlled. Some urban vagabonds were shipped to northern missions and forts. In the general administrative reorganization of the 1770s, the army was greatly strengthened, the militia was organized, and intendents were appointed to preside over individual provinces.[14] The causes and effects of such important changes are still under review by scholars. No doubt they led to fiscal efficiency, bolstered national defense, and stimulated the economy. They also provided considerable low-level employment, but at the same time they removed ranking colonists from favored positions to make way for new delegates from Spain. As hacendados purchased military commissions and organized their own militia, they further strengthened their hand—for or against the crown. Suffice it to say, the reforms cut both ways and further unsettled society. Ideas of the Enlightenment and the French and American revolutions found the fissures. An increasing number of colonists thought of themselves as Mexicans, not as Spaniards. Criminality increased. The administrator of the post office at Huautla lost 1,697 pesos to robbers in his home. At Zimapan, not far from the capital, bandits took 11,000 pesos from a mule train. Such brigandage nonetheless remained the exception. The environment was not yet conducive to aggressive opportunists who lacked capital and connections. But judging by the way so many Mexicans took to brigandage during the wars for Independence, aspirations for self-betterment must have been building during those good business years near the close of the colonial era.[15]

Although considerable shuffling took place in the upper echelons of colonial society as the elites jockeyed for demonstrable gain, it is difficult to assess how ordinary Mexicans viewed their possibilities for improvement outside of their traditional villages and lifestyles. Wage labor at the northern mines was well paid and in demand, and Indians from central Mexico responded. Others, whose ancestors had not even known the horse, became superb cowboys on expanding cattle ranches. So there was movement in society. Men who joined the army went from their villages to garrisons and in the process had their eyes opened to the change going on "out there."[16]

As time went on, the mobile, marginal group certainly increased in size. Economic development absorbed some people, but could hardly dent the surplus created by population growth, economic displacements, and those who voluntarily left their homes in search of change. Racial considerations further muddled the milieu. Although time and capitalism had blurred race distinctions, the increasing number of mixed bloods found no security in a business community reserved mainly for whites or in Indian villages still largely intact. Undulations in development led to layoffs and more uncertainty. The European wars cut off quicksilver needed to refine ores and the paper required by the tobacco industry. Big operations shut down, turning loose their workers. The Independence movement began about this time. It offered elites and the reasonably well-to-do the chance to shuck Spanish controls. To many other aspiring Mexicans it meant employment and opportunity, and they took it as soldiers, patriots, guerrillas, bandits, all of them interchangeable.[17]

The balance between order and disorder is always precarious, and advocates of either can easily justify their position—in the name of justice, the national good, the Almighty, or the People. The aura of the king and his royal authority legitimized order in colonial Mexico and maintained the degree of domestic tranquility that existed. It took a special determination to disrupt the king's peace, although rural villagers sometimes vented their grievances by attacking local crown officials. Still, respect for legitimate regal authority remained a formidable social control. When the king disappeared in the Napoleonic Wars, disorder took over the colony. There were also institutional props to the psychological presence of the crown. The king himself was not beyond the call of the common man, and as ultimate patron he demonstrated some care for his peons, although more for some than for others. The colony's judicial system provided an avenue of possible relief. An official could always be found to hear a complaint against another authority. Certainly the church, working in tandem with the crown, reinforced order, despite some disruptive priests in the provinces. Instruments of official repression also existed: the Acordada, the army, the militia, and local strongmen. Blanketing the entire system was the law. All through the nineteenth century, through turmoil and dictatorship, Mexicans yearned for the certainty and justice of the former Spanish law. Security in the law yields compliance and domestic peace.[18]

Chapter 3
The Spoils of Independence

Everything is possible in war, and Mexico had not had widespread warfare for some three hundred years. So the people took advantage of the unprecedented opportunities for self-advancement offered by the breakdown of authority in the turbulence of the Independence movement that began in the Bajío in the fall of 1810. New power bases were established and defended against competitors. Material wealth was redistributed by force. The rebellion has been called conservative, because the colonials who supported it tended not to seek fundamental change; that is, they wanted to retain much of the colonial structure but to put themselves in charge. Because there was relatively little room at the top, and national spoils were limited, a protracted struggle followed over who should chart the country's course. It lasted more than half a century and was very expensive, not only in human and property loss but also because it prostrated the nation before the onrush of aggressively industrializing world powers.[1]

The insurrection may have lasted longer than it had to, but the profit-taking was so great on both sides that the combatants were reluctant to forge a conclusion. The priest Hidalgo's initial endeavors failed because elites that could have supported him feared that they could not control the outcome in their favor. They may have sensed a race war in the making, or perhaps they recognized in Hidalgo's ranks those aspiring mixed bloods from the Bajío who intended at whatever price to make a place for themselves in any new order. Be that as it may, the people with resources abandoned the curate, and the war developed into nearly a decade of guerrilla and counter-guerrilla activities. Christon I. Archer has discovered that people on both sides deliberately kept the war going because it

25

offered so much easy plunder, all in the guise of patriotism. For instance, Agustín Iturbide, the royalist turncoat who was instrumental in completing the Independence, earlier sold exit permits to Spaniards who feared death from the disturbances. His profits depended on continued disorder.[2]

Haciendas were looted and burned; cattle stolen and dispersed. The followers of bandits nicknamed "The Crate," "The Castrator," and "Colonel of the Colonels," along with the Ortíz brothers and Pedro de Negro, became infamous for their crimes. Royalist generals looted along with the guerrilla nationalists, and all changed sides at will. New commercial interests developed. Due to the insecurity of the roads, merchants had to hire military-like units to protect their goods in transit. Domestic commerce depended on the army and the bandits, who took advantage of the disorder to enrich themselves. Brigands sold plunder to royalist merchants who marketed the goods in cities like Guanajuato. Bandits like the notorious García ran wild. He joined the Spaniards at Orizaba, but when their resistance slackened he returned to brigandage. The Mexicans complained about his brutalities, and in response García buried his victims alive. He was eventually captured and exiled to California, where he resumed his robberies. García in his excesses was certainly not the average bandit. But clearly, colonial values, ethics, and morals were in most quarters being shaken. With the superstructure of Spanish regalism in flames, compliance drifted into dissent.[3]

When the Spanish Liberals saddled their king with a constitution in 1820 but evidenced little intent of sharing their new-gained power with the colonists, middle-level Mexicans opted for independence. They arranged for imperial army officers to treat with the guerrilla-bandit nationalists, and the colony shucked its parent. The Spaniards, embroiled in their European rivalries, lacked sufficient strength to restore their imperial authority. Mexico was adrift, directionless. After a brief flirtation with monarchy, a clique of leaders settled on a federal republic, to a large degree forced on the country by the realities of national disorder and confirmed in the Constitution of 1824. Then began the armed debate among the power brokers. With no effective institutions to mediate their differences, Mexicans suffered eight hundred revolts between 1821 and 1875.[4]

By no means did all the powerful aim to be national leaders. Some of the strongest wanted only to be left alone to rule their regional fiefs. Men like Juan Alvarez in Guerrero, and others such as the Zacatecan Francisco García, were willing to compromise with a central government, even to serve it, as long as they were allowed to retain command in their states. A few of these caudillos—and the best-known is Antonio López de Santa Anna—aspired to the presidency, and he, by a combination of military strength, charisma, the control over customs revenue at Veracruz, and the support of those who benefitted by his presence in the capital, became President of Mexico eleven different times. But not only caudillos demanded their freedoms. Long encumbered by the hegemony of Mexico City, cities and districts snapped the old colonial bonds. Guadalajara used trade routes that by-passed the onerous middlemen protected by monopoly in the capital. The northern tier states developed closer economic ties with the southern United States. Silver miners at Alamos cut costs by importing goods through Guaymas instead of distant Acapulco, as required in colonial times. Tampico insisted on retaining revenues that might have passed into the federal treasury at Veracruz.[5]

Local chiefs, called caciques, also intended to guard their unfettered liberties, acquired during the Independence wars, including the right to tax. Smugglers working the port of San Blas wanted no part of federal inspectors. Agriculture slowly recovered from war's devastation in central Mexico, and the agrarian capitalists sought to avoid taxation and regulation. Disorder shielded rural interests from central encroachment, so federalists induced unrest. They tore up and otherwise refused to repair roads that approached their enclaves. And not all centralists were as appalled by the chaos as those who were trying to impose administrative control. Other centralists, looking on and waiting their chance to take power, knew that continued disturbance paved the way, so they contributed to the anarchy. The national government pleaded the need for domestic stability but had no means to enforce it, and so received scant compliance from the provinces.[6]

How much rural strongmen deliberately stirred up the Indians lodged in communal villages in order to fuel disorder is difficult to gauge, but agrarian unrest was common during the era. The constitution, with its emphasis on individualism and equality, had removed the crown's protections of native villages, including the right to designate and work property for the common good, as the Indians did with pasture lands, water resources, and wooded patches needed for making charcoal. In accordance with the constitution, states began to force the natives to break up their communal patterns, but the Indians were not about to lose their holdings in the name of some abstract ideal. So they resisted—in Michoacán, in Oaxaca, in Puebla, in the state of México—all of which experienced native upheavals. Turmoil wracked the country. Disorder was the order of the day.[7]

The specter of a full-scale caste war also arose. The continuing struggle of Sonora's Yaquis had long had a racial tinge. Juan Ignacio Jusacamea in 1826 used a tax issue to raise his Yaqui comrades. It took more than a year for security forces to pacify them. When Jusacamea surrendered, he explained that he had not realized that Independence had been won. He had been, all along, fighting Spaniards, not Mexicans. The excuse served, and he was appointed chief justice of the Yaqui territory. Five years later he was back in rebellion, this time to be defeated and executed. But new conflict between the whites and natives erupted in 1842 in the fertile contested area between the Yaqui and Mayo rivers. The quarrel crested during the Porfiriato.[8]

Barbarism prevailed in Yucatán, where the Mayans in the 1840s launched a bitterly revengeful caste revolt, but no racial conflict threatened white Mexicans more than that which in 1847 rumbled through the Sierra Gorda, which dominates the heartland of the nation. The Sierra runs through five north-central states that are vital, because of their communication routes and resources, to the geographical and economic unity of the country. The main mountain chain encompasses more than half of Querétaro and parts of Guanajuato and Hidalgo. So strongly did the Pames, Ximpeces, and Jonaces Indians who inhabit the range fear and distrust whites that Spanish imperial power had hardly penetrated the region. Armed expeditions failed to pacify the Indians. The Church had only sightly better fortune. So the natives entered the Independence period with substantial confidence and solidarity. Merchants, miners, and hacendados lured to the region by commercial opportunity soon began to subvert this native self-satisfaction, and by the 1840s the Indians had become agitated. And a small, personal dispute among the natives themselves suddenly escalated into a race war.[9]

Francisco Chaire, in August 1847, deserted his Guanajuato army post and returned to his Sierran village of Xichú. The mayor, no friend of the Chaires, arrested Francisco, who was subsequently freed from jail by his brother, assisted by a family servant, Eleuterio Quirós. The mayor called in the army to track down the escapee and his accomplices. The Chaires surrendered and were later pardoned, but Quirós determined to resist; precisely why cannot be determined. Remarkably, this former servant ignited a caste war. His sense of immediacy was good, and Quirós knew the issues: no more government interference in Sierran affairs, by taxation or in matters of public order and justice. He demanded land redistribution through confiscation, guaranteed employment on haciendas, and the termination of Church intrusions. These were old grievances never resolved, and Quirós formalized them in a published plan that rallied hundreds of campesinos to the fight.[10]

San Luis Potosí officials lightly brushed off the rebellion as "socialist," a catchword used by outsiders to characterize Indian anger and unity, but with reports of caste war in Sonora and Yucatán, the nation's whites, even many mestizos, became deeply concerned about the possibility of a combined effort by the Indians to expel them from the country. Few doubted their ability to do so, if the tribes ever united their efforts.[11]

The bands of Quirós ravaged the Sierra well into 1849. Whites were driven from some regions; others fled. The time had come to settle scores; the results were often savage. Local authorities preached conciliation with Quirós, but more distant policymakers advocated annihilation. When a Durango newspaper called Quirós a bandit and advised him to crawl back into his dark cave, the rebel heightened the violence. Army battalions moved in to cauterize the uprising before it spread. No less a personage than a former president, General Anastasio Bustamente, organized the strategic offensive, but it took a native son of the Sierra, General Tomás Mejía, to track down Quirós and in December 1849 to certify his execution. But a martyr's death rarely brings peace.[12]

Politicians, both national and state, debated during the next two years the best way to subdue the rebellious Indians of the

Sierra Gorda. Suggested solutions ran from extermination to land redistribution. Compromise prevailed. No haciendas were to be subdivided for the natives, but they were given some land to farm, considerable tax relief, and a promise that they would not be force-drafted into the army. In a move to win their political support, the federal government founded three colonies for the Indians and gave them provisions and cattle for subsistence there. Hundreds of Indians agreed to the resettlement. Then, as one of the minor ironies of history, the French invaded Mexico, and General Mejía, still a Sierran despite his assault on Quirós, won the support of the Indians for the monarchists. What he promised them is not known, but Mejía died on the Hill of the Bells, executed next to Maximilian, and the natives of the Sierra Gorda were enveloped, although not completely pacified, by the national economic development that followed.[13]

Banditry, village uprisings, predatory armies, caste wars—they all combined to maintain rural Mexico in turmoil. No property was safe, no trade route secure. The two forces most responsible for sustaining the turbulence were the bandits and the army, and they often worked together, selling stolen goods for their mutual profit. The bandits had emerged from the Independence strife in small gangs from disparate backgrounds united by a common desire to get ahead. They had pillaged as both monarchists and republicans during the war, and when it ended they would not go back home. They meant to deal with the new power brokers. The brigands were reinforced during the strife by peons who had been handed weapons and told to fight. After victory, these commoners refused to surrender their rifles, and when the national treasury could not afford to buy their continued services turned to banditry. So did others determined to protect from centralistic encroachment the land they had occupied during the upheaval. All these people became kinds of rebels, determined to redistribute prestige and goods in their own favor, although not in accord with any ideology.[14]

These new brigands were not yet strong enough to regulate business by themselves; they were not like the Plateados at midcentury. So a lot of these earlier brigands settled for partnerships and became retainers for competing regional interests. No common cause existed in provincial Mexico, unless it was a mutual determination to keep central authority at bay. Rural strongmen were frequently at each other's throats—for economic advantage, political influence, and social prestige. Often, the number of guns that a man could count on determined the victor. The relationship between the outlaws and the people of power resembled a partnership more than an employer and employee arrangement. Hacendados normally would rather hang a brigand than treat with him, and they proved it later when backed by the dictatorship of Porfirio Díaz and his rural policemen, but, given the uncertainties of post-Independence conditions, the propertied had to make their deals with brigands for commercial service, protection, and retribution. Merchants also courted bandits out of fear and gain. Like the hacendados, they would have welcomed effective policing, but none was available. So they sold to the robbers the goods that they needed to sustain their bandit activities. When they did so, the local authorities and propertied people looked the other way. If the outlaws did not fulfill their needs one way, they would do it another. Governors also treated with brigands. As in Brazil, backland banditry depended in part on gubernatorial politics. Lampião openly consorted with ranking officials, and in Mexico a traveler complained that the governor of Tlaxcala had deliberately arranged for him to be robbed on the road to Puebla. Small farmers also encourged conflict, in the hope of extending their holdings during the unrest. So too did the tenant farmers in search of their own land. People previously assigned to an inferior social status began to look for improvement, and outlaws both contributed to and adapted well to the new mood.[15]

Brigands also served the armies raised by politicians in pursuit of power, even the presidency. Bandits who welcomed the chance to plunder within the bounds of a political cause were much more reliable recruits than Indians, who might desert an army to return home to plant and harvest their corn. If their side won, so much the better for the bandits. If not, common practice pardoned the defeated and perhaps rewarded them in the hope of buying their allegiance. That was the kind of insurance that suited bandits; later it gave them police work in the service of the state.[16]

Mexico's army personnel gained promotions, profit, power, and an entree to politics through disorder. The army was the best available means for upward social mobility. It was not a profes-

sionally military corps of soldiers but a conglomeration of competing political interests whose leaders had, in the main, gained
their military rank through political appointment (or self-appoint-
ment) during the confusions of war. A few had been former royalist
officers. Factions within the service constantly jockeyed for favor
with caudillos, civilian leaders, and other military troops. The
most successful schemer became president—but not for long. In the
thirty years between 1821 and 1851, military men, meaning individuals with army rank, held the presidency in all but three years.
Stability would have curtailed their ambitions.[17]

Promotions were the political norm, so the army was larded
with generals and other top rankers. Following Independence,
common men who alleged important services to the republic
received rank and promotion. The losers had meanwhile been
promoting their people to keep them loyal. Winners amnestied
their foes to earn their compliance and allowed them to keep their
rank. Army units naturally considered revolt as the means to
promotion. The officers had to be paid good salaries and be permitted additional rake-offs in order to cement their allegiance. No
pay led to rebellions, each of which helped to pick the federal
treasury clean.[18]

Simple country people became colonels. They had no allegiance to the national government and regularly pronounced
against it not only for promotion but to loot on a march to nowhere
across a rural sector or to steal a payroll assigned to their troop.
This is what occurs when there is no penalty for defeat. Army
generals got rich during disturbances, so they kept banditry alive
to justify their campaigns. In fact, they themselves robbed like
bandits: horses and food from campesinos, money and weapons
from hacendados. The local authority who called on the army to
dispel trouble chanced much worse from the soldiers. So the officials learned to work with the bandits, who were hardly more
scrupulous.[19]

Military people who led these forays not only stole property for
themselves but seized people as recruits for their ranks. The forced
draft was notorious, and desertions rife because of it. Men fled their
homes to avoid it and turned to brigandage.[20] But a substantial
number of Mexicans volunteered for service, and among those who

put on uniforms a fair percentage liked service well enough to stay. Mexico's common soldiers compiled a decent record for endurance and steadfastness in combat. Their record was partially due to the peon's customary obedience to authority, especially to the person who rewarded and punished him, but it was also due to the fact that the ordinary soldiers were comparatively well paid and could accumulate booty along the way. They joined for personal reasons, too: adventure, their leader's charisma, to get away from home, to see the big city—all shades of motivation were present. Santa Anna, supported by wealthy interests in and near Veracruz, paid his soldiers, even though on one occasion pay did not prevent his arrest by the troops he commanded, when they experienced a sudden political change of mind. The Pintos of Alvarez ravaged their way from Guerrero to the capital.[21] Soldiering, then, could provide betterment for humble people burdened by lives of boring subsistence.

Hence, an important contradiction: although the army in its diversity of interests helped to maintain regionalism and separatism from central control, it also unraveled individual Mexicans from their tightly-knit and resistant traditions, which were a paramount barrier to nation-building. When Santa Anna swept those campesinos out of the lowlands of Veracruz and introduced them to the plateau and Mexico City, he broadened visions that had been restricted to village life. Perhaps it was only a blink, but that was a start. Imagine the Pintos on the loose in the capital. How many of them returned to the mountains of Guerrero to stay? Their bond to the soil had been slackened, even if a good many still returned for harvests. In 1800 there were an estimated nine thousand soldiers in New Spain. At the end of Independence there were seventy-five thousand. Under Mexico's first ruler, Iturbide, the army totaled some sixteen thousand men. Santa Anna in 1855 had more than sixty-four thousand soldiers. That is a 400 percent increase.[22] These statistics indicate a good deal of movement in lower society. As succeeding presidents assumed control, there was always the problem of paring down the army that had brought them to power. These veterans were not all docile peasants; they had become demanding soldiers, driven to some extent by their superiors, who could use armed and disgruntled regulars to support their own ambitions. At the same time, individuals experienced personal breakthroughs as opportunity and mobility began to loosen their traditional restraints.

Throughout, the central government, such as it was, insisted that domestic peace should be the responsibility of the individual states, municipalities, and entrepreneurs. The federal government granted authority to the states to create a wide variety of militia and police units, although these were usually small, ill-trained, and poorly equipped. Few officials had the resources to recruit and professionalize any sizeable unit, so the countryside became dotted with vigilante-like outfits short on justice but quick on the trigger. They frequently contributed to disorder. A leading Liberal politician, José María Luis Mora, noted that their interest lay more in robbing than in protecting private property. Britain's minister called them the "dregs of society." But backed by a hanging judge like José M. Aguirre in Saltillo, local forces did eliminate a few bandits. Ballo Arriero and his eighteen gang members, who had terrorized Coahuila, were captured by irregulars in 1831 and executed on Aguirre's orders. More often, however, governors like Juan Múgica Osorio of Puebla complained of their inability to curb brigandage even with a proliferation of security units. It was, of course, the nature and not the number of these police-like units that mattered: too many of them deserved the designation bandits-and-lawmen to provide any measure of domestic tranquility, especially when so many powerful people really did not welcome it.[23]

The corps that were best developed tended to protect and promote the political interests of their creator rather than to involve themselves in disciplined law enforcement. Governors had their militia, a municipal president his police, and an hacendado his private troop of retainers. Petty politicians found that the best way to promote their careers was to establish a personal armed unit that could be used to counterbalance or, if necessary, batter a rival. Power, more than ideals or even justice, builds a constituency. Finally, these units represented something tangible and useful to be donated to the cause of a caudillo or a governor or a rebel general in the expectation of substantial return. Simply said, a man needed a troop of his own to get ahead.[24]

Porfirio Díaz knew the locus of power. As a young man, his Liberal tendencies won Díaz an appointment as political chief of a small Oaxacan district. He immediately began to organize a personal militia, purportedly because of his affection for the military. But his regional superior recognized the power ploy and ordered Díaz to disassemble his troop on the spurious ground that the Indians were too ignorant to be security police. Díaz acquiesced—ostensibly—but secretly he continued to mobilize, enticing recruits with minor privileges. Those militiamen who committed civil offenses were not jailed like common criminals but were permitted to loaf away their sentence at the municipal building, around Díaz himself. He gave them their own gymnasium and sponsored closed dances to build esprit de corps. When disgruntled citizens threatened to storm the regional capital, Díaz unveiled his troop, intervened, suppressed the riot, and became a local hero. It was his first military-political victory, and it revealed his ability to seize the moment. A long-time acquaintance, Benito Juárez, soon after became Oaxaca's governor and gave Díaz permission to organize a national guard in his district. Díaz quickly mounted a powerful retainer-like troop that guaranteed his political stature. He was now a man to be heard from and reckoned with. Not many, of course, achieved the presidency, but plenty started off like Porfirio Díaz.[25]

False starts toward creation of these irregular militia units abounded. States did not generate sufficient revenue to attract recruits and then equip them. Militia units therefore came and went in accordance with a governor's immediate political needs. Only one state seems to have developed a noteworthy troop: Zacatecas, under its intelligent governor Francisco García, who colonized land-hungry campesinos in several districts, supported their welfare with terrain, seeds, and cattle, and then proclaimed them his militiamen. Of course, García could afford a superb militia. His state was the country's leading silver producer for three decades after Independence. Zacatecas led the world in silver production in the 1830s. Santa Anna wanted that revenue for himself and the central government, and he demanded that García disband his militia. The governor mobilized four thousand irregulars to defend his interests, and called for other states to join in resisting the attack on their sovereignty, but their promised help never materialized. So García stood alone with his famous militia. As it turned out, the organization's reputation exceeded its abilities, and when faced by army regulars the militia disbanded in headlong flight. Santa Anna took over García's state finance company, which promptly agreed to loan the dictator one million pesos and to grant him a share of the mining profits. Out of grace with the federal government for the moment, García took refuge on a distant hacienda, but soon returned to the capital as a national minister. Disorder often moved politicians like pawns in and out of office.[26]

Leaders like Santa Anna also laid plans during this period for the establishment of a civic militia based on the Spanish model, but the Mexicans stood the Spanish program on its head. Whereas Spanish Liberals advocated the militia in order to protect local government against overbearing central authority represented mainly by the army, Santa Anna thought that allowing the formation of state militias would encourage provincial strongmen to support his central regime against an ambitious, unreliable, and politically divided army. He offered the governors militiamen in return for support. So whereas the Spaniards aimed to advance their goal of municipal autonomy with a civic militia, Santa Anna wanted to cement an alliance with regional bosses through armed forces that would guarantee their respective political positions. The Spaniards wanted decentralization; the Mexicans sought a modus vivendi that would allow them to centralize. The great federalist Juan Alvarez said as much in 1833: "The bad men are the generals, and remedies ought to be energetic; the states need the aid of the executive."[27] And the executive wanted the aid of the states. Under the proposal, governors would control their militia without legislative restriction, and presidents could, with state approval, employ the militia for their own purposes outside the whims of a frequently obstructive national congress. No wonder Santa Anna pressed for creation of a civic militia. It would have given him a provincial constituency to counterbalance both the undependable army and a balky congress. But the project foundered for political and financial reasons, so Santa Anna began to experiment with several rural police corps along the route to

Veracruz, supposedly to combat banditry but really to maintain a lifeline to his power base in the port city with its customs house, the major source of national revenue.[28]

The fractured nature of the republic became painfully evident during the Mexican-American War. Mexicans fought Mexicans as much as they battled the American invaders. Some Mexicans sought to ally themselves to the foreigners, even while others died, some heroically, resisting them. The quick amputation of one-half of the national territory by the victors further discredited the government, and respect for authority, on the decline since Independence, largely disappeared. Its demise could be seen in the change of style and new intensity of banditry. Brigands now took the initiative. If they formed partnerships with more respected citizens, they did so on their own terms. It seemed as if the bandits went out of their way to show their contempt for authority. They certainly displayed no pride in being Mexican. The war had eroded all such morale, and in disgust and frustration ex-soldiers became brigands.[29]

Officials and foreigners became fair game along with any others worth looting. Ministers of state riding a stage near Querétaro in 1848 were robbed and their escort killed. The national congress could not meet because deputies feared to travel from their home districts on brigand-infested roads. Bandits looted and killed a Frenchman and his son at Ayotla in the state of México in 1852. As there were no banks in the republic, people kept their money at home, something bandits understood. One brigand, dressed as a priest, gained entrance to the house of the Swiss consul on the fringe of the capital. With two accomplices he then killed the consul and stole 10,000 pesos from his residence. Some forty deserters from the United States Army joined the spree and stayed in Mexico to pillage in Hidalgo. Brigandage flourished in the breakdown of society.[30]

National near-disintegration also stimulated violent demands for social reform and encouraged the armed settlement of long-standing rural disputes. More than four hundred Tarascan Indians marched with their picks, swords, and clubs to the state capital at Morelia in 1855 to demand land distribution, and tax complaints ignited a riot in the Veracruz village of Coatepec, where rebels

sacked the town, burned its archive, and then turned to loot nearby
haciendas. A priest, or someone masquerading as one, pillaged
freely around Tenancingo in the state of México, proclaiming the
advent of "The Political Generation." He meant a new political
generation, one that could regenerate the stricken country,
although, like most of the others, he offered no vision of how
regeneration could be accomplished.[31] But some others did—a
group of politicians less bound to a colonial past and more attracted to modern ideals. They called themselves Liberal reformers
and advocated the kind of republicanism, individualism, and
capitalism that had energized countries like England and the
United States. Whereas Conservatives sought a foreign prince to
patch up the old social fabric, the Liberals aimed to reweave things
to their liking. They were not radicals; they did not intend to tear
out the seams; but they did mean to reduce sharply the thick
strands of the army and the Church.

The issue was joined in 1854, and the Liberals amassed
substantial provincial strength to seize tenuous national control
with a loose coalition of frequently conflicting ambitions. Despite
their weakness at the core, they unleashed their promised reform
through a politics of confrontation, although they insisted that they
did not wish to be harsh with their adversaries. To establish the
new order, they had to vigorously attack the old one, not only the
army and the Church but also the whole system of the post-
Independence period with its caudillos, bandits, and deliberately
sustained rural disorder, and the Indians with their traditional
communal priorities. Paradoxically, the Liberals plunged their
country into unmitigated disorder in a frantic search for peace. To
them, peace equaled progress, yet they needed disorder to establish
their order of things—their system. Disorder is not privy to the poor
and dispossessed. Elites, too, know its value. But Mexico's Liberals
learned that disorder, once encouraged, is not easily curbed, and
that restoration of domestic tranquility can exact a high national
price.

Chapter 4
Bent on Being Modern

Mexico's reformers set their sights on modernizing their country along classical liberal lines: republicanism, capitalism, and individualism. These aims were to varying degrees soon adjusted by self-interest and other realities. Republicanism drifted toward dictatorship and central police. Capitalism invited foreign economic domination. Individualism wandered further and further from social responsibility. Still the Liberals plunged ahead: Church and army privileges would have to be pared down in the name of social equality, and those formidable regional caudillos would either have to cooperate or be eliminated. Indian communal properties would be redistributed into private hands, and the natives scrubbed of their Indianness for the sake of national integration. The reformers made domestic order their first priority; they incessantly talked about pacification. At the same time they pursued policies that could only induce disorder. Their adversaries had to fight because alternatives to strident opposition were slow to appear.[1]

Leaders of the Reform arose from diverse social backgrounds and blended considerable time in public office with their mainly military, law, and journalism careers. They were neither single-minded nor united in purpose, and their differences of opinion, some acute, soon surfaced. Their leader, Juan Alvarez, was run out of the capital soon after his arrival because his men so enjoyed their looting. Alvarez was not much interested in reform anyway. During one week in Mexico City he doled out army commissions at the rate of forty-three a day.[2] Nothing new about that, but other reformers planned substantial change.

Fearful of tyranny and protective of their individual am-

bitions, they opted for a republican government with a president of
limited powers tied to a strong representative legislature tempered
by an independent judiciary, and they wrote all those political
models into their Constitution of 1857. It soon became evident that
a much stronger chief executive would be required to hammer out
Liberal political and developmental intentions. So began the drift
toward dictatorship, and the judiciary became a dumping ground
for patronage. The principle of municipal independence had long
since been discarded. The Liberals openly compromised with
Mexico's realities, and some grew rich doing it. Competition for
the yield of capitalism clouded social consciousness as the reformers exchanged individual liberties (of others) for a semblance of
domestic peace (for themselves) and otherwise adjusted their
principles and lofty goals to meet their times and their needs.[3]

The newcomers saw the army, Church, and Indians as serious
obstacles to their aspirations, and early on they attacked the long-
held privileges of those sectors. The army, Church, and merchant
guilds lost their special judicial rights; henceforth their members
could be tried in civil courts along with everyone else. Indian
villages and the Church were ordered to divide their corporate
holdings. For the natives that meant that their commonly-worked
pastures and woodcutting reserves would be disposed of, along
with their scarce water resources. The Indians could not live
without their property, so as always they fought hard to protect it.
They would do so again.[4]

The Liberals also sniped away with edicts that remade various
ecclesiastical ceremonies, such as those attending birth, marriage,
and burial, into civil obligations, a measure that assured the
animosity of the parish priests, who were remunerated by just such
religious services. And the acting president, Ignacio Comonfort, in
1856 guaranteed the army's hostility by demoting to common foot
soldiers a group of well-known generals for their attempted coup
against him at Puebla. This was the politics of confrontation at its
best. The military, the Church, and the natives proved up to the
challenge, but were in no way unified, even within their respective
ranks, which is why the Liberals eventually triumphed.[5]

What did the Liberals hope to accomplish by their assault on
those corporations, and by their emphasis on equality, even if

tinged with selfishness? First, they sought to create a political constituency to maintain themselves in power. By making institutions like the army, communal life, and the Church less attractive, and by forcing common people from their traditional securities, they expected to attract broad-based support for their regime. Private property was intended to create civic-mindedness and an appreciation for the government's program. When bathed by civilization (as the Liberals interpreted it), illiterate rural Mexicans would shed their stoicism, ignorance, fatalism—indeed, their culture—and become, it was dreamed, more like us, the Liberals. A Liberal legislator put it clearly: "In order that the light of civilization can penetrate these [Indian] towns, it is necessary to dissipate the clouds of their Indianism."[6] Among their other characteristics, many Liberals never tired of teaching good citizenship; they were also racist and egotistical.

As experienced politicians, the Liberals understood the need to wean the natives from the influence of the parish priest and the local cacique in order to win their allegiance to the national government. Although there were communal aspects in the Indians' culture, they had always lived within a hierarchy that had its authorities. Social egalitarianism was rarely if ever present, and the rulers meant to retain their power over the ruled. The strength of this structure may be measured by the success with which the Indians resisted the immense pressures exerted by Liberal capitalism.[7]

The Liberals who were so determined to break apart the Indian political and economic structures also thought that they could forge public peace. The availability of cheap private property would induce bandits and would-be troublemakers to settle down as yeoman farmers. It would also deliver land to more responsible Mexicans, meaning themselves. Landholders, they knew, would fight to protect their holdings and would even pay taxes to finance police protection. Individualistic agrarian competitiveness, with its prospect of gain, would burn up the disruptive energies that fueled brigandage. New opportunities within the law would sponge up illicit behavior outside of it. Mexico would become a nation.[8]

National integration would itself contribute to domestic tranquility through its aura of equality and unity. It would also stimulate economic development by creating a national market and freeing the flow of commerce. Foreign investment would generate industrialization of the country, and colonized European farmers could teach Mexicans the value of disciplined hard work and profitable agrarian practices. Other obstacles to economic growth, the Liberals insisted, would be removed when laissez faire worked the wonders it had already worked in Western Europe and in the United States. All these reforms would result in the greatest good for the greatest number. Nothing of the sort happened, of course, which is one of the reasons why there was a revolution in 1910. Reformers and revolutionaries have yet to reconcile the need for individual freedom with that of significant restructuring, and the price for this failure is terrible human suffering.[9]

Reaction to the Liberal reforms, as imbedded in the Constitution of 1857, was immediate. The Church employed various schemes to protect its holdings. The Indians tossed land surveyors off their property, and the army went to war. General Félix Zuloaga pronounced against the constitution in the capital, sent Comonfort packing into exile, and named himself acting president. Meanwhile, some seventy congressmen fled north, recognizing as president the legitimate constitutional successor, Chief Justice Juárez of the Supreme Court. Mexico now had two presidents, each of whom raised his army through promises of patronage, and, because the two presidents had no revenue with which to pay their soldiers, the two chief executives had to let the troops pillage. As custodians of the capital and therefore nominally in charge of national affairs, the Conservatives were charged with domestic order, while the Liberals encouraged disorder to keep the centralists at bay—and the Juaristas knew just how to do it. They incited bandits to roam in the guise of patriots, and they issued even more radical political decrees. Brigand chiefs like Aureliano Rivera received army commissions and were encouraged to loot in the name of the constitution. Other bandits more expediently named themselves generals and pillaged under whatever political standard suited the moment. Because they assumed that the Church financed Zuloaga, the Liberals nationalized virtually all Church property, although there was no way to enforce this edict in the midst of civil war. Furthermore, they asserted that priests who did not publicly advocate adherence to the constitution could be shot. Such threats and the bandits effectively fed national discord.[10]

The horrendously destructive civil war lasted three years. For most of that time the Conservatives kept Juárez on the run, but they never possessed the military strength to mount the counter-guerrilla action necessary to crush their opponents. In fact, neither side had the financial resources to sustain an offensive, so the war settled into a defensive clawing between the major adversaries. But bandits thrived in the unsettled atmosphere, and so did many others who used the excuse of unrest to settle old scores. Time finally ran out on the Conservatives. Counter-guerrillas who quite quickly won their first battles might still lose the war, and as the resources of the Conservatives ran thinner, support shifted toward the Liberals.

The contenders changed sides briefly in 1861, when the Liberals occupied the capital and drove their rivals into rural skirmishing. Now responsibility for internal tranquility fell to the Juaristas, but they had little opportunity to impose any program before French interventionists, paving the way for Maximilian, forced them into an even more desperate holding action in the provinces. Once installed in the royal palace, the surprisingly benign and understanding archduke, now emperor, offered amnesty to his opponents and peace to the nation. Juárez naturally refused, and so did thousands of other Mexicans, some of whom were patriots, while others used the turbulence for personal betterment. Tossing out the foreigners became a special license for rampant disorder, which eventually caused Maximilian to commit a blunder that controverted his true liberality. The emperor's sponsor, Louis Napoleon, declared in 1865 that this was "not the time for liberalism or clemency," and Maximilian reluctantly concurred, issuing his Black Decree of October 3, which permitted the prompt execution of any Mexican who joined or shielded an armed troop that was in conflict with the government. The law opened the sluice gates for personal denunciations and witch hunts, and quickened the pace of resistance.[11]

French military planners finally turned to pacification through militarization in accord with the highly regarded Prussian

Plan, which gave almost all males a military obligation. On second thought, the French questioned the capacity of Mexicans to imitate Prussians. To the French, Mexicans had a character defect. Decades of unrest had made them naturally rebellious, and no amount of French regeneration could ever tame them.[12] Yet what French civilization under Maximilian could not accomplish, capitalism eventually secured. When it became worthwhile for Mexicans to settle down, a sufficient number of power brokers designed a pattern of domestic peace in their own best interests. Tranquility, of course, did not arrive evenly or overnight. Another twenty years passed after the French had withdrawn and the monarchists had been defeated or coopted before the Mexicans worked out their political and profit-making arrangements. Even then it took a highly visible constabulary like the Rurales to hold the loose-fitting pieces in place.

The Liberals had long understood the desirability of a tough rural police force. No matter that they preached federalism, they aimed at centralism and needed a vehicle to carry their intentions into the countryside across the nation. They also wanted to counterbalance the presence of a hostile military. Moreover, the Minister of the Interior, José María LaFragua, a sophisticated and intelligent creole lawyer who directed public security matters, had a model. Spain's new horse troops, the Guardia Civil, effectively served central government and even enhanced its ability to withstand political overthrow. Mexican Liberals sought the same ends.[13]

Spain, after its guerrilla war against Napoleon I earlier in the century, experienced a long period of instability marked by institutionalized banditry. Monarchists vied with liberal factions for political power, and in 1833 progressive liberals took control, opposed by both the moderate sector of their own party and by the royalists. The major contention between the liberal factions concerned municipal liberties. The progressives wanted towns and villages free to run their own affairs, defended by a local militia, but the moderates feared anarchy and advocated a centrally-managed national life. Both sides distrusted the army. In parallel circumstances, Mexico's Liberals sided with the moderates. Years of upheaval had led them, also, to despise chaos more than they

Stagecoach travelers in mid-nineteenth-century Mexico seemed disappointed if on their journey brigands did not rob them at least once. *Instituto Nacional de Antropología e Historia, Secretaría de Educación Pública, México*

Chucho el Roto, the phantom bandit, evaded arrest through ingenious disguises, here as a woman. *Instituto de la Enciclopedia de México*

Highwaymen were often celebrated members of Mexican society, remembered in paintings and praised in popular folk songs called *corridos*. *Instituto Nacional de Antropología e Historia, Secretaría de Educación Pública, México*

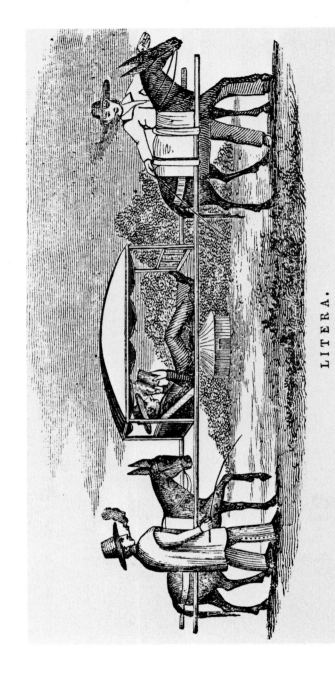

LITERA.

Before the stagecoach, travelers jounced across Mexico's rugged countryside on decorative litters uneasily suspended between two burros. *Brantz Mayer, Mexico as It Was and as It Is (New York: J. Winchester, New World Press, 1944)*

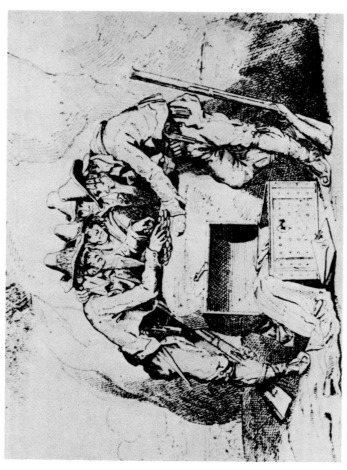

Bandits were petty entrepreneurs who, despite the risk, often grew rich dividing their booty and selling their loot to more respected people. *Instituto Nacional de Antropología e Historia, Secretaría de Educación Pública, México*

The "Thunderbolt of Sinaloa," Heraclio Bernal, won nationwide acclaim as a social bandit for his daring bedevilment of federal authorities in the 1880s. *Instituto Nacional de Antropología e Historia, Secretaría de Educación Pública, México*

ARRIEROS.

Through much of the nineteenth century, commerce in Mexico depended largely upon the strong backs of burros and the skills of the muleteers to keep the beasts moving. *Brantz Mayer*, Mexico as It Was and as It Is *(New York: J. Winchester, New World Press, 1844)*

To emphasize their dedication and skill, the Rurales frequently posed for photographs with the outlaws they captured. *Amon Carter Museum, Fort Worth, Texas*

loved liberty, and this disposition caused them to favor a centralized police force over the militia as the means to political
socialization.[14]

Police are structurally the offspring of politics. They arise out
of political need and effect political education and control. They
are no doubt shaped by economic and social realities, but they
remain in essence a political instrument of the state. But why do
they arise at a certain time in a certain place? May common factors
be found in the origins of Italy's carabinieri, the French gendarmerie, Germany's state police, or the British "bobbies"? David
H. Bayley concludes that differing forces were at work in those
European countries when their state police, more or less as known
today, were founded. Mexico too had its peculiarities. But Bayley
also determined that certain factors more than others seemed to
stimulate the formation of state police. Population growth, ur-
banization, industrialization, rising criminality, a foreign threat,
or even an ideological crusade—all, to some degree, might influence the formation of police. Yet a more general and powerful
propellant has been the consolidation of national power, with its
new priorities of law and order. France and Italy each founded
their constabularies at the time for a new concentration of political
power. Prussian landowners gradually lost their traditional police
functions as the state gathered strength. Thus, as Mexico's
executive acquired power, the Rurales became the president's
police.[15]

But Mexico's Liberals were at the outset not convinced of their
own power and direction. Their desire to buttress the government's
authority conflicted with their ideal of community participation
and led them to develop a hybrid federal-state police force with
mixed responsibilities and controls. The states basically handled
city and village security with pedestrian patrols of militiamen,
while the central government financed a constabulary for rural
enforcement. The government explained the details and functions
of the organization in a decree that made it official on January 16,
1857. The militia-like town units also aimed to teach civics, and
the rural police would crack through barriers to national
unification—like the bandits—and link rural districts to the
capital. Mexico City was out to regain its colonial hegemony, but

that could not be done by force alone. Only when it became more worthwhile to join the federal government than to fight it would regional strongmen agree to central direction.[16]

Interior Minister LaFragua also intended that the new police forces should counter the influence of the unpredictable army, and he imposed military discipline on them to shape the militia and the rural police. Army-like regulations governed training, equipment, promotions, and punishments, and LaFragua recruited ex-soldiers to fill the ranks of the new force. But problems arose at once. For example, both civil and military authorities, from generals to judges, had emergency powers to utilize the police for pacification, an unwelcome temptation to abuse and separatism. The minister floundered; his project needed rethinking and reworking. Before he could reform the militia, bandits forced his hand.[17]

Some thirty brigands raided the prosperous, Spaniard-owned hacienda of San Vicente, near Cuernavaca, in December 1856. Five Spaniards died resisting the assault, at the very time Mexican diplomats were in Madrid trying to improve relations with the mother country. Worse yet, rumors had it that the reform leader Juan Alvarez himself had ordered the attack, an especially delicate assertion. Other Spanish property had recently been looted in Morelos and Guerrero, where the greedy Pintos of Alvarez liked to plunder. A thoroughly embarrassed Mexican government sent five hundred additional army troops to Cuernavaca, along with a special judicial investigator, to get those bandits. Alvarez agreed to return to Guerrero, and, as a final measure of good faith, LaFragua introduced his new security force, ready or not.[18] A couple of undermanned and underfinanced Rural Police units were organized to guard the roads around Mexico City, but the enterprise soon collapsed in the turbulence of civil war. The Liberals had nevertheless established a precedent that they meant to follow, if and when they won the war.[19]

The Juárez regime and the Liberals eventually won the struggle against Zuloaga and his Conservatives and then against Maximilian and the monarchists. Within a few months after each victory, one in 1861 and the other in 1867, the government turned its attention immediately to public security and renewed its determination to establish a rural police force. However, the pacification problem had assumed a new, highly serious dimension in the 1860s. What could be done with the guerrillas-turned-patriots-turned-bandits-turned-guerrillas who had made those two Liberal triumphs possible? Earlier, LaFragua had not been forced to grapple with this situation, so critical for successful revolutionaries everywhere. In the mid-1850s, many of the opposition's generals had quietly retired to their homes. Others, as professional soldiers, made an orderly transfer to the Liberal standard. As for the victors, many of the leaders supported the Reform only to ensure their regional dominance; they collected their armies and returned to their strongholds. Alvarez took his Pintos to Guerrero, Manuel Doblado took his soldiers to Guanajuato, and Santiago Vidaurri led his men to Nuevo León, where they could protect his lucrative economic ties to the United States.[20]

The civil war and foreign intervention had, however, forced the republicans to ally themselves with bandit gangs for survival. Now, in return for services so splendidly rendered, the bandits wanted well-paid jobs, preferably in government. They, like everyone else, searched for security, but brigands, if not properly compensated, could continue as brigands, and many did so.

The bandits emphasized their demands with an upsurge in pillaging after the official termination of hostilities against both the Conservatives and the French. Newspapers like *El Siglo XIX*, in the capital, commented on the change in the accustomed bandit style. Whereas brigands had formerly been "kind, often attentive, and limited themselves to stealing from transients," the post-Intervention brand had become kidnappers—a clear sign to the paper of national degeneration.[21]

Despite *El Siglo's* gloomy observation, Mexico was not necessarily on the decline. The boldness of the bandits simply signaled their position of command, and their actions could be outrageous. In March 1868, peons on the Manzano hacienda in Zapotlán, Jalisco, warmly welcomed the arrival of four itinerant missionaries dressed in vestments of the St. Vincent de Paul Society. The priests assured the workers that their living conditions would soon improve, heard their confessions, and gave them communion. Then they visited with the well-to-do hacendado.

They ate Manzano's food, drank his wine, kidnapped him during the night, and delivered a ransom demand to his laborers the following day. Manzano's fate remains unknown. Newspapers did not report his ransom, release, or murder.[22]

Such kidnappings were not in any way limited to the countryside. The bandits also braved downtown Mexico City. They took a wealthy French national, Bassot, from the flourishing mill where he worked, blindfolded him, and then crammed him into a grave-like hole beneath the floor of a country shack. A twelve-year-old boy periodically opened the tomb to feed the victim. Bassot was on several occasions allowed out only long enough to sign a succession of ransom notes dictated by his abductors. After a desperate escape, Bassot implicated five men and the youngster in the crime. One was killed resisting arrest. Two others and the youth received the death sentence, subsequently commuted to life imprisonment. The other two escaped.[23]

Kidnapping remained a sensation of the times, and Mexicans speculated on its originator, perhaps Alexandre Dumas in his novels or, more likely, they thought, José María Cobos, who had terrified the *New York Times* correspondent and who mixed his banditry with Conservative politics.[24]

National disorder was exacerbated by the need to discharge thousands of nonbandits who had joined the Liberals with the promise of bettering their lives. Many were latecomers to the cause, men and women whose patriotism took shape after the result of the struggle had been determined. They joined the republicans as the French army withdrew and the fate of Maximilian became certain. These come-lately loyalists also wanted recompense and steady employment, or they too threatened to become bandits.

The government could not afford a large army, for both political and financial reasons. It had to release its soldiers and hope that they would return to their former subsistence living, but they knew that the country's war-stricken economy could not possibly absorb them all. Juárez turned loose some forty thousand of these ex-soldiers in 1867. The subsequent upsurge in brigandage not only disrupted commerce and the social order but also rattled the regime politically. Presidential rivals, like Porfirio Díaz, stirred the pot by assuring the former soldiers that they had been cheated by the Juárez government and by openly questioning the ability of the administration to enforce peace.[25]

The Juaristas, however, had not forgotten LaFragua's experiment with a national police force. The new Minister of the Interior, Francisco Zarco, understood brigandage to be the expected outcome of prolonged civil strife, and he had warned critics in 1861 that a weak national treasury inhibited the government's ability to control it. He had promised some relief, nevertheless, and the administrative organization of Mexico's Rural Police Force had quietly taken place on May 6, 1861—quietly, because so many powerful Mexicans were bound to protest the establishment of a political police controlled by the president.[26]

The plan called for the creation of four corps of rural policemen, each with its commander, paymaster, 18 officers, and 255 enlisted men. The government named the senior officers, who then selected their subordinates. All men were to be volunteers, no *leva* (conscription) as with the army. Pay son.ewhat higher than military wages would attract personnel. The men would finance their horses, uniforms, and equipment through a complicated system of daily deductions, an investment that would also help to teach responsibility and self-discipline, in other words, make the corpsmen good Liberals.[27] Considerable internal debate took place over which ministry should control the police—War or Interior. To give them to War would only strengthen the army, but the guards needed to be controlled by military-like procedures. The Interior minister, on the other hand, might use the outfit to manipulate the elections he oversaw, yet public security was part of his job. The planners straddled the issue, for the time being, by giving administrative responsibility for the corps to Interior and letting War direct the field activities. Soon after the Intervention ended in 1867, the organization expanded to seven better-organized corps, and the entire operation became a dependency of the Interior minister, an adjustment that rescued the constabulary from intra-cabinet rivalries and confirmed its political and public order functions.[28]

In fact, Juárez the federalist, under the impact of civil war and congressional challenge, moved steadily to the right. Domestic order seemed to demand it. To fill the ranks of the fledgling outfit the government sensibly converted bandits into policemen. Or, better said, some bandits agreed to become policemen. It was their choice, not that of the administration. Well-known brigands, along with any number of suspect characters, became rural policemen, but many of them also kept a hand in banditry, and as a result order and disorder developed still another blend.

Chapter 5
Bandits into Police—
and Vice Versa

What king or country has not had sense enough to attempt to turn bandits into policemen? To let the lawless enforce the law? What better way to attain domestic tranquility than, as Hobsbawm suggests, to convert the poachers into gamekeepers? Bourbon kings in Spain's century of enlightenment, the eighteenth, pardoned bandits and inducted them into royal service. Russian tsars and lords gave the Cossacks land and privileges for police protection. The Khonds of India's Bengal area, displaced by British capitalism, plundered openly and in good conscience until many turned to law enforcement for the imperialists. Bandit leaders around Palermo in mid-nineteenth-century Sicily had special charge of public security. About that same time, the astute Mexican Liberal lawyer Manuel Doblado, clever enough to become Guanajuato's governor even before reaching the constitutionally legal age, is said to have built his Mexican power base with brigands-turned-lawmen. And Lampião, the most famous of Brazil's cangaceiros, in January 1926 negotiated with federal and state authorities to help track down the communist Prestes column that was prowling the country's Northwest, even though Lampião may have been more interested in securing government weapons than in joining the manhunt.[1]

Former outlaws figured among the best lawmen who brought order to the American West. Terrified town councilmen lured gunslingers to their side by putting a tin star on their vests. But such badges did not always effect the intended cure. A member of Billy the Kid's gang drifted into Kansas to become marshall of Caldwell and ended up at the end of a rope, for bank robbery. Burt Alvord, raised in Tombstone, Arizona, was a deputy sheriff and

51

cattle thief. He guided criminals to safety in Mexico for pay but, if
they were broke, turned them in for ransom. Despite his record as a
highwayman, or maybe because of it, Henry Plummer was elected
a Montana sheriff and soon organized one of the most notorious
brigand outfits in the region. He stationed deputies around gold-
mining camps to learn about their shipments; then he plundered
the train. Wyatt Earp and Bat Masterson worked both sides of the
law, and Gregorio Cortez, who killed a couple of South Texas
sheriffs and was pardoned by the governor, ended up in Mexico's
Rurales.[2]

Bandits became policemen for as many individual reasons as
there were people who made the change. The process was
facilitated by the aspirations of so many outlaws to become
lawmen. A nineteenth-century French intellectual who studied the
bandit-to-police metamorphosis wrote that bandits knew that they
entered their business at substantial risk, so that, when they
became proficient, they joined the state as policemen, which was
where they had always wanted to be. As he concluded, "when one
knows from one's own practice the crafts and dodges of the
blockade runner, it is better [safer and sufficiently rewarding] to
devote oneself to repression."[3] Eric Wolf noted that in their
alliance with rural gentry, brigands easily adapted to the habits
and style of the gentry, and "then they adopted those norms."
From the viewpoint of a government, especially one that is weak or
inefficient, robbers must be conciliated like any other armed force.
Hobsbawm explains how kings first pursued outlaws but, unable to
vanquish them, took them into royal service.[4] Scholars continue to
search for Robin Hood in royal documents that may authenticate
wages paid to an R. Hood by the king.[5] Police evolved from former
ruffians who prowled the edges of forests where they could jump a
trader or a traveler with the demand, "Your money or your life."
The bandits had to be paid. Eventually they were bought off to
protect, not to rob. "Taxes were the subscription, the premium
paid by the robbed to the robbers. Joyous and grateful, the
plundered placed themselves behind the knights of the highway,
and proclaimed them the supporters of order . . . , consecrated
them a legitimate government."[6]

Brigands in mid-nineteenth-century Mexico similarly forced the government's hand. Pacification required assimilation of the bandits into a police force, so brigands like Abraham Plata were amnestied into service as corps commanders. Not only did the practice help to ensure a semblance of public order, it also removed, or at least eroded, a major obstacle to political centralization and national integration. The Juárez government aimed at organizing a tough political police force to carry out its program, to counterbalance the quarrelsome, factionalized army, and to provide decent employment for ex-guerrillas, not all of whom had been bandits. With these objectives in mind the Liberal administration of Benito Juárez founded Mexico's Rural Police Force in 1861.[7]

His uniform distinguished the Rural. It confirmed his transition from bandit to lawman, since the Rurales dressed much like the most powerful bandits of the time, the Plateados. Both wore the *charro* outfit, and everyone understood what it meant: its wearer could outride, outrope, outshoot, outdrink, and outwomanize any other cowboy, from whatever land. The Rurales rode and strutted in dove-gray bolero jackets and suede-leather, tight-fitting trousers embroidered with ornate braiding and studded with silver buttons. On their heads they wore the heavy felt sombrero that had emerged from the heat of the Mexican countryside to become a national symbol. Each sombrero bore the number of the corps to which its wearer belonged. The sombrero became for Mexico's Rurales what the tri-cornered hat had become to Spain's Guardia Civil, the clear symbol of authority. But the sombrero also emphasized the idea that "This man is a MAN."[8]

The distinctive uniforms also firmly separated the corps from the army. The British deliberately did the same with their police "bobby" dress. In Mexico the village people, especially, regarded the army as an outside force come to crush resistance and independence. The police, though representatives of the state, tended to settle into a community and tried to convince the populace to follow the law. The Rurales might coerce; the army hammered. The Rural Police were meant to be the emissaries of a firm but just, and occasionally even kindly, patron. Image-building enhanced their presence. The Rurales rode in magnificent holiday parades in the capital on patriotic dates; they staged fabled shows of riding at international expositions; the president toasted them annually at a lavish banquet; they received praise in *corridos*. But despite the fact that during the Díaz dictatorship almost all the corpsmen were former campesinos and artisans, the public still imagined a bandit heritage. For example, according to one Mexican newspaper, "The Arab and gaucho horsemen cannot equal, cannot even be compared to, those valiant Plateados of our Rural Police Corps."[9]

An international incident propelled the Rurales into action. An English sea captain and two of his officers were returning by stagecoach to their ship, anchored in Veracruz harbor, after an inspection of British mining interests in central Mexico, when bandits waylaid them near Córdoba. The sea captain had gotten off to an early morning start without armed escort. In his safekeeping on the stage were the niece of a British consul, her three children, and a French lady, Eugenia Maison. The group succeeded in traveling unscathed through heavily-infested bandit country during the first part of the journey, although the captain, his officers, and the seaman who rode a high seat up front next to the driver kept their weapons handy. But the captain's arrogance undermined his prudence.

The passengers were dozing just before dawn when the stage jolted to a halt, tossing the occupants into a heap of bodies and luggage. They soon realized their plight. Three mounted bandits were lined up on each side of the coach, their rifles poked through the curtained windows. The captain drew and fired his pistol to defend the party, but the gun misfired. The sailor outside had better luck; his rifle fire caused the bandits to back off. Still the brigands peppered the coach with bullets. The captain struggled to get out, but as he opened a side door a bullet hit his leg and tumbled him onto the muddy roadway. Madame Maison was also seriously wounded and collapsed near the captain. The officers climbed out of the other side of the stage and engaged the robbers in a lively firefight. The travelers finally forced the outlaws to flee, and the battered group proceeded to the next town for medical attention. There the French woman died. European powers, including the French and British, had already been demanding that the Juárez government pay off its debts to them, so this incident could not have occurred at a more critical time for the shaky government of Mexico. Since it appeared that the administration could not safeguard foreign interests, a show of force, or even intervention by the European powers, might be justified.[10]

Juárez did what he could to counter European outrage. The government in Mexico City ordered army troops to capture the bandits who had attacked the stage and to judge them in accordance with extra-official powers that permitted the execution of brigands. At the same time the central authority hired two mercenary outfits—private security units that had supported the Liberals for a price—to patrol the highway from Mexico City to Veracruz. The best constabulary force, two hundred strong, was headed by Rafael Cuéllar, who may have had bandit antecedents. Cuéllar became the Inspector General of Rurales in the 1880s, but, before that, he had helped to quell anarchist-influenced land reform movements near Chalco in the state of México. In the process, Cuéllar openly sold government-owned arms and ammunition to hacienda owners for his own profit. Eyewitnesses testified to his corruption, and investigations followed, but Cuéllar had the political influence necessary to rebuff the charges. Aureliano Rivera, a genuine bandit-revolutionary-patriot, captained the second Rural Police unit, and soon both he and Cuéllar functioned as well-paid emergency security forces for the government.[11]

By the autumn of 1861, four official Rural Police troops functioned around Mexico City. Bandits gave them no rest. Manuel Quesada's First Corps, assigned to the Cuernavaca district, simply declined to dispute the Plateados, and when the Fourth, under Francisco M. Salazar, ran into nearly a hundred bandits at Tula, it quickly broke ranks and ran for cover. Thirty died in the slaughter that ensued. The government brought Salazar to the capital to explain the disaster but then vindicated the commander. It was no time to chance sending a disgruntled commander into banditry.[12]

With important Conservative generals like Leonardo Márquez and ex-president Zuloaga still active in the countryside, contingents of these earliest Rurales frequently served as scouts for army divisions and as anti-guerrilla units. Quesada's force proved especially effective at flushing out enemy ambushes, and his corps thoroughly impressed the young general in charge of the army's advance guard, who was Porfirio Díaz. When Díaz became president, he put simlar units to his immediate political use.[13] But now there was no opportunity for the administration to shape its new constabulary, for French imperialists threatened the very existence of the republic. The Liberals no longer wanted domestic peace. They needed to foment disorder, and they turned loose the bandits on the French.

Juárez had reservations about an alliance with proven bandits. He apologized for such a necessity to the government of the United States, which was friendly to his republicanism. "I regret the excesses of Rojas, Carbajal, González Ortega, and Pueblita," the beleaguered president professed, "but it is necessary to tolerate them, or else they will abandon us, and I have made our allies [the Americans] understand that such guerrillas operate in order to take all sorts of supplies from the enemy."[14]

The brigands certainly did plunder at will, not only the enemy but all citizens, and in the name of national need. No doubt they helped to save the republic from the monarchists, and with peace in 1867 the outlaws demanded what they maintained was their due. Banditry had expanded the economic horizons of these people, and had swept or enticed them to leave a dreary life for one of adventure and opportunity. It put them in touch with others, people with big ideas, and it awakened them to new possibilities. In sum, banditry released individuals from their traditionalism.

Not all of these aggressive self-seekers tried to find recompense from the government. Any number preferred to continue their looting, not just for profit but as a way of life. A Juarista general, Simón Gutiérrez of Jalisco, known as "La Simona," had a short stint as a kidnapper before he was captured and shot. Luckily for Juárez, French counter-guerrillas, before leaving Mexico, exterminated two of the more notorious bandit-patriots, Antonio Rojas and Manuel García Pueblita, who would have been difficult to control under any post-war circumstances. Juárez could forget those two, but he invited others into Rural Police service, where they could enjoy both the official protection of a nation still too weak to enforce discipline and the chance to maraud outside the law. The bandits-policemen extracted their toll as part of the price to be paid for domestic peace, and perhaps only the looted thought the cost too high.[15]

Complaints of dereliction of duty among the Rural Policemen poured into the capital. One detachment of Rurales arrived at a town they were supposed to patrol in the company of brigands. Together they raided the village. Six Rurales on another occasion got drunk, robbed several stagecoaches assigned to their protection, and headed for the mountains as out-and-out bandits. An army officer arrested four corpsmen detached to patrol an hacienda; instead, they burglarized it. Another policeman was jailed when he turned up with goods stolen from a traveler. A company of the Third Corps, thirty-five men, joined a remnant of the imperialist troops to justify their looting as political dissent; next year, in 1870, the entire Second Corps rebelled against the government and rode into banditry. In 1872, the commander of the Seventh Corps converted his men to brigands to rob the government he was sworn to defend, and a special detail organized to terminate the defiance of the great Nayarit cuadillo, Manuel Lozada, ended up joining his camp.[16]

How much more could be expected from corps commanders like León Ugalde and Antonio Carbajal? Ugalde had been an unmitigated and unmerciful bandit chieftain in Querétaro during the Intervention. Police chased him into Michoacán in 1865, where the Liberals received him as a bulwark against the French. Ugalde preferred to plunder, so the republican governor, Vicente Riva Palacio, ordered him shot. Army forces under Lieutenant-Colonel José Acevedo dispersed Ugalde's band, but the leader escaped and eventually received amnesty, provided that he return to Querétaro and raise a troop among his homepeople to fight the French. Ugalde agreed, organized the contingent, and returned to Michoacán. After several spirited encounters with the invaders, Ugalde lapsed into his old ways. He really did not want to fight the French; he wanted to pillage. Riva Palacio again issued a death warrant for the brigand, but Ugalde's fighting fury was critically needed against the enemy, and so his robber band ended up in the regular army, where it could be watched if not trained. He lasted out the war and its immediate aftermath, fighting here, looting there. He became commander of the Fourth Rural Police Corps on April 1, 1872, where his brother, also an experienced brigand, joined him as a ranking officer.[17]

With his unit's payroll now in hand, Ugalde seems to have lost some of his bandit fervor. Maybe not. Some find peculation more desirable than kidnapping and pillage. Ugalde's men complained that they were not being paid by their commander and that he had set up a high-priced store that he forced the guards to patronize. Brigands often made good capitalists, which is what they wanted to be all along. One of the country's leading newspapers, *El Monitor Republicano*, investigated the allegations against Ugalde and concluded: "The services that Colonel Ugalde lent the country in the past are a guarantee of his continuing good service as commander of the corps." No one wanted Ugalde back in the field as a bandit.[18]

General Carbajal made a career of recruiting bandits to political service, and his brigade lent the Liberals important strength both in the civil war and against the Intervention. The War minister in early 1861 ordered him to trim down the size of his unit and to weed out the criminals, but with banditry spiraling because unemployed ex-servicemen found work where they could, the minister once again allowed Carvajal to pack his troop with a new bunch of brigands. In 1867 these men formed the nucleus of the Third Rural Police Corps. Cuéllar's commercial security guard became the Second Corps.[19] Aureliano Rivera, another patriot-guerrilla-bandit, also took his Defenders of Liberty in and out of government service, depending on his prognosis of chances for personal profit.[20]

In 1875, more than a thousand Rurales, circulating in forty-two detachments, patrolled the countryside, mostly in the central valley of Mexico. They were easy to fault for their bad discipline and excesses, but, if it really does take a thief to catch a thief, the corpsmen proved it could be done (which does not mean that all enlistees were robbers). The rural guards killed the famous Tlaxcalan bandit "Chato" Cruz and destroyed nests of brigands in Jalisco. They pursued Miguel Negrete in Puebla, Paulino Noriega around Pachuca, and Luis León in the state of México, all of whom cloaked their depredations with political complaints against the regime. Negrete was especially prone to issue political decrees motivated by anarchist sentiments. The line between brigand and agrarian reformer can also be quite thin.[21]

In October 1875, in Michoacán, Rurales shot down Colonel Máximo Molina, a long-time and respected Liberal who had rendered important military service to the republic. Rumor had it that Molina was trying to surrender, and newspapers charged political murder, but the administration labeled Molina a bandit and rewarded the policemen who had hounded him down. Centralization was on the march.[22]

Sometimes the Rural Police got in over their heads. When a bandit gang of nearly four hundred kidnapped two officials from the isolated village of Tejupilco de Hidalgo, in the southwestern corner of the state of México, the Rurales demanded the unharmed return of those authorities or else Tejupilco would be ravaged, its remaining inhabitants killed, and property ransacked. The bandits immediately responded. They sent back their victims dead, viciously mutilated and strapped across the backs of mules, to emphasize the contempt of the bandits for the police. So far as is known, the Rurales took no revenge on the town. Such incidents undoubtedly made the corpsmen think twice about whom they chased where.[23]

At best, an unregulated, uneven performance marked the corps, whose acts were too aggressive at one time and too hesitant or indolent the next. Stagecoach passengers reported that the corpsmen refused to chase bandits who had divested the travelers of their personal belongings. The governor of the state of México alleged that guards along the Toluca road settled into their siesta long before the 1:00-p.m. stage had reached their checkpoint. Puebla's governor complained that the guards displayed a surly contempt for local citizens and their officials. They had even beaten one municipal official with belts after robbing a townsman of four pesos and his blanket.[24]

Such charges, and many others brought by public officials against the corps, were rather carefully investigated by the organization's administration and, at times, by federal inspectors. Denials and rebuttals followed. Some urged the creation of state security units to replace the federal Rurales. Others counseled patience.[25] Most important, the complaints indicate the extent to which the Rurales by the mid-1870s were beginning to be considered as formidable agents of central government. State and local authorities naturally resisted their intrusions. Similar conflicts ran right through the dictatorship of Porfirio Díaz during the uncertain scramble for patronage, profit, power, and security that accompanied development.

Brigands and Rurales remained an important part of the milieu, despite the disappearance of the Ugaldes, Carvajals, and Riveras. No more Plateados appeared. But bandits with perhaps even greater social influence came to challenge the government and to raise common hopes for personal betterment. Nor could the Rurales be purged of their drive for self-improvement outside the law. Greatly changed national conditions in the Porfiriato altered the relationship between bandits and policemen but never did eliminate their overlap.

PART II

TOWARD THE
WESTERN MODEL

Chapter 6
Order, Disorder, and
Development

When Mexico's bandits became Rurales, they remained in large part brigands. Bandits and policemen: they are not really the antagonists they are assumed to be. They are fluid and interchangeable—even as one dominates, the other is actively present. They are double agents of order and disorder. Thus, the relative domestic order that succeeded the French Intervention was rife with disorder. Order, in fact, only began to make some headway when it became more profitable for the disorderly to embrace peace. Even then, pacification bred new forms of discontent.

The dilemma for Mexico's modernizers was clear: the power brokers viewed capitalistic development as the means to peace, power, and profit, but potential investors declined to risk their money in such a turbulent environment. To both Mexican politicans and foreign investors it seemed that peace and progress required strong central government. For more or less two decades—1867 to 1887—Mexico edged toward integration, toward political centralism and a national market. These so-called hallmarks of modernization met with great resistance. Gaining in fits and starts, the process advanced more through compromise than forceful direction. Regional and quasi-military strongmen did not necessarily capitulate to central demands; they agreed, rather, to cooperate because they had more to gain through partnership than through autonomy. All of this took some doing. Those in power naturally declined to relinquish political office, their avenue to income and patronage. Revolution therefore remained the only way to pry them from office until other sources of profit and status were found outside the government.

Four presidential administrations—those of Juárez (1867–1872), Lerdo de Tejada (1872–1876), Díaz (1876–1880), and González (1880–1884)—all bent on modernization but in competition for the proceeds, contributed to changing the national framework until international conditions finally confirmed Díaz in power. Juárez was conciliatory toward the Church and the imperialists, inaugurated tax reforms to fund a treasury needed to pay off the military, and attacked state taxation that funded municipal and regional independence. But he lacked the political and financial strength to develop consistency in his program.[1]

Lerdo created a legislative senate that had broad authority to intervene in the affairs of the states. A senate gave him the means, within the law, to hand-pick governors and other officials. Anxious to dramatize his program of internal order, the president in 1874 organized a pompous journey, escorting foreign diplomats and Mexican dignitaries through the once turbulent valley of Cuernavaca to a lavish banquet inside the bandit-infested state of Guerrero. Lerdo proudly pointed to the presence of his cabinet and eight governors, and asked how such a gathering was possible except in times of guaranteed tranquility. Guaranteed, all right. The diplomats certainly had welcomed the large cavalry escort that guarded their excursion, and also the detachments of Rurales stationed in every village and town through which they had passed. They felt far from recommending investment in Mexico.[2]

Lerdo could claim some accomplishments for his administration—inauguration of the Veracruz-Mexico railroad (1873) and the elimination of the rebellious Indian caudillo Manuel Lozada—but the country was by no means quieted. Political rivals like Porfirio Díaz intrigued for his job. The Church was riled up over the president's enforcement of the Reform Laws, and bandits still ravaged much of the countryside at will. Yet Lerdo's overall intentions matched the national direction undertaken by the Liberal reformers, and he exploited regional rivalries to get rid of Lozada, the fearsome Tiger of the Sierra of Alicia.[3]

For twenty years Manuel Lozada dominated the economically attractive Tepic region north of Guadalajara with his fearsome Cora and Huichol Indian guerrillas. Lozada's personal intentions are still under review. He was given to compromise with central authority but perhaps only to wring concessions for his district. He supported Juárez against the Conservatives and then the imperialists against the republicans. He espoused radical land reform, but so did others in search of adherents. Without a doubt Lozada meant to preserve regional autonomy for his people, but the Liberal reformers would have none of that.[4]

Juárez severed Tepic from the state of Jalisco and made it a federal entity so that he could order the army to go after Lozada. Agents provocateurs then goaded the chieftain into a direct confrontation with his most formidable rival, General Juan Corona, the military governor of Jalisco, who lamented the loss of Tepic. There stood Lozada in that January of 1873, poised at the gates of Guadalajara with his populist army—warriors, their women, dogs, chickens, and belongings—to insist on regional autonomy and radical agrarian change. Romantic. Magnificent. But Corona had the artillery and quickly dispersed the native multitude back to its mountain lair in ragged defeat.[5]

Army soldiers captured Lozada, betrayed by two of his lieutenants, as he bathed in a mountain stream, and executed him under congressional authority that had suspended judicial guarantees for bandits. It was outright political murder in the name of progress, and others were to follow, even that of Juan Corona. At his death the Tiger protested only his concern for the people of Tepic—and his followers remembered.[6] Rurales spent the next forty years unsuccessfully trying to impose order on the district. Elsewhere the centralists had better luck, for when the hacendados, caciques, and merchants opted for an alliance with the federal government, they sapped brigandage of its sustenance. Banditry did not evaporate, of course, nor did bandits sever all their connections with rural strongmen, but capitalistic development rent apart the brigand curtain that had so thoroughly shielded major rural interests from central controls. Even the bandits-turned-Rurales came to support the new system.

Porfirio Díaz tried twice through elections (1867 and 1869) and once by revolution (1871–1872) to achieve the presidency before he attained it in 1876 by his Tuxtepec revolt. Although they did not especially welcome his earlier rebellion, Juárez and Lerdo realized its benefit. Bandits, including the ferocious gang around Chalco, had joined the Díaz movement, looking to sack their way right into the capital. Their adherence to the rebels gave the administration the chance to lick the brigands and Díaz in one encounter.[7]

Lerdo was not so fortunate in 1876. An odd assortment backed Tuxtepec—dissatisfied militarists, provincials who sought to retain their fiefs, the Church in search of a modus vivendi with government, Indians who held land grievances—and the combination swept Lerdo into exile. But the triumph brought Díaz no peace; it only unleashed a new struggle for booty and a determination to redress grievances. Pledges Díaz had made in search of a constituency now came due. On the eve of military victory he had said, "In the age-old battle of the people between the forces of the people and the hacendado, I shall be on the side of the people, when I achieve power." Indians probably did not believe him but still took him at his word, and the country was wracked by some of the most bitter agrarian unrest since Independence. The states of Michoacán, Guanajuato, Oaxaca, México, Sonora, Querétaro, and Hidalgo all seethed with property disputes. By 1879 the virus had spread to Veracruz and Yucatán. Many such conflicts had more to do with local autonomy than land, but they served notice on the planners of national development that rural interests intended to state their case. And when firebrands like Juan Santiago and Alberto Santa Fe spoke up, the government had to listen.[8]

Juan Santiago in July 1879 traveled from his native village near Tamazunchale in San Luis Potosí to the capital to discuss land distribution with federal officials. When he received no satisfaction, he returned to his townsmen with an invented assurance that Díaz had appointed him the governor of the district with authority to recover native lands lost to hacendados. To prove their intent, more than six hundred Indians attacked the police station at Tamazunchale. Soldiers under Colonel Bernardo Reyes, later a presidential aspirant, brutally put them down, but the revolt spread to neighboring states, where it developed racial overtones. The horde burned and pillaged numerous haciendas. More troops, along with government promises of land relief, finally broke the rebellion. The promises, of course, were not kept. The uncertainty of his political base had at this time forced Díaz to compromise. Later he hammered such opposition.[9]

A more direct political challenge came from radicals like Colonel Alberto Santa Fe, a professed socialist who offered his *Law of the People* to lower-class Mexicans. Santa Fe knew how to write an appeal. He advocated, among other reforms, land distribution, municipal independence, sharply limited military recruitment, and government factories to provide jobs. Indeed, proletarians began to be heard from during the first Díaz administration, and if the workers united with the campesinos, then what? But rural Mexicans generally remained skeptical of outsiders and their ideas for change.[10]

Banditry also flourished as the first Díaz administration failed to meet the promises of Tuxtepec. Dissatisfied ex-soldiers took to the road. Bandits robbed and murdered Congressman Carlos Aristi at Zapote, Jalisco, and *El Monitor Republicano* reported that the infamous robber base at Río Frío, once cleared out, was by 1878 again in the hands of brigands. More than two hundred bandits attacked an hacienda on the Puebla-Guerrero border at 4 o'clock one morning in 1879 and spent the next six hours sacking the premises. Employees lost their clothes and other possessions. Those who resisted were murdered. The hacendado became an object lesson; he was shot ten times and then chopped up with machetes.[11]

An entire mule train that carried 30,000 pesos in proceeds belonging to merchants in Zacatecas and Guanajuato was looted by brigands at Venta de Bata, near Tula in Hidalgo. Investigation indicated that they had accomplices in respected circles, although the names never became public. Several of the bandits were captured in Hidalgo and suffered the "ley fuga"—executing a prisoner on the faked excuse of his attempted escape. Others were sentenced to death in the capital, but officials recovered only 6,143 pesos of the stolen money.[12] Authorities in another case found 15,000 pesos' worth of silver stolen from a stagecoach near Tultepec, state of México, hidden in the home of a well-to-do resident of the town. He was reported shot while trying to flee his house. More ley fuga. Rurals later arrested a municipal official of Tlalnepantla along with several wealthy residents of Mexico City in connection with the Tultepec affair. Bandits still had no difficulty finding collaborators among respected citizens.[13]

These were hard times for Porfirio Díaz. Rebellions and banditry abounded. Restless workers further threatened stability. The United States refused diplomatic recognition to his regime until he secured their mutual border against Indian raiders, cattle rustlers, and contraband. In 1877 Díaz gave the clean-up job to one of his most formidable political challengers, Gerónimo Treviño, who accepted because it gave him control of illicit trade from which he could surely profit. The president, meanwhile, turned American aggressiveness to his own political advantage. He appeased the sharp political partisanship that characterized his own administration by appealing to patriotic sentiment, the need to remain united against foreign threat, principally the United States. "No more 1848s" became a slogan. Where he could, Díaz employed a variety of pressures to ease friends into office, like Ignacio Pesqueira in Sonora and Rafael Craviato in Hidalgo, but he dared not challenge others such as Trinidad García de la Cadena in Zacatecas. Some who received no political payoff turned to rebellion: Canuto Neri in Guerrero, Filomeno Bravo of Colima, and Juan Corona in Jalisco.[14]

Díaz barely hung on. He invested 55 percent of Mexico's revenue in military and police services, and another 30 percent to maintain a contented bureaucracy. Still, domestic peace eluded him. Unexpected help, however, was on the way. The industrial revolution had slowed down in the more developed countries along with profits on manufactured goods. Foreign capitalists searching for other possibilities savored Mexico's potential for profit. The Mexican government further whetted the appetites of the capitalists with a variety of incentives, and, anxious to boost its declining economy, the United States government increasingly cooperated with U.S. businessmen abroad.[15] With foreign risk money available as never before, Mexico had only to tidy up its politics and establish a semblance of domestic order. The profit motive soon spurred achievement of those goals.

Mutual economic opportunities even sealed a detente with the mistrusted United States. Former President Ulysses S. Grant visited

Mexico in 1880 to assure the native elite that his country had no annexation goals and that Americans looked to invest in a railroad network that would firmly tie Mexico to its northern neighbor. Díaz, for his part, emphasized his nation's eagerness to pursue the Western world's example of progress. Together the governments labored to fabricate an inviting climate for investment, and the itchy capitalists welcomed reports of a stabilized Mexico. Look at those elegant Rurales as they paraded before the celebrities at the Zócalo, the capital's main square! U.S. Cavalry Commander Phil Sheridan favorably compared the corps to the world's best. Then he toasted them: "With that cavalry I could encircle the globe!"[16]

Such accolades made sensational reading in the Mexico City press, helped to cement foreign relations, and engraved a handsome invitation to capital; but actually the Rurales, along with so much else, had given Díaz a great deal of trouble since his ascendancy to power. The Rural Police problem for the president was two-fold: 1) to divest the corpsmen of army influence so that they counterbalanced military pressures on the presidency and made any attempted coup more risky, and 2) to ensure their loyalty to the president himself. He knew the political in-fighting would get ever rougher after his revolution triumphed, so, even before victory had been assured, Díaz assigned a political convert, Colonel Pedro A. González, to cast the Rural Police in a Porfirian mold. The republicans had imprisoned González, an ardent imperialist, at the close of the Intervention. Pardoned by Juárez, González repaid the favor by joining the first Díaz rebellion against the government. Defeat, another amnesty, and Tuxtepec followed. González saved Díaz's life in a firefight and in reward became Inspector General of Rurales.[17]

The power of military commanders like Treviño in the north and Manuel González in Michoacán made it difficult to wean the Rurales away from the army. Police corps commanders, for their part, did not often relish separation from the miltiary, which promised a known quantity of corruption and promotions beyond lieutenant colonel, highest rank in the Rurales. Subordinates frequently resisted Inspector González's insistence that his subordinates do Rural Police business with his office. Victorino Torrentera, First Corps commander, complained to Díaz himself that González threatened to eliminate his entire unit from the constabulary simply because Torrentera had discussed supply shortages with an army officer. Third Corps Commander Prisciliano Arteaga levied similar charges against his boss. Díaz mediated. He normally backed his hand-picked inspector but rarely criticized the complainants. It was the famous Díaz conciliation at work, but at this point based on weakness rather than dictatorial strength.[18]

Political demands finally forced Díaz to abandon his inspector general. High-placed government officials criticized González for not using military personnel to prepare formal regulations for the Rural Police Force. A former cabinet minister charged him with building "a little war ministry" for himself and Díaz. The Interior minister expressed reservations about the potential political use of the rural policemen, and labor newspapers remembered the bandit background of the guards. Congressman Francisco Menocal demanded abolition of the corps. Finally, in June 1880, the Interior minister fired González. It came at a time when Díaz was in the midst of a difficult presidential political campaign. He himelf was not a candidate, but several contenders vied for his support, and a serious public question concerned the extent of Díaz's influence on the next administration. Under the circumstances, he could not afford to defend the beleaguered González.[19]

The president, however, did not abandon his Rural Police. By 1880 he had expanded the force by 90 percent to 1,767 men and had won a 400-percent budgetary increase out of the congress. More important for his future, in a dramatic way Díaz began to weld the constabulary to the presidency. When a company of the Fifth Corps revolted in Veracruz in support of a minor political adversary of the administration, the president not only ordered the traitors caught and punished but even erased the entire Fifth Corps from the ledgers of the force. Members of the Fifth who had remained loyal were transferred to other units, and at a series of formal full-dress assemblies, corps commanders ceremoniously read the disgraced Fifth out of the service. The press wondered if Díaz was not overdoing the matter, but it was only the beginning.[20]

Second Lieutenant Rafael Piz, who commanded an Eleventh Corps detachment at Xalostoc, state of Tlaxcala, revolted in mid-

1880 against Díaz's endorsement of General Manuel González as the presidential successor. Piz induced some sixty corpsmen stationed in units around the Federal District to join him. The guards who did so suspected no political implications. Most thought they were headed for routine patrol duty. Others understood the defection but went along because they had been cheated of pay or because of some other grievance against the corps.[21]

Díaz ordered army and Rural Police units to track down the deserters at all cost. Two weeks later they caught up with some of the rebels in Hidalgo. Piz escaped, but sixteen of his men were apprehended. The president ordered them tried immediately by special military court martial at Zumpango, north of the capital, and appointed a special prosecutor to ensure that the defendants be found guilty and sentenced to death. When *El Monitor Republicano* reported that "the government has bad intentions toward the Rurales who rebelled," it understated the matter. *La Patria* noted that the policemen were civilians and not subject to military justice, but still predicted that the corpsmen would be shot. *El Combate* challenged the president to recollect his own rebellious past. They even reviewed it for him and could not understand his "disgust and anger" with such a minor revolt in light of his own rebellions against Juárez and Lerdo. Criticism rolled in, but Díaz meant to deliver a lesson in political discipline.[22]

The tribunal that heard the cases stunned everyone, including Díaz, when it sentenced to death only three noncommissioned officers judged to be co-leaders of the conspiracy. It exonerated the other guards on the grounds that they had only followed orders.

Díaz considered the court's decision insubordination. He ordered the freed men rearrested and consigned them to the army death battalions on diseased Yucatán. They were held incommunicado from their families and shipped in closed railroad cattle cars to Veracruz, then by fetid prison ships to their final destination. The Eleventh Corps commander and his second-in-command were discharged from service for failure to properly supervise their subordinates, and a firing squad eliminated the three sergeants, who insisted their actions were in no way politically motivated. Then Díaz punctuated the affair: the three judges, all respected army generals, were humiliated. One lost his professorship at the military college, the second his commission in the War ministry, and the third his seat in the national congress.[23]

Newspapers in the capital exploded. "We assume that if some colonel had pronounced death sentences on all of the accused, he would have been promoted to general," wrote *El Monitor Republicano.* "Never has society been so disturbed as it has . . . by the official assassination of three unfortunate Rurales by the government." *La Patria* doubted that the government had selected good examples for improving army morale by executing Rurales who had legitimate complaints against their organization. It asked if the government intended to terrorize anyone who entertained thoughts of rebellion.[24] Not everyone. Conciliation remained an important part of Porfirian policy, but, with the Rurales, no compromise. They belonged to the president.

Manuel González may have succeeded to the presidency on the endorsement of Díaz, but once in office in 1881 he proved to be his own man. And it was González who in large part laid the foundation on which Díaz later built his dictatorship. Gonzáles did much of the hard and unpopular work. He destroyed the hegemony of regional strongmen in Puebla, Zacatecas, and Jalisco, and by bringing men like Treviño into his cabinet he forged a link to the north that had escaped Díaz. He amnestied rebels and gave them substantial jobs. General Sóstenes Rocha, who had vigorously defended ex-President Lerdo against Díaz, became director of the military college, and Miguel Negrete, occasional radical reformer in and out of revolt, received a senate seat. Frantic railroad construction under González allowed Mexico City to regain a political, economic, and social prominence it had not known since colonial days. Professionalization of the army and the Rurales brought them into closer line with the administration. The military academy produced specialists in up-to-date warfare, and a new Rural Police code aimed at institutionalizing the constabulary to make it more efficient, more modern, more businesslike. Furthermore, the establishment of a national bank, along with a series of new commercial and civil codes accompanied by tax and fiscal reforms, created an environment for economic development. For the first time in the country's history, congress budgeted more money for economic advancement than for the military. The González administration, in sum, erected much of the infrastructure of a capitalistic society. Corruption, payoffs, and kickbacks existed, of course, but they seemed to be the price paid for peace. At any rate, the beneficiaries of the mounting progress would not have had it any differently.[25]

The great majority of Mexican people also paid for progress. Under new laws, those who could not produce legal title to their property lost it to a public fund, where speculators, surveyors, hacendados, and commercial entrepreneurs gobbled it up. Railroads sliced through other holdings. And, under the impact of development, traditional groups of country people began to break up, not all by brute force, and not always through the greed and rapacity of the dominant groups. Growing cities, enlarged markets with their variety of products, new factories, reawakened mining, greatly facilitated physical mobility, and simply the obviousness of change all combined to beckon numbers of common Mexicans to the new opportunities, or what they perceived as new opportunities. Development created a desire to see, and in doing so it expanded the restricted world view of thousands of Mexicans formerly trapped in the stifling boredom of their isolated lives. Nothing spectacular, just their old world wearing away. Romantics then and today may lament the passing of that traditional village life. Most of them never had to live it. But among those people who did, a good many wanted to get out, and the quickening of the national pulse gave them the chance. If nothing else, they welcomed the freedom to choose.

The most visible aspect of development concerned railroads: the 550 miles of track in 1880 became five times that amount only four years later, including a line from the capital to El Paso, Texas. The building pattern was kaleidoscopic, determined by whim and immediate economic potential. The emphasis was on short-term windfalls rather than long-term gains, and the railroads, built with urban capital, served special interests.[26]

The rails and the accompanying telegraph lines did not really integrate the country. Main lines connected only major commercial centers and the export-import depots. They never conquered Mexico's topography or tamed its distances. Large areas

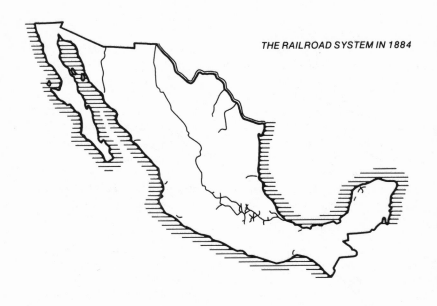

THE RAILROAD SYSTEM IN 1884

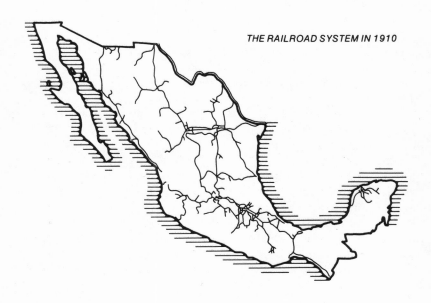

THE RAILROAD SYSTEM IN 1910

in the south and along the Pacific coast lay entirely outside the network. Feeder lines had little to do with population: they tended to be financed by individual entrepreneurs who needed to get their products to a major transport route. Railroads could have been constructed to bring many more Mexicans into the national life, but González and later Díaz were not the nation-builders they are thought to be. Railroads did not make the country modern, only capitalistic.[27]

That great enemy of capitalism, recession, caught up with González in 1883 and gave his enemies a crevice to exploit. As profits dropped, impatience with the president rose. His proposals to renegotiate a British loan and to modernize the nation's small coinage were economically vital but also politically explosive and ineptly presented. The opposition made the creditable plans look like a program for personal enrichment, and the charges against González launched a crusade to recall Díaz to the presidency. Mexico needed Díaz. Only Díaz could assure the peace. International investors trusted Díaz. An American newspaper editor wrote Díaz: "Your friends and the friends of Mexico in the United States regard you more and more as the Messiah of your country."[28] Whether the masses of Mexicans craved Díaz or not is another question, but it did not matter, because they had no share in making the nation's political choices. The ballyhoo in 1884 lofted Díaz virtually without challenge back into the presidency. Within three years his dictatorship had been secured by a pandering congress that rewrote the promise of Tuxtepec, not to mention the national constitution, to permit an unlimited number of terms for presidents and governors. The long, desperate quest for a national political institution to replace the one dismantled by Independence was finally realized by the dictatorship of Porfirio Díaz. Not everyone, of course, embraced the new order, and forces of disorder soon enough emerged.

Chapter 7
The Limits to Dictatorship

Porfirio Díaz managed México for a quarter of a century, thanks to international capitalism. The order was capitalism, with Díaz as top administrator. Handsome returns available outside the presidency relieved pressures on the office or at least undermined potential support for those who aspired to it. Díaz was never free of challengers. Moneyed interests willingly surrendered regional freedoms, so vigorously defended against previous presidents, for a personal dictatorship that could keep the peace and promote further economic gain for the power brokers. Yet the dictatorship had limits. Business competition and the fluctuations of capitalism influenced the president's policies and affected his ability to pull the strings of government. Díaz himself instigated bureaucratic infighting to keep his political enemies at bay. A classic example: he fomented disorder to re-enforce his order. He was not without a dictator's usual obsession with sedition, and he stamped it out with a vengeance, although over all he found that conciliation and compromise best preserved his regime. At times, such compromise was against his better judgment, but the elements of disorder had stated such a strong case that they had to be pacified in order to protect the dictatorship.

The new wave of capitalism did not suddenly wash over Mexico. It arrived in uneven ripples and distributed itself in geographical patches. Parts of the country felt an immediate effect; others had hardly been touched by the end of the period. Some regions remained anchored in tradition while others were gripped by change. Modern communications surrounded places like San José de Gracia in Michoacán, but not even mail service reached the village itself. Although development came with a great flourish, it remained dependent on world economic conditions, which fluc-tuated in ways that have always characterized the process. The convulsions and revulsions of yesterday are the recessions and depressions of today.[1] By the 1870s a gradual decline in profits from their industrial revolution had driven the manufacturing nations into a genuine recession and stimulated a worldwide scramble for new markets—consumer, raw materials, and in-vestment. Mexico proved to be of only limited importance to the new European economic expansion: only 5.5 percent of Europe's total foreign investment to 1910 went into Mexico, although by then 62 percent of all foreign money in the country was European, mainly British and French. But United States capitalists lodged nearly one-half of their foreign investments in their vulnerable neighbor. Not that Mexico resisted. The dictatorship encouraged the trend with risk-reducing inducements including tax breaks, subsidies, loans, and immense gifts of real estate. Such advantages made bandits and disorder of less concern to the businessmen.[2]

Entrepreneurs earned mixed results. Railroads and govern-ment bonds generally resulted in losses, but mineral and agri-cultural exporters profited. Manufacturers did well enough in the 1890s, when they earned a 20-to-25-percent dividend, but a series of business downturns after 1900, along with increased market competition, declining terms of trade, and inflation, created an instability that was reflected in bankruptcies, unionization, and a desperate search for a secure livelihood by large segments of the work force.[3]

So although increasing tax revenues and import duties in 1894 balanced Mexico's budget for the first time, and public works projects showed off material progress, and exports occasionally created fortunes, the economic venture in overview remained spotty, even risky. It did not take much to rattle its timbers. Subject to fluctuating international market conditions, uncontrollable economic cycles, and the vagaries of business psychology, Mexican development could only suffer the overall gyrations of the capitalistic system. And, as a dependent partner, Mexico felt the turbulence much more severely than more developed nations, which could cushion the plunges at the expense of their "colonies." Nor could much be done about the developmental shortcomings of

Mexican geography or resistant cultural traditions, although money eroded the latter much more readily than it changed the former. Yet, despite the odds against success, becoming modern was (and is) an addictive idea, and Mexico plunged ahead.

Electrification created a need for wiring that in 1894 unleashed copper fever in Mexico, but within a decade mining booms in Chile, the United States, Japan, and Rhodesia had cut deeply into Mexico's bonanza. Mexican copper that yielded 24.4 cents a pound in 1880 dropped to 12.9 cents in 1910. Tobacco production fell from 400 tons in 1898–1899 to 110 tons a decade later because of Dutch East Indian and Cuban competition. The rot-resistant and insect-repellent characteristics of henequen brought prosperity to Yucatán, especially when the new Mc-Cormick reapers in the United States began to eat up binder twine by the ton. War in the Philippines in 1896 eliminated a major competitor, and henequen became Mexico's leading agricultural export. But the Filipino conflict ended, and that country's cheaper and better henequen recaptured its markets. Mexicans got 12 cents a pound for their henequen in 1904 but four years later only 8 cents. A storm battered Brazil's coffee crop in 1886, affording Mexican planters sudden inroads into that commodity, and a chewing gum fad in the United States demanded chicle from Yucatán's chicozapote trees, but the Brazilians were soon back in business with their fine coffee, and Americans chewed only so much gum. The health of Mexico's economy depended heavily on the fashions, tastes, and whims of others.[4]

Cuban Independence in 1898 released that country from Spanish trade restrictions and opened a market for Mexican garbanzo beans and cattle. The Cubans, however, soon repaired their ravaged farms and ranches to care for their own needs. Mexican sugar exports decreased in the 1890s when the industrialized countries favored sugar beets. When sugar producers agreed at a 1902 conference to drop their protectionist policies, world sugar production doubled (encouraging Mexican planters to exert new pressures on the campesinos of Morelos). Mexico's sugar exports surged in 1904–1905 but within three years had tumbled back down. In general, prices on Mexican exports rose 28.7 percent during the Porfiriato but 51 percent on imports. Attempts to close that gap squeezed already lean workers, and the nature of Mexican development precluded the mapping of a strategy that might have alleviated social discord.[5]

Two broad international economic trends greatly influenced Mexico's plunge into capitalistic turbulence: a shift in the world's terms of trade, and the decline of silver. Until 1881, countries that provided raw materials to manufacturers had somewhat the better of things in terms of trade. Raw products acquired a healthy return in manufactured goods. Just as Mexico entered the competition, the terms changed. Manufacturing countries gained the trade edge. Mexican exports of copper and lead lost much of their purchasing power, even though the nation's henequen fibers, coffee, and a rubber product called guayule unexpectedly retained favorable world markets.[6]

Compounding the downturn, silver, Mexico's standard of monetary exchange and its primary mineral export, declined sharply in value as the world settled on the gold standard. Exports that had expanded by 8 percent from 1891 to 1899 dipped to 5.4 percent from 1900 to 1910. Weakened foreign exchange naturally affected domestic production, the availability of subsistence and consumer goods, financial resources, purchasing power—and eventually the public peace.[7]

Better-off Mexicans paid higher prices for their wines, vehicles, and chemicals. They also charged more for their own products and spawned an inflation that sorely burdened the great majority of their countrymen. Factories pressed workers to produce more at lower wages. Commercial farmers expanded their land holdings to gobble up those of neighboring campesinos and diverted production of domestic food staples to profit-bearing exports. Farm wages had increased 25 percent between 1885 and 1895 but fell 17 percent from 1895 to 1910. Measured in purchasing power, these wages sank in 1908 to what they had been in 1800, although the effect of the decline depended on the extent to which a campesino's well-being was tied to monetary exchange. By all reports, many people agonized. Pay for miners and skilled cowhands contined to show overall improvement, but the textile workers barely held their own. It took an estimated 65 pesos a month in 1910 to decently support a family of five. Many could get by fairly well on half that amount. Rural people grew much of their own food, and urbanites doubled up in their shelters. But the average Mexican earned less than one peso a day.[8] No use to talk to him or her and their children about peace, development, and progress. Disorder, for some, promised possible relief.

Capitalism also forced, enticed, and encouraged Mexicans into entirely new living experiences. The tenacity of accustomed security should not be underestimated, but neither should the lure of change. It is impossible to gauge the number of Mexicans unwillingly propelled into their new environment as against those who welcomed new opportunity. Suffice it to say that there were many of each. Change, even for the willing, rarely equaled betterment, and so people moved on to something else, or they just drifted in and out of work, into city slums, back to country farms. A number tried the Rurales, but too much discipline or not enough rewards caused many to desert. Regardless, there they were, in motion, looking for employment, advancements, security, subsistence, excitement. Frederick Jackson Turner noted that "mobility is death to localism." If traditional Mexico did not fall apart under the impact of capitalism, it certainly strained at the seams.[9]

The role of money in dislodging agrarian people from traditional lives is controversial, but a significant number of Mexicans apparently welcomed industrial jobs that paid two or three times what they received on farms. The Tlahualilo cotton enterprise in Laguna during the early 1890s attracted two thousand permanent and six thousand seasonal workers paid daily in cash. Other capitalists in the district cursed Tlahualilo for raising the region's wage scale. Sonoran farmers complained that high wages in the mines were draining off their hands, and competition for workers in the industrializing district of Puebla-Tlaxcala forced hacendados to raise pay for their free laborers and to strengthen their grip on their debt peons.[10] Mexicans by the thousands made that awesome leap from a subsistence to a wage economy. They began to see their work in terms of pay rather than survival. They were, in short, becoming modern.

Change created movement. Campesinos fell into new labor arrangements with hacendados, some better off because of it, a great many more not. People found work as carpenters, brick masons, painters, and railroad builders, while along the old wagon routes muleteers, innkeepers, smithies, and merchants lost out. Between ten thousand and a hundred thousand—accounts greatly vary—annually crossed the Rio Grande in the first decade of this century to work in the United States, not only on the border but in restaurants in Chicago and hotels in San Francisco, on farms in Wyoming, and on railroad construction across the Midwest. Tarascan Indians from the Zacapu region of Michoacán, driven from their rich farmsites by commercial interests, cut sugar cane in Jalisco and Colima and picked cotton in Texas. Tropical plantations in Veracruz drew labor from Puebla and Oaxaca. Factories employed thousands, and their products put artisans out of business.[11]

Coahuila reported in 1895 that 26.4 percent of its inhabitants had been born elsewhere, a percentage that increased to 31.3 by 1910. On the eve of the Revolution, 13 percent of the city of Puebla's population had been born outside of the state. For Orizaba it was 20 percent. Torreón had fewer than a thousand residents in 1877 but twenty-three thousand in 1900. Monterrey increased from fourteen thousand to sixty-two thousand in the same period. Morelia, León, and Querétaro lost population in central Mexico, perhaps because their new industries could not absorb the artisans displaced by urban machines. Aguascalientes, Guadalajara, and Toluca gained in the migrations. As populations rose and fell, so did the quality of life.[12]

Much of the population movement was circular. The Tarascans returned after several months of cutting cane elsewhere, and three years of back-breaking labor in the United States was enough. Some Mexicans who migrated to the United States sooner or later came home. After a stay, many headed back north. Industrial foremen noted that their workers tended to return to their former villages for planting and harvest.[13] Their lives had long been associated with farming cycles, and they were also drawn back by personal attachments and the security of the village fraternity. How many stayed home is another question. One thing is sure: their return stirred the stale air. All the people who went back to their old surroundings proved by their presence and their stories that change was possible. That alone can be big news in a traditional community and can stimulate further migration. It became another blow against the old structure of society.

Patterns emerge and then disintegrate as students of the Porfiriato sift through data and formulate hypotheses. Friedrich Katz finds regional differences in employment patterns. Substantial underemployment in central Mexico's farm belt with its seasonal fluctuations released a surplus that spilled northward toward the mines and the United States and seeped into already overcrowded cities. Yet there were regions of chronic labor shortage. Workers had to be drafted by force for tobacco and henequen plantations in the south. Asians were imported for farm work in Sinaloa and Veracruz. Debt peonage and security measures increased where labor was short. Overages in central Mexico fostered a variety of modes of employment: day laborers, live-ons, sharecroppers, tenant farmers, and seasonal workers. For some, such an arrangement represented advancement, for others, degradation.[14] It has generally been said that 60 percent of all Mexicans lived on the verge of starvation as the Revolution approached, but James Coatsworth has found them eating differently but not less than their accustomed fare.[15]

Fewer Mexicans, without doubt, owned land, not that very many ever held property, but the 20 percent who possessed tracts in 1895 had been reduced to only 2 percent by 1910. The despoliation of land from ordinary Mexicans by the most powerful is a sordid story best told by Wistano Luis Orozco, a specialist in jurisprudence, who warned of its consequences at the time of the rape. Land tenure questions, nonetheless, remain infinitely complex. Despite the obvious concentration that took place in some regions of the country, Moisés González Navarro has discovered a remarkable increase of ranchos or smaller farms in central Mexico during the period, and estimates that 40 percent of the Indian villages in the region survived the land-grab intact. Jan Bazant reports the fractionalization of large Church holdings in accordance with the Reform Laws. And although some hacendados may have put their land and water resources to poor use, or no use at all, and others may have drained an entire area of its economic vitality by soaking up its assets and investing them elsewhere, haciendas around Toluca stimulated market activity and exposed residents to new forms of sales and purchase. Orozco even found a few campesinos who grew wealthy farming in the shadows of a great hacienda.[16]

People who were released from their land and old work habits, for whatever purpose, scattered in all directions. Development swept a few Mexicans up the social scale and dumped some others down it. For many who had been attracted or shoved out of their traditional security into a new and unsettled world of frequently frustrated possibilities, disillusionment and genuine hardship set in. Modernization proffered advantages and then denied them. It was not so much a matter of whether one's life was better before or after capitalism: the new order made promises it did not honor. It preached betterment that it did not deliver. In so doing it trained the soldiers of the Revolution. Some boldly challenged the Porfirian order long before outright rebellion engulfed the country. Unionizing workers did so, along with radical politicians despairing of dictatorship. Others had all along resisted the encroachment of capitalistic development on their customary ways. Banditry persisted and assumed new forms. Beneath the façade of Porfirian order there was a very definite rumble of disorder for anyone who dared to listen.

Díaz the dictator was no totalitarian. He made no effort, like the great twentieth-century totalitarians, to mobilize mass support or even to develop a political party among elites. Nor was he a military dictator. The army never controlled national affairs and never was able to run them to its benefit. Just the opposite occurred. Díaz expended a good deal of his ingenuity and budget to keep the military off-stride and satisfied. He used army commanders he trusted to manipulate other military people and civilians in and out of positions of power. The army never developed a common purpose that set it apart from civilians. It was, at least until the end of the century, still a conglomeration of old-fashioned caudillos and a few professionals. Daniel Cosío Villegas notes in his study of Porfirian politics that although in 1889 only seven of the country's twenty-nine governors were civilian (i.e., without military rank), only three, Manuel González, Ramón Corona, and José Ceballos, had reputations as soldiers. By

1903 the ratio had almost reversed itself. There were twenty-one civilian governors, and only eight who held military rank.[17]

Most of the important generals who had supported Tuxtepec were dead by 1902. Only Treviño and Francisco Z. Mena remained, and they backed the regime. The passing of the old-time military caudillos meant that Díaz had survived the most disruptive element of an entire era. He came to power just when traditional power groups were on the wane and new ones had not yet garnered much strength. Díaz simply outlived most of his early competitors.[18]

Institutional chaos characterized the Porfirian system. Like other authoritarian administrators, it only appeared to be decisive, but in fact was rife with bureaucratic disorder. Assertions concerning discipline and order only masked the confusion instigated by the dictator. Díaz created this commotion, rivalry, and backbiting so that he could stand above it as arbiter. His decisions were pragmatic, arbitrary, and frequently contradictory. The lack of standards for performance left everyone dependent on the dictator. The president fired local authorities to ensure the allegiance of campesinos at the same time that he authorized the harsh repression of factory workers. He encouraged subordinates to circumvent their superiors in order to correspond directly with the dictator. Charges, countercharges, rumors, gossip, intelligence, secrets, all reached Díaz, who stirred the pot to his liking.

A favorite tactic was to advise a petitioner to proceed at his own discretion, which left the president free to praise or criticize the result. Newsmen, hacendados, municipal officials, foreign investors, labor leaders, and ordinary soldiers all corresponded directly with Díaz, never sure of how he might respond. The president promised what he could to almost everyone, and in this manner kept people hopeful if not satisfied. Governors asked him to revoke a decree issued by a cabinet member or to annul an agreement made between a government minister and a private party. When Finance Minister Manuel Dublán requested troops to remove stubborn Indians from their property in Michoacán, that state's governor urged that the petition be denied, and Díaz concurred. Army commanders asked the president about field maneuvers. Rurales complained that their officers had short-changed them. Díaz was called on to make judicial decisions. Should captured bandits be shot, consigned to the army, or referred to civil courts? Sonoran Governor Luis Torres wanted to crush his opponents, and Díaz counseled against it. A long-term military officer requested commutation of his death sentence for murder. Díaz changed it to life but refused later appeals. A local politician asked mercy for army deserters and disaffected peons who had rebelled in Puebla, and Díaz returned the deserters to the army and the campesinos to their farm work. He ordered that a militant labor leader not be inducted into the army, so that the administration could maintain a pipeline to dissatisfied workers. A governor who thought the land laws too harsh was warned, "The law is the law," but Díaz later arranged to alter a state constitution to permit that same governor to continue in office. He approved the removal of a regional political authority in Guanajuato, but told the governor of that state to find good employment for the ousted politician, "because we must have him content."[19]

Concessions and incentives went to numerous friends, investors, and potential troublemakers, but even relatives were on occasion sharply restricted or, like his nephew, "exiled" to some minor diplomatic post.[20] Díaz never stopped reminding all Mexicans that he was boss. Yet he disciplined with compromise more than force, and not always because he wanted to. Personal dictatorships are among the least stable forms of government, and Díaz felt it, even if he did not know it.

Regionalism did not just evaporate under the impact of dictatorship and development. It took until 1892 to foist Porfirian governors on Michoacán and Chihuahua. Querétaro and Coahuila also proved politically difficult. And, unlike the dictators, governors frequently faced substantial opposition to their reelection. Some managed to retain office for substantial periods, in Michoacán and Veracruz for eighteen years, but others lost out in their first reelection bid. Guerrero had five governors in twenty-two years. Although the governors were certainly subordinate to Díaz, no question about that, they were not all subservient. Their allegiance to the president often betrayed more than a tinge of self-interest, which the dictator had to satisfy.[21]

The same was true of those political officials called *jefes políticos* (political bosses). The *jefeturas* had been established early in the century by Spanish liberals anxious to strengthen local government against central power. Díaz stood the institution on its head. Jefaturas became patronage positions to ensure local support for his government, meaning himself. They had different functions in the various states, but they generally enforced laws, decrees, and judicial decisions, issued a variety of permits, recruited soldiers, and did much of the administration's dirty work. Because they had such power to reward and punish and because they were normally outsiders to the community where they worked, they were often mistrusted and were centers of controversy; often enough they were feared and hated. But they could not afford to be too arbitrary with municipal authorities or local strongmen, because it was their connection to them that made the job of jefe so lucrative. The jefes therefore often shielded influential people from the inquiries or complaints of the central government; this could put the politicos at odds with the rural policemen stationed in their towns, and did cause the president to shuffle the jefes about. When the Revolution of 1910 erupted, the jefes were notable for their lack of aggressive concern for the stricken regime. They did not raise the troops that Díaz needed to defend himself. After the dictator had been exiled, a number of districts petitioned the new government for the return of their Porfirian jefe, who had all along been more one of them than a man of the ex-president.[22]

The same held true for local judges. Their remuneration lay with the people they judged, not the dictator, so they frequently declined to do the president's bidding, as, for example, with army recruits. The Mexican constitution prohibited forcing people to work against their will, so when some were levied into the army, they went to court and won their release often enough to nettle Díaz and to cause War ministers to rant. It was not, of course, the common soldier who made such appeals, but employers who needed labor or patrons protecting their extended families and thereby their influence, in other words, individuals who counted in the judge's district.[23]

Judges in a similar way found loopholes for dismissing criminal charges against locals who had power or protection. They helped to make banditry succeed. Díaz himself was not unmindful of the law, but his use of it had little to do with justice. Law was an important political tool for him. Reliance on the law, when he saw fit, became another way by which the dictator tried to rein in his assistants. He once told the governor of Veracruz to stop sending petty criminals to the death camps on Yucatán, and thereby made himself look beneficent. He also advised subordinates to refer for trial only those cases for which they had substantial proof, because dismissals made his system look weak. Arbitrary law enforcement was also another form of the approved corruption that everywhere greased the Porfirian machine. It bred loyalty, salved discontent, and, in general, allowed Díaz himself to be the ultimate law.[24]

Despite his use of various dodges, the dictator was rarely free of direct challenges. The constitutional change that gave him unlimited succession rights passed congress on December 21, 1890. It was the high point of the dictatorship. Within two years, reformists were campaigning for press freedom and judicial independence, for cutting fat from the army budget, and for broadening the electoral process. But those who wanted to deter or depose Díaz were by no means united in thought. They were all Liberals, but of different stripes. Although they remembered the fundamentals of the Constitution of 1857, they could not forget the decades of domestic disorder. So they split on the vital issue of the limits of authoritarianism for their country. Some campaigned for individual freedoms, others for centralistic controls. Their debate suited Díaz, for it divided his challengers. He even brought some of them into his government as quasi-scientific planners and managers of national development. Díaz also used these "científicos" to buffer the political and business aspirations of others outside their circle. The president deliberately ground his competitors against one another. Friction burned off their strength and eroded their will. Díaz never constructed the kind of efficient bureaucracy necessary to effectively centralize a country. His was a one-man show, and Porfirio Díaz was a remarkable manager.[25]

The dictator combined optimism with scare-tactics to forge a national mood that led Mexicans to desire and respect a strong hand at the helm. He reminded them of the recent past—the debilitating anarchy, the loss of Texas, the Mexican-American War, the French Intervention—and he assured them that the

United States harbored further designs on Mexican territory. Indeed, the United States army did have a contingency plan for an invasion of Mexico, although the officer who prepared it warned that Porfirian Mexico would be harder to defeat than the Mexico of 1848.[26]

Díaz also boasted of the country's progress, its unaccustomed high standing among civilized nations, and its historic ascendancy from a noble past. Nationalism became a bulwark against disorder. Nationalism blamed the country's ills on an easily identified outsider, a tactic that had special impact in a Mexico that well remembered its painful experiences with the United States in 1847–1848 and later with the French. Nor was Díaz modest about his own contributions to a regenerated Mexico. The president in this manner became a symbol of a progressive and respected Mexico, which made him difficult to attack as a man and dictator. Dictatorship depends less on laws and institutions than on the psychology of leadership. A dictator, to succeed, must obtain recognition as the leader of his nation. Díaz did just that. He earned some such acceptance at all levels of society through force, manipulation, and his persuasive personality. But, most important for him, influential people proved willing to trade political recognition for the creation and maintenance of conditions in which they could get rich. To them, peace-equaled-progress-equaled-profits. To many others, however, the Porfirian kind of peace offered much the opposite—if not degradation, certainly no noteworthy improvement—and increasingly Mexicans turned to disorder in their search for betterment.

Chapter 8
A Kind of Peace

The *pax porfiriano*, or Porfirian peace, was more imagined than real, invented by those who stood to profit from such an impression. So the minister of the Interior bragged in 1900 that his countrymen had not only been pacified but civilized, that ordinary Mexicans had come to love work more than revolution.[1] Such assertions were, of course, narrowly based. Peace meant having the same president in office for so many years. Civilization equaled improved transportation, modernized agriculture, and technical progress. As for love of work more than of rebellion, that was a wishful boast that the minister would soon have to swallow.

A veneer of peace had indeed been laid over the country as a new generation of ambitious Mexicans made their marks as lawyers, commercial farmers, shippers, and bureaucrats rather than as rebels. Some old styles of disorder had also been diminished by telegraph lines, electricity, stronger safes, the Rurales, and the breakdown of a regional system that had been maintained by disturbance. Some Mexicans, such as the lawyer and journalist Ireneo Paz, even lamented that revolutions had lost their creditability and that so many of his generation had sacrificed their individual liberties for peace.[2] But the former founts of disorder certainly did not just dry up, and they were soon abetted by new ones created by dictatorship and development.

No sooner had Díaz assumed office in 1885 for his second term than it seemed like the 1850s all over again. Faustino Mora in 1885 attracted some four hundred villagers in the Córdoba district of Veracruz with promises of land relief and free religious expression. By this time, however, Conservatives, including the Church, were in league with Díaz and supported order. Army soldiers and Rurales killed Mora at Omeapa in Veracruz and dispersed his forces into Oaxaca. Antonio Díaz Manfort rebelled in late 1885 at Jalacingo, Veracruz, under the well-worn banner of "religion and privileges," but he was cornered within three months and eliminated. The old battle cries seemed to have lost their appeal, but in fact the Porfiriato promised sufficient returns to the Church and the army to enlist their support of the regime.[3]

Development, however, by no means absorbed all traditional concerns. It irritated old ones and raised new ones. Indians in the valley of Papantla, Veracruz, in 1891, understood the implications of those visiting land-survey teams. Investors wanted the Indians' property for coffee, cocoa, rice, and sugar, all of them potentially profitable exports. Although Díaz assigned Rurales to protect the surveyors, the Indians resisted. Bloodshed summoned the army, and soldiers devastated the native villages and took command of the region.[4]

El Monitor Republicano carried the cause of the Indians to the public and won promises of relief from the government. By mid-September the once-rebellious natives were drinking toasts to their tormentors at a government-sponsored banquet. Díaz even sent a special commission to Papantla to investigate the issues and suffered some embarrassment when the local military commander arrested the commissioners because they agreed with the natives. But their prompt release did not resolve any questions for the inhabitants, nor did a committee of Indians who went to Mexico City in December to see the president.[5]

In June 1896, five years after their initial protest, the natives ran out of patience with the government's delays. Encouraged by a local entrepreneur who did not welcome government intervention in the valley's economy, they rampaged against local authorities, killing and looting to emphasize the measure of their anger. Díaz, who had planned to colonize the valley with foreigners, ordered the army to retaliate. He also played on local Indian rivalries, raising contingents of natives to help subdue the rebels, and gave General Rosalino Martínez a free hand to mop up the remnants. Relentless repression followed. Reports had it that thousands of Rurales, along with army troops, labored strenuously to exterminate the natives and that the stench of putrefying corpses madé the valley uninhabitable for a month or more. This is an exaggeration—the Rurales did not even participate in the 1896 affair—but such tales nonetheless pointed up the reputation of Díaz himself. Mexicans were learning what to expect from his administration. Papantla belonged to the capitalists, although native resentment continued to erupt in periodic violence. But the scars that government repression left on the national mentality were soon to be multiplied.[6]

Events at Tomóchic, even more than those at Papantla, most deeply stirred Mexicans in this decade and firmly confronted them with the realities of Porfirian authority. The tragedy at Tomóchic underscores the complexities of personal dictatorship. Díaz attempted conciliation, but refusal by the villagers and a military setback forced his hand. He had either to prove his strength or admit his weakness before the nation.

Some three hundred peasant farmers in 1892 had long made their home in Tomóchic, a village cradled in a valley formed by precipitous mountains in southwestern Chihuahua. Silver and gold mines dotted the district, creating an active commerce that crisscrossed the mountain range from Hermosillo in neighboring Sonora to Chihuahua City. Volunteers from Tomóchic won favorable government recognition in the late 1850s when they marched from their village all the way to the state of Hidalgo to defend Juárez and the Constitution. In recompense, Tomóchic received from the government two pieces of field artillery, useless by the 1890s but still symbols of autonomy.[7]

The moderate policies of succeeding governors allowed Tomóchic's people to pursue their farm work and muleteering without encumbrance. The villagers also fiercely venerated as a saint Teresa Urrea, whose worship took them on long pilgrimages to the mystic's abode in Cabora, Sonora. An itinerant priest who served the village caused discord when in 1890 he demanded devotion to God and himself rather than La Santa de Cabora, but the residents of Tomóchic simply ignored him and went about their chores. The controversy simmered. In the following year, bandits assaulted a mule train carrying silver near Tomóchic, and state security forces executed without trial five suspects who lived in the district. The natives turned to Teresa for advice, and when the priest ridiculed them for their beliefs, they banned him from town. Chihuahua's governor demanded an apology on behalf of the

priest, but the villagers professed obedience to no authority but
Teresa and Jesus Christ.[8]

Such defiance was tantamount to open rebellion, but Díaz kept
calm. He sent a state legislator from Hermosillo, known and respected by the mountaineers, to offer amnesty in return for allegiance to the state. No luck. The defenders of Tomóchic protested
their independence, and when a small state militia troop tested
their will, they drove it off. The legislator returned with corn seeds
needed for spring planting, but the people of Tomóchic placed
their independence even above food. The government then decided
to call out the army. Some sixty rebels challenged the advance of
nearly four hundred federal soldiers on September 2, 1892, outside
Tomóchic. Eyewitnesses estimated that the guerrillas were 80
percent effective with their shots. They picked off the uniformed
officers and drove the regulars into disarray. Twenty-nine soldiers
died and the natives wounded and captured forty others, including
Colonel José María Ramírez, second in command. The rebels
brought doctors from larger towns to treat the soldiers, although
they preferred to use traditional herbs and ointments on their own
wounds. When Colonel Ramírez did not respond to treatment, they
freed him to go to a city doctor. Ramírez later testified to the
respect he held for his adversaries as fighters and the treatment
they accorded him as a human being and suggested compromise.
Bargaining, however, was no longer possible for either side. The
natives rejected the government's pleas for surrender, as the federals knew they would. Four battalions of soldiers, supported by
artillery, marched on Tomóchic. The general who led the attack
was not vengeful, but his reputation was at stake.[9]

Hostilities began about where they had left off. Straw dummies
placed by the rebels in advanced positions drew the rifle fire of the
infantrymen, who then became easy targets for the guerrilla
marksmen. But the numerical differences, 104 versus 1,600, had to
tell. In one madly romantic dash to capture the commanding
general, four guerrillas fell near his position. The others grudgingly
retreated to the village church, where the elderly had gathered
with those too young to fight in a prayerful plea for succor from
Santa Teresa. Federal artillery shells chewed chunks out of the
masonry, but resistance continued from the doors, windows, and

tower of the church. The tower collapsed, then the roof and a wall. A boy of fourteen, who rushed from the church to confront the enemy, was later found sprawled dead on the bodies of five soldiers he had killed, one with a dagger. A mother, 68 years old, urged her sons to fight on. If they fell, she would continue the battle, and did.

Hostilities ended on the third day. There was no surrender, but the federal commander agreed to spare the women and children. The male natives took up their last stand in the house of their leader. All died there in hand-to-hand combat. Only forty women and seventy-one children survived, and perhaps three hundred federals perished in combat.[10]

The bloody work of the dictatorship did not go unreproached. *La Patria,* a Porfirian newspaper, explained that the repression had been necessary to preserve order, that the principle of authority had to be upheld, but *El Diario del Hogar* reported what many Mexicans must have deeply felt: that the people of Tomóchic had in defense of their rights been "trampled by a government that has little love for its people."[11] Such notoriety gnawed at the dictatorship. And when the Revolution of 1910 sputtered to its start, mountaineers from the Tomóchic region sustained the movement in its most difficult, touch-and-go days and encouraged a mounting insurgency that eventually toppled Díaz.

Papantla and Tomóchic contribute only two examples of continuing native insistence on traditional rights. Less spectacular or less known revolts unsettled agrarian Mexico throughout the dictatorship. They were another facet of the disturbance that development foments. Although the process chipped away at the solidarity of some villages and dissolved others, any number tenaciously resisted. Such opposition had diversified causes often linked to a town's peculiar circumstances. Tomóchic had its religious fervor and Papantla the concerns of local businesspeople. Others could hardly be expected to welcome changes that disrupted securities on which their lives depended. It made no sense to try something new, and, as they always had, outsiders preaching progress continued to represent taxation and forced military recruitment and possibly worse. Therefore, many commoners stuck to the surest bet they knew and defended it.

Banditry as a means to betterment contributed another

element to the disorder. Gone were the great bandit gangs of the past, like the Plateados. The socioeconomic conditions and political atmosphere in which they thrived had been altered. Development had shunted them aside, and brigands could no longer make demands on authority as they did in their heyday. There was no pressure on Díaz to convert the likes of Rivera, Ugalde, and Carvajal into policemen. The dictator had the guns to force compliance, although he did not discourage reports that bandits were being remolded into Rurales. Those who wanted to fabricate the aura of an orderly and safe republic welcomed and embellished such propaganda.

Banditry, however, did not evaporate during the Porfiriato. Technology, of course, impinged in a crucial way on traditional bandit territory, especially in the form of railroads and telegraph lines that began to tie regions to central authority. Bandits tore up tracks to derail trains and get at the contents, but they also burned trestles to preserve their way of life. Regional strongmen frantic to protect their interests must have encouraged the brigands, and they also knew how to stir up the natives to feed the disruption. It was not only that robbers on into the 1890s regularly derailed trains to get at their contents, but that poor people along the rights of way repeatedly ripped up the rails and wooden ties for sale or for their own use. Or they tore down the telegraph poles to burn as firewood and peddled the copper wiring, which was in great demand at the junk shops. It was not only the money incentive that agitated these people. Turnabout seemed like fair play to them. The railroadmen regularly cut down trees along the rights of way to fuel the locomotives, and they used tons of rocks from the vicinity for the roadbeds. Sparks that belched from the engines ignited crops, and so for many reasons—including the outright loss of their land— rural people harassed the railroads. United States bandits also traveled south for easier pickings, and Mexican officials called on American anti-train-robber specialists to help them stem the tide.[12]

These conditions caused the Mexican congress to pass a Draconian law that required immediate punishment, even death, without formal trial for those who tampered with rail and telegraph communications. For a while a nightmare of arbitrary authority prevailed. Local officials used their new power to threaten rivals, eliminate troublemakers, and please the dictator.

The jefe político at Irapuato sentenced a teenaged boy to five years in prison for simply stealing a bolt that connected two standing railway cars. Another jefe sentenced two men who had robbed a third on a public roadway to five year terms each under the new law. Appeals of these cases went all the way to Díaz, who both feared the repercussions of unreasonably tough enforcement and understood the political gains to be made by juxtaposing presidential compassion and the harshness of local officials. Díaz referred the boy to a municipal judge on grounds that his theft had not impeded the flow of traffic, and sent the robbers to judicial authorities because the new law supposedly referred only to railroads. Still, the drastic statute stayed in effect and its misapplication continued.[13]

How much the new law deterred bandits is difficult to determine. They continued to knock an occasional train off the tracks throughout the Porfiriato, although armed guards, often Rurales, rode the trains to maintain order among passengers and to blunt any brigand raids. Trains and telegraph lines helped to speed assistance in emergencies and thereby contributed to the overall peacekeeping. Díaz, however, came to rely on them too much. When the rebels religiously interdicted the lines in 1910–1911, they cost the military its mobility, sorely needed because of the army's small size. The dictator should have been building all-weather roads along with the rails. Good roads would have provided only limited economic advancement and certainly would not have guaranteed his tenure, but they would have further integrated the country and permitted better political and military control.[14]

For the brigands, though, raiding a train and escaping to fence the goods became a major operation, and only a few of them had the wherewithal and contacts needed to succeed. Bandits who kept to older patterns had better luck, although their take was limited because so much of what was worth stealing was transported by rail. Such realities revamped Mexican banditry and gave rise to social bandits like Jesús Arriaga, alias "Chucho el Roto" ("El Roto" is a monicker for humble people who like to dress elegantly); Heraclio Bernal, the Thunderbolt of Sinoloa; and Santana Rodríguez, simply Santanón to the multitudes excited by his audacious challenge to Porfirio Díaz.

Mexico's social bandits do not so snugly fit the mold designed by Eric Hobsbawm.[15] They may or may not have been campesinos, although they were all ordinary people. At least Bernal and Santanón had a sharp political sense. The Mexicans mostly chose banditry rather than being propelled into it, and they did so more to join the new system than to oppose it. Banditry was their means of social mobility, although this was much harder to accomplish in the Porfiriato than it had been earlier. Rural commoners at times shielded these bandits from pursuit, but they were also instrumental in hunting them down in league with authorities. Middle-level Mexicans also appreciated and romanticized these brigands and even tried to protect the reputations of the robbers from official assault.

There was something different about these Porfirian brigands. Mexicans had long celebrated their bandits, but more for their group power and haughty regional control. The Plateados were more admired as stern rulers than as troublesome subjects. But the social bandits were lauded for the way in which they burlesqued established order and for the verve and wit with which they challenged authority, even though they were tragic figures doomed to defeat and early death. These bandits seemed to express an independence that many Mexicans sensed they had lost or had never enjoyed, and the popular culture of the time, specifically the folk ballads called *corridos*, clothed the bandits in a legitimacy that augered danger for constituted government.

Chucho el Roto (Arriaga) was a low-income mestizo cabinetmaker in the capital who supplemented his income through banditry. Rumor held that frustrated love had driven him into brigandage. In a moment of passion he kidnapped and raped the young lady he loved, but could never possess because she was of elite status.[16] A myth, quite likely, but one that underlined the real and uncrossable gap between rich and poor.

His crime supposedly forced Chucho into full-time banditry, more as a gentleman Robin Hood than as a murderous desperado. Arriaga boasted that he never killed a victim, and the public believed him. The Church provided a favorite target. He kidnapped priests and sued the bishop for ransom, or he simply picked the pockets of wealthy patrons attending mass. Chucho insisted that he was a Christian. A jefe político in the state of México of-

fered 2,000 pesos for the bandit's life. Arriaga upped the ante:
3,000 pesos for the life of any available jefe and a bonus of 1,000
more for the head of this particular adversary. Again probably
myth, the tale indicates where jefes stood with the populace. They
were undoubtedly the *bêtes noires* of the regime.[17]

Mexico City's *El Correo de Lunes* in 1884 called Arriaga a
"civilized bandit"—sociable, cultured, elegant, and well educated,
and noted that Mexican high life was full of Chuchos, all of them
after money but none so frank or impudent as the bandit. The
newspaper admitted that he was no angel but knew plenty of
Mexicans anxious to join his financial paradise. The paper even
nominated Chucho for congress. Why not? The brigand possessed
an independence and wit that escaped the present legislators.
Furthermore, it suggested that a bust of Arriaga belonged in the
Palace of Justice, so that, in whatever governmental position,
Chucho el Roto would be at home, like the others, wallowing in the
national treasury.[18]

Arriaga, described as a short, husky, bearded man with a kind
face, was captured at the age of forty in Orizaba, where his cabinet
shop was said to be a front for the intended robbery of a local cigar
factory. Police found him in the company of three other bandits,
one the well-known Francisco Valera, and in possession of a
considerable cache of weapons. But prison could not long hold
Chucho, and his escape in 1882 made people swear that he was
more mirage than human. Three times he fled imprisonment, once
outfoxing two hundred soldiers guarding the jail. After each
recapture several of the capital's best lawyers handled his legal
defense. Middle-class Mexicans cherished their relationship with
the bandit. They even tried to shield him from prosecutions. *El
Monitor Republicano* even complained that authorities tried to
saddle him with a number of unsolved crimes, and demanded
proof of his involvement.[19]

The famed poet Manuel Gutiérrez Nájera more than half-
seriously used the example of Arriaga to advocate prison reform.
He wondered at the brigand's general intelligence and ability for
scientific reasoning. Chucho, he thought, might even make a good
minister of the Interior. But if he had learned the difficult art of
delinquency after only a short term in prison, how much more

could he have gained by a longer sentence? Jails seemed to be fine learning institutions. If revamped along European lines, Mexico's prisons could teach morals and do so scientifically. People would be glad to stay in them, where they could sleep well, eat better, grow fat, and live a hygienic life. True, they would lack liberty, but so did soldiers, sailors, the sick, and many others. If Chucho el Roto had learned brigandage in prison, more acceptable manners could be taught in the same environment.[20]

Jesús Arriaga was caught for good in 1884 in Querétaro, where he had lived with his woman for two years, making cabinets and picking the pockets of the populace, at times disguised as a female. He had come to Querétaro dressed as a Turk, and got started in business by selling rosaries to the city's residents, whom he described as "very Catholic." He also robbed loan houses, but later asked a reporter: "Since when is it a crime to rob usurers?" How had he been discovered? "Damn it. My love of art." Theater art at that: Chucho was apprehended in a theater. His picture had been circulating for some time, and he was recognized by a scar on his hand, the result of a carpentry slip. Some had previously surmised that he had fled to the comforts of Europe, that he was bathing in the sea at Biarritz, but Arriaga proclaimed his patriotism. He intended to die in Mexico, and he declined to elaborate on reports that he robbed mainly to finance a daughter's education in Brussels. If Chucho could not be bourgeois, he at least wanted such well-being for his daughter.[21]

The bandit assured newsmen that he soon would be released from prison and shaking hands with old friends, but Arriaga died in 1885 in the dankness of San Juan de Ulúa. Rumors that he had been beaten to death inflamed public sympathy and caused an official investigation into his death. The final verdict: dysentery. But Chucho el Roto outwitted his captors after all—he survives and cavorts on Mexican television today.[22]

The Thunderbolt of Sinaloa, Heraclio Bernal, toiled as a youth in Sinaloa's silver-mining district. He knew the harshness of that life, but state politics nudged him into banditry. After the French Intervention, Sinaloa split politically between President Juárez and his challenger, Díaz. Heraclio, like his father, supported Juárez. With the advent of Tuxtepec, Bernal's political opportunities evaporated, and he turned to banditry. The foreign-owned mines of Sinaloa and Durango offered easy targets and great rewards. Smugglers awaited stolen silver along the Pacific Coast. With local success, Bernal's regional reality ballooned into a national myth.[23]

Politics permeated Bernal's banditry. Teasing Sinaloa's Porfirian governor made great sport and attractive headlines for the brigand. When the governor sponsored a state dinner for a visiting official, Bernal organized in a rural village an even more sumptuous banquet for his followers. He once invited the governor to a dance that he had sponsored for friends. The governor, as expected, sent troops, but the Thunderbolt was long gone. Mexicans loved Bernal's pranks, even the imagined ones. No prank was intended, however, when he raised Sinaloan support for adversaries of Díaz in the 1880 presidential election. The movement produced some heat but no fire, so he returned to brigandage. "Here comes Heraclio Bernal" became a popular national slogan that suggested terror, justice, jest, respect. Bernal played any role but loser.[24]

In 1885 the Thunderbolt of Sinaloa apparently made a bid to enter government service. He got word to Díaz that in return for his loyalty he wanted to be named the jefe político of a Sinaloan municipality. He also demanded 30,000 pesos to finance himself and a security unit, and the release of gang members held by the government, including his brother. The president scoffed at such presumptuousness. Díaz did not have to bargain with robbers. Bernal might be pardoned if he surrendered, but there would be no promise of employment. The rebel rejected such adverse terms. He would undoubtedly have made a fine policeman, but instead he remained a good bandit.[25]

With a band that may have fluctuated up to one hundred strong, Bernal dominated parts of Sinaloa and neighboring Durango. He forced loans from the wealthy residents of the towns he raided, attacked armories, and sold contraband silver to finance his operation. He fined the administrator of one hacienda 25,000 pesos for daring to oppose him. When the administrator could not raise that amount, Bernal made him sign a promissory note. Then he took 9,000 pesos and a hostage just to make sure that the note would be honored. Despite the governor's threat to punish those who aided Bernal, the brigand sustained substantial business ties. Local people in one sense had no choice. To denounce Bernal invited reprisal, which the state had no resources to prevent. Better to cooperate with him than to risk everything to his mood. Besides, even policemen and soldiers understand that there is profit in selling guns and ammunition to brigands.[26]

Throughout, Bernal's political ambitions never diminished. If Díaz would not let him weasel into his administration, he would have to overthrow it. He joined revolts against Porfirian rule, with no success, and in 1887 produced his own political platform, which called for adherence to the Constitution of 1857, in particular the section prohibiting reelections. But a constituency that at one time might have supported such a proposal now favored the retention of Díaz. Bernal's challenge was simply too late. His days were numbered.[27]

The end of war against the Yaquis in Sonora permitted the federal army to concentrate on Bernal. To assist the military, anti-guerrilla forces were raised among those who knew his habits and territory. No peasant solidarity existed here. Ordinary Mexicans declined to follow Bernal's revolutionary instincts and joined the manhunt. The governors of Sinaloa and Durango put a 10,000-peso ransom on Bernal, and two of the bandit's gang members took the bait. They helped set the ambush in which Bernal died on January 5, 1888. His gang split up, and several members apparently joined the notorious brigand Ignacio Parra, who is said to have tutored Pancho Villa. The federals killed Bernal but not the Thunderbolt of Sinaloa. Newspapers printed an epitaph that he supposedly wrote for himself on the eve on his death. Incredibly, it lamented his failure to discover a place for himself in Mexican society. What irony! People admired Bernal for his stance outside social structures, when all the time he wanted to join the administration. But Bernal has finally acquired his niche inside the system. Nicole Giron, who has recently studied Bernal, the man and the myth, found him celebrated in thirteen songs, four poems, and four motion pictures, some adapted for television. Mexicans seem to yearn for his return.[28]

Santanón, another acclaimed bandit, earned his nationwide notoriety on the eve of the Revolution. For more than a year he eluded the heralded Rurales, who by reputation always got their man but could not get Santanón—nor in reality, many more like him. Narrow misses bloated the myths that people wanted to believe about the brigand. Durango's *La Evolución* concluded in July 1910 that the Rurales must be shooting blanks instead of bullets at Santanón. It was the only explanation for the bandit's hairbreadth escapes. Or perhaps the Rurales did not shoot very straight, but no one dared say that, let alone believe it—even though it was true.[29]

Santana Rodríguez Palafox (Santanón) grew up an illiterate and unruly mestizo on a sugar plantation near his home town of San Juan Evangelista in Veracruz. He hated his bosses, let them know it, ran off, was captured, and ended up literally shackled to his miserable work. Rodríguez's obstreperousness got his consigned to an army infantry battalion in Oaxaca, but he deserted in 1903 and returned home, where he found his mother in some way mistreated by authorities. One report had her beaten to death, a detail perhaps concocted to legitimize his depredations. Others said that he fell in with gunslingers as a restless young man, or that he lapsed into banditry out of grief at the death of his young wife. Some insisted that he left decent plantation labor to become a cattle thief, or that he was unjustly accused of stealing cows and then consigned to the military.[30]

Santanón's frustrations, whatever their source, drove him into banditry, aimed mainly, but not exclusively, at foreign sugar planters and owners of sugar mills in southern Veracruz. He murdered the American manager of one mill and attacked several others with a band of only seven companions. Failure to apprehend him fed the public fancy. Santanón, they insisted, used no firearms, only a machete. He was a centaur protected by the shadows of night. No one had really seen him, no one knew him. Moreover, he was amphibious, which explained how he raided river-going cargo ships without detection. The facts of his adventures spread as rapidly as the fiction. Santanón did not shy from the murder of exploiters, but he also force-recruited supporters from Indian villages and put them up front as cannon fodder when he attacked a target. He also shot deserters. It was for good reason that vengeful natives joined the federal forces in hunting him.[31]

Porfirio Díaz became seriously concerned about Santana Rodríguez when he learned that the brigand might be flirting with the ideas of radical Liberals, who from exile in the United States advocated overthrow of the dictatorship. The president hurried sizeable reinforcements to Veracruz, consisting of Rurales, a battalion of soldiers, and field artillery. Get Santanón.[32]

Liberals in Veracruz, with connections to the exiles, had indeed tried to recruit the bandit. They had even named him commander of a nonexistent Liberal army. Whether Santanón had any ideological affinity for the cause is not known, but he should have welcomed support from any quarter. Later reports placed Liberal plans for insurrection in the brigand's possession, but that may have been a government ploy to justify repression of radicals throughout the country.[33]

A federal deputy, Salvador Díaz Mirón, better known for his poetry than his legislation, was, in a moment of presidential fancy, given army units to track down the brigand. There you have it: poet versus bandit. Mexicans could scarcely contain themselves. Many rooted for Santanón. *La Evolución* called him an outlaw but praised his outrageous defiance of authority. It headlined the story about him, "Hero of the day."[34]

Rurales finally caught up with him at Mecayopán in October 1910. Rural Police scouts flushed him and twenty-six companions from a campsite, and a fierce firefight ensued. Nearby army units, quickly on the scene, sent the brigands packing after a six-hour fight, and the bandits left behind eight dead, including Santanón. The Rurales received credit for the kill, because their commanding officer, Lieutenant Francisco Cárdenas, galloped to the nearest telegraph to report the triumph to his superiors in the capital. (Cárdenas in 1913 murdered President Francisco Madero. For his role in the Santanón affair he earned a promotion to captain.) Most probably it was a regular army soldier who shot the brigand, and it is doubtful that the Rurales could have weathered their encounter with the bandits without army support. Such claims were, however, part of the image-building process that sustained the Rural Police Force far beyond its performance.[35]

Campesinos from the district helped federal soldiers to pursue the remnants of the brigand's band. Santanón was hardly a hero to all commoners in the region where he had marauded. Yet death enhanced his stature. Veracruz admirers in 1932 renamed a village in his honor, and, as has occurred with almost everyone who in some way defied the dictatorship, he has been declared a precursor of the Revolution. That label ill fits him, but he did ruffle the Porfirian peace. Now Santanón, like other social bandits, has finally found a pedestal inside the social order.[36]

The overall impact of social banditry on Porfirian Mexico is difficult to assess even in retrospect. Rather than disrupt the social order, it may have reinforced it. At least, it cut both ways. The brigands certainly reflected some of the ambitions and frustrations of those times and generated some desire to resolve them. Yet they stirred no movement, only emotions. In their imaginary capers with the brigands, the populace wasted energies that might have been harnessed to more effective ends. Bandit myths, after all, did not satisfy rebellious Indians who craved land. They did not strengthen unionizing workers who demanded betterment, or assist radical Liberals preparing to invade the country. They did not in any meaningful way affect local authorities who resisted central restraints, nor could the bandits influence the oscillations of international capitalism that made national policies and planning irrelevant.

Myths, on the other hand, are important tools for social control, and Díaz invented some of his own. One of his most carefully constructed and highly successful myths concerned the Rurales. Along with compromise, Díaz needed force to maintain a strong sense of domestic order, a kaleidoscope of police and military troops to watchdog each other while keeping public peace. The president kept the army at a lean twenty thousand men or fewer, although it was budgeted for nearly twice that number so that commanders could skim off the overage as payment for their loyalty. Díaz was not about to arm too many campesinos. Governors and municipal officials raised irregulars as needed to care for their political purposes and emergency police needs. Few towns and villages beyond state capitals had many permanent policemen, only a few guards at the major municipal buildings and the jail. Capitalists often policed their enterprises with private forces. Special units handled specific missions. The "Mad Rus-

sian," Emilio Kosterlitsky, was, for instance, assigned to cooperate
with United States authorities along the Sonoran border in patrol
work that included the harassment and arrest of anti-administra-
tion radicals trying to penetrate the republic.[37]

To maintain himself in power, Díaz depended most heavily on
his Rural Police Force. They were his peacekeepers, but, much
more important for the dictator, they were his means for political
centralization, and they represented his determination to have his
will obeyed. They also assured national security for capitalistic
investors and became the showpiece of a modernized Mexico. How
deliberately the dictator built their image! Here are the famed
Rurales, toasted annually at an elaborate presidential banquet in
the capital, with all Mexicans, and many people of other nations,
looking and listening:

> Is there anything more national,
>> More ours, though he be proud and hard,
>> Than this wise warrior
>> Whom we call Rural?
>
> From that immortal epoch
>> In which some brave country people
>> Defeated the Zouaves [French] . . .
>> Our memory recalls the Rural.
>
> Are there, tell me, more typical
>> Soldiers in our troops?
>> Gentlemen, raise your glasses
>> To them, to the Rurales:
>> To the Rural soldier,
>> To his happy future:
>> For them no wine is made,
>> But only reddish pulque.[38]

PART III

A POLITICAL POLICE PERFORMANCE

Chapter 9
Constabulary of Campesinos and Artisans

Perhaps there were no more bandits-turned-Rurales, for times had changed, but Porfirio Díaz still siphoned off some of the nation's potentially more dissident elements into the Rural Police Force. The new recruits were mainly artisans and campesinos from central Mexico, untied from customary tasks and surroundings by development, some enthusiastic about the change of events, others distraught, but most at loose ends. They did not flock to become Rurales. Few Mexicans viewed rural police service as a career, or one taste of it proved to be enough, since fewer than one-tenth of the corpsmen reenlisted. Nor did they join with much expectation of upward mobility: only 8 percent were ever promoted and even then rarely past corporal, hardly up the ladder. Pay was 1.30 pesos daily, higher than that of most ordinary laborers, but deductions for horses and equipment decreased any benefits. So why enlist? For many, service apparently provided a stopgap job until something better came along, or an easy chance to rip off a government rifle, a horse, or other property. Deserters so frequently sold their equipment and then reenlisted under an assumed name that the administration ordered that physical descriptions of deserters be circulated so that corps commanders could spot and weed out violators.[1]

The corps offered its members official authority and reasonable security if the Rural could adapt to the regimentation. Half could do so, and completed their rather long enlistment, which was four years prior to 1890 and five years thereafter. But 25 percent deserted, the great majority of them in their first year, and another 15 percent had to be discharged as incorrigible. They simply could not or would not take the regimen of inspectors, barracks life, and orders from superiors who could be extremely abusive. Those killed on duty and discharged as hardship cases made up the final 10 percent. No genuine screening of recruits took place, because the constabulary had to take the men it could get. Yet all enlistees volunteered—at least none was levied into service—and in sum they probably joined for as many personal reasons as they were individuals. Significantly, they enlisted more because of the persuasion of the field commanders who recruited them than to serve the dictatorship.[2]

More than half (53.6 percent) came from the Bajío, which had been so thoroughly disrupted by the regime's land and labor programs. Another fifth were from Puebla and Tlaxcala, where sporadic factory employment created an uneven flow of insecure workers. Similar industrial conditions, together with urban poverty and overpopulation around the federal district, induced another 11.7 percent to try the force, and the mineral districts of San Luis Potosí and Zacatecas provided the remainder, not miners but farmhands and craftsmen. The corps did not attract membership outside of its operational area. The presence of the constabulary itself drew volunteers, but it carried no further. It lured no vaqueros from their freedoms and better-paying jobs in the north and encouraged no defections among debt peons in the south.[3]

Those who enlisted between 1880 and 1910—and more than thirty thousand men experienced at least some Rural Police service during those years—were ordinary Mexicans, half from the country, the rest from towns of more than five thousand and from larger cities. Most were illiterate; two-thirds were bachelors. Not particularly young men in search of a start, their average age was in the mid-to-late twenties, and after 1890 more than 40 percent of the recruits were well into their thirties. That means that when they completed their term, they were approaching forty years of age. They must have worried about where to head next.[4]

Nearly one-third of the recruits were artisans: shoemakers, bakers, candle, soap, and harness makers, woodcutters, brickmakers, and crafts helpers. Manufacturing had dislodged them from their old work. Machines eliminated jobs and poured out cheap goods that replaced handicrafts. One-fifth of the corpsmen

José Guadalupe Posada, Mexico's renowned graphics artist who pointedly commented upon his times, depicts the involuntary nature of labor recruitment. *Fondo Editorial de la Plástica Mexicana*

General Jose M. Rangel

JEFE DL LA

Campaña de Temóchic,

The blundering General José María Rangel led the ponderous federal army against the heroic mountaineers of Tomóchic. *Fondo Editorial de la Plástica Mexicana*

A Rural, splendid in his *charro* outfit and seated on a saddle adorned with silver, is ready for parade on a national holiday in Mexico City. *Amon Carter Museum, Fort Worth, Texas*

To increase their public visibility, Rurales frequently rode trains and were steadfast in their defense of the dictatorship. *Amon Carter Museum, Fort Worth, Texas*

Families, girl friends, and an assortment of hangers-on accompanied the Rural Policemen on patrol and at their duty stations. *Amon Carter Museum, Fort Worth, Texas*

The "Mad Russian," Emilio Kosterlitsky, was commissioned by President Díaz to direct a special Rural Police constabulary to safeguard public security along the sensitive Arizona-Sonora border. *Reproduced, by permission of the author and the publisher, from Cornelius C. Smith, Jr.,* Emilio Kosterlitsky: Eagle of Sonora and the Southwest Border *(Glendale, Calif.: Arthur H. Clark Co., 1970)*

Enemies of the Porfirian Peace are about to be executed by a contingent of Rural Policemen. *Amon Carter Museum, Fort Worth, Texas*

Political campaign gatherings occurred, but under the concerned vigilance of Rural Policemen. *Amon Carter Museum, Fort Worth, Texas*

were campesinos, driven or attracted from their farms by so-called modernization. Underemployment in towns and urban settings provided other enlistments. One-sixth had been petty merchants and another sixth had possessed a trade. They were carpenters, blacksmiths, and printers. A gathering of domestics and custodians sought better jobs as Rurales, and muleteers put out of business by the railroads needed new work and tried the corps. The constabulary did not attract any significant numbers of factory workers and miners; only one-tenth of the corpsmen were former proletarians. And practically none of the men—only one percent— were ex-soldiers, although a number of soldiers were former Rurales.[5] Captured deserters ended up with an army battalion in the hellholes of Veracruz and Yucatán, but most who deserted were never captured or even pursued. Although the corps paid a heavy price in terms of discipline, it was cheaper to enlist new men than to track down deserters.[6]

Fluctuations in recruitment patterns indicate how seriously the inevitable but unforeseeable fluctuations of international capitalism unsettled the country's work force. Annual enlistments from the Bajío's farmlands increased 22 percent between 1880 and 1910, but they decreased 43 percent in more industrialized Puebla and Tlaxcala. More than 40 percent of the recruits between 1880 and 1885 were former campesinos, but that decreased to 22.4 percent in the final decade of the dictatorship. Artisans went from 20 percent in the earlier period to 33.4 percent between 1900 and 1910. Overall enlistments in the Federal District dropped 13 percent in the final decade, and the initially heavy recruitment of artisans and campesinos from San Luis Potosí and Zacatecas leveled off in the 1890s. Regional differences by time periods probably help to explain the percentage differences. As the home district of the majority of Rurales, the Bajío deserves special attention. An unusual amount of racial mixture, petty entrepreneurship, commercial exchange, and personal mobility characterized the Bajío even before Independence. Increasing numbers of people migrated between Tlaxcala and Puebla between 1900 and 1910, but fewer of them joined the constabulary from these industrialized states. Mining declined in Zacatecas after 1880 and in the process weakened the tie between hacendados and peons, and this could relate to the influx of campesinos into the corps at that time. Thanks to foreign investment in smelters and other industries, San Luis Potosí experienced a business boom after 1900 that affected Rural Police recruitment in that area. Further explanations of recruitment trends will appear with new regional studies, but certainly the statistical surges and steep plunges that marked the constabulary confirm in human terms the severity of the rootlessness that accompanied the Porfiriato. Instability existed throughout the heartland of the country. People moved in and out of jobs, but nothing seemed to satisfy them. Large numbers of unemployed artisans, people who tend to be somewhat more political than campesinos, were especially in evidence. And police have long noted the propensity of artisans to challenge authority and to disrupt order. The increasingly dramatic movement of individuals in the last decade of the period indicates how discontent turned to desperation. The government had to recruit more than twenty thousand Rurales in those final ten years just to maintain the twenty-four hundred budgeted, five-year positions in the constabulary.[7]

The Rural Police Force could not escape the nation's escalating frights and frustrations in the last years of the dictatorship. Desertions after 1900 rose 10 percent over those in the previous decade. Now far more than one-third of the Rurales were deserting. By comparison, the Canadian Northwest Mounted Police had a 6-percent desertion rate. The United States reported its army desertion rate at 6.7 percent in 1909, while the British had only 1.7 percent. Not only did more Rurales desert, but they did so more quickly. Of the men who between 1885 and 1890 left the organization within six months of their enlistment, 45.5 percent had deserted. After 1900 it was 56.3 percent, among them a lieutenant who ran off with his detachment's treasury.[8]

In other important ways the same trend toward dissolution permeated the constabulary in that chaotic final decade. The incidence of those cited for drunkenness after 1900 leaped 37 percent, and the corps responded by dishonorably discharging an increasing number of men as incorrigibles. Although slightly under 10 percent were dismissed as habitual offenders between 1885 and 1890, the percentage jumped to 13.3 percent in the 1890s and to nearly 20 percent at the turn of the century.[9] Missed roll calls and bedchecks, insubordination that equaled direct challenge to authority, drunken brawling, all increased as the dictatorship began to totter. Their soaring disregard for regulations indicates how little the Rurales respected their superiors and their mission, and how far rot had advanced in the Porfirian system.

Declining completion rates confirmed the slippage. In the 1880s almost 60 percent of those who joined fulfilled their four-year enlistment. In the next decade it dipped to 29 percent, partly because of the increased enlistment term and also because overall discipline tightened. These were also the most expansive economic years of the Porfiriato, meaning that more attractive labor opportunities existed outside the corps. The national downturn after 1900, however, drove the constabulary's fulfilled commitments down to a miserable 13 percent. The majority of the others either deserted or were discharged for malfeasance. In 1910, after assessing the performance of the men, including the officials, a federal inspector could only conclude: "The Rurales are costing Mexico a lot of money and are not living up to expectations."[10]

In the last decade of the dictatorship, when the turnover rate in the constabulary substantially increased, recruitment teams had to scour the countryside for replacements. Whereas it took an extra four hundred men a year to maintain the force at regulation strength between 1885 and 1890, and six hundred men in the following decade, the organization had to attract more than two thousand newcomers annually during the final ten years of the dictatorship just to keep the corps at full strength. It took an average of seven men to fulfill only one enlistment in these years. That is a 50 percent increase over the requirements of the previous decade. And in finding replacements in the final years, the constabulary paid distinctly less attention to regulations concerning age, literacy, background, and recommendations.[11] The compromise showed up in poor discipline and desertions. No doubt this late joiner was a different kind of "volunteer." In earlier years the corps attracted people more eager to leave their traditional settings—men who welcomed the new opportunities of development and who, if they left the constabulary, often did so to take better employment elsewhere. But as capitalism bored more deeply into

Mexican society, it dislodged individuals less anxious to leave
customary securities. Their restless dissatisfaction and personal
instability showed in their Rural Police performance.

Officers joined the corps because it offered an unfettered
chance for personal gain. Díaz personally approved the re-
assignment of army personnel to the corps. He also enlisted
cronies and friends, some of them too old and infirm to work. A
lieutenant at Chalco in 1910 had a mutilated leg that left him
immobile. Another on duty was paralyzed. A third was eighty
years old (three decades beyond mandatory retirement) and too
sick to function. But almost all of the officers were robust and
vigorous, if not always engaged in legitimate police duties.[12]

Díaz paid well for loyalty. A complicated accounting system
offered the officials easy peculations. The corps commander had
his built-in payroll overages. The budgeted annual salary of corps
commanders was a respectable 3,000 pesos at the end of the
Porfiriato. On top of that, the commanders skimmed off a
budgeted surplus.[13] Each corps was financed for fifteen sergeants
but averaged only eight, twenty-four corporals but had only fifteen, and a hundred and sixty privates but normally counted a
hundred or fewer. In terms of the 1907 pay scale these disparities
represented a monthly bonus of 3,610 pesos, or more than the
commander's yearly pay.[14] All of this had been going on for some
time. Officers regularly did not report deserters or immediately
pay new enlistees in order to create overages that they could
pocket. The corps assigned to Tepic in 1882 was budgeted for a
hundred and eighty-eight guards, seventeen more than were actually enrolled, which amounted to a neat 663-peso monthly
supplement for the commander. And this occurred at a time when
the commander's annual pay was 2,522 pesos (compared to the
1,810 paid army officers of the same lieutenant colonel's rank) and
was supplemented by a monthly federal gratuity of 8 pesos to show
the government's appreciation for not conspiring against it.[15]

Junior and noncommissioned officers raided other Rural
Police funds they administered, such as housing and horsefeed
accounts, as well as the personal deposits of the ordinary corpsmen. These subordinates claimed payment from Mexico City for
lodging and forage that had already been donated by private

citizens in exchange for police service. Or they forged reimbursement chits with the names of junior noncommissioned officers. One such scheme fell apart when a lieutenant signed repayment vouchers with the name of a subordinate who could not read or write.[16]

The government intended to furnish the constabulary with the latest models of weaponry, such as Remington carbines from the United States and French cavalry swords, but supply officers often sold the new equipment to local people and let the corpsmen get along as best they could. One corps carried the same useless soggy bullets for four years. Other policemen cornered several bandits in 1899 but lost them when the brigands realized that the rifles being held on them were too old and dirty to shoot.[17]

In the Juárez days, Rurales were expected to bring their own rifles and horses with them into the service, but that led to such an extraordinary collection of weapons and animals that Díaz abandoned the system. Moreover, Porfirian recruits were not bandits, and many did not own a horse or gun, so the administration devised a complicated system of pay deductions that allowed the men to finance their matériel over time. When discharged, they could resell their equipment to the quartermaster at a mutually agreeable price. Illiterate guards were somehow supposed to keep records of their deposits and deductions, but bookkeeping was hardly their forte. Therefore, officers who controlled the procedures enjoyed another wide-open route to cheating.[18]

The corpsmen were not necessarily docile in the face of abuse. Their charges against the officers became so numerous that in 1895 the Inspector General of Rurales told them to be more specific and to sign their allegations. When they did, the result was a thick catalogue of offenses logged by the corpsmen, and not all of them involved money matters. The detachment in Monterrey complained that their commander had assigned them to the personal charge of a local politician who treated them like servants, beat them like slaves, and forced them to pimp for him. Another officer, who had become the lackey of United States sugar planters in Veracruz, imprisoned a corpsman for fifteen days because he had borrowed a file from the Americans to sharpen his machete. The specific charge: unnecessarily bothering a foreign entrepreneur. In another instance, a physician employed by the corps refused to give a sick guard medical attention, and the corpsman's superior ordered the ill man to cut fodder by day and gave him guard duty at night. In none of these cases was the offending official reprimanded or punished. Investigators came down on the side of the officers.[19]

No wonder the corpsmen did not seem to care much about their duty. A sergeant who inspected the detachment at Cantera, Michoacán, found the corpsmen drunk in a neighboring village. He ordered them to their quarters. While returning, one drunk guard fell off his horse; the animal then toppled over and nearly killed him. The inspector took no disciplinary action in this case, but he was not often so lenient. A lieutenant ordered a sergeant to arrest a criminal in a nearby town; when the enlisted man did not return, the officer investigated and found the sergeant drunk in a saloon. That sergeant was discharged, as were the corpsmen assigned to patrol a Mexican Central train, who arrived drunk in Acámbaro, Guanajuato, and cussed out the municipal policemen sent to meet them. The men who in 1896 drank up pulque worth 400 pesos of the thousand entrusted to them for safe escort to a depository received the same punishment.[20]

The incidence of such offenses is difficult to estimate—plenty of them are recorded in the constabulary's ledgers—but there is no doubt about the drinking. An inspector reported in 1910 that chronic alcoholism afflicted much of the organization. Nearly half the policemen committed offenses serious enough to be included as part of their service record. Commanders handled many others informally. A good third of the infractions written up involved drunkenness on duty, and another 25 percent mentioned missed formations. Officers also cited guards for lack of military spirit, abuse of confidence, spreading malevolent rumors about their commander, criticizing the corps, and contracting debts. And those punished with restrictions, extra duty, or jail were by no means only single or double offenders. Almost 30 percent committed five or more violations. Espiridón Vera piled up twenty-six offenses over three years until he deserted in 1891. Antonio Velásquez finished his enlistment the preceding year with twenty-three violations. The record, however, must go to Eduardo Martínez, a 24-year-old married hatmaker from the Federal District, who enlisted in 1887 and had nine offenses before being promoted to sergeant second class. He managed two more at that rank before reenlisting. After another couple of infractions he was promoted to sergeant first class. He somehow committed another twenty-two offenses—abusing his authority, mistreating his horse, and the usuals—before being discharged as "habitual" in 1896.[21]

The administration in the capital tried to alleviate these conditions by issuing a series of written decrees that circulated among the corps commanders, but lax supervision and follow-up by that high office meant that the orders were ignored. Inspector General Francisco Ramírez, more colorful than capable, noted in 1895 that commanders most frequently completed their banditry reports by stating that the brigands had escaped. He advised more diligence, but did not tell his men to produce or else.[22] He also urged the upgrading of recruits and suggested that his officers attend military classes. A few did, but the efficiency report of one lieutenant still read: "Capacity: none. He did not learn anything inside or outside the military academy. Aptitude: none. Performs duties slowly and ineptly. Civil conduct: frequents prostitutes and gets drunk. Military conduct: sets bad example for subordinates." But it concluded that the lieutenant showed respect for his superiors, and that was apparently enough to secure his position. Or he knew someone up top.[23] Formal education and training really did not matter much. Evaluators of one officer found him stupid and noted he had attended only rural primary school. Yet they concluded that he was "useful for the Rurales" because he understood how to reason with and control country people, meaning both his men and those among whom they policed and politicked.[24]

An honor council of officers, established to examine charges against fellow officials, found officers unwilling to testify against each other. They followed a code about such matters prevalent among police, criminals, and profiteers. Inspector Ramírez also decreed that small, unsupervised detachments be eliminated, a regulation rendered moot in 1903 by the necessity of spreading detachments among a greater number of factories.[25] A variety of circumstances largely hamstrung the inspector's endeavor to improve the corps, although his biggest problem was his own failure to pursue aggressively his stated intentions.

Detailed reports concerning personnel, logistics, and duties, some due every four days, deluged the central administration with paper. Everything demanded a written report: those bound bundles still lie in Mexico's National Archive. When a guard tossed a rock at a bucking horse and slightly injured the animal's eye, a long explanation ensued. The inspector eventually told his men to file only the "most urgent" messages and then to "use the least possible number of words." Even so, it was necessary to increase the inspector's civilian assistants from six to twenty employees during the Porfiriato, and they were complemented by ninety corpsmen relieved of field duties to help out. Along with those engaged in administrative duties at the unit levels (assigned to do so by officers shirking their own responsibilities), it took 20 percent of all Rurales just to keep the organization's paperwork moving.[26]

Paper naturally did not improve the constabulary, and it is doubtful that it was ever intended to do so. Chaos and corruption behind a paper curtain was typically Porfirian and a characteristic of other personal dictatorships. But after the economic crisis of 1907 and the political reverberations that succeeded it, Díaz became more concerned about his Rural Police Force. Army inspectors detailed to investigate it returned with reports crammed with details concerning peculations, alcoholism, nepotism, dilapidated equipment, spent horses, misused and abused personnel, and overall indolence. And they named names. None of these charges was new, but they added up to a stinging indictment of the organization, or at least of those units under review.[27]

The performance of Mexico's Rurales should not have been, and probably was not, unexpected. In his analysis of the modern origins of four European police forces, David Bayley concludes that although some broad generalizations might blanket them all, their national peculiarities are far more evident and significant. The shape and style of each is most determined by the political and cultural heritage and contemporary ambience in which it emerges. The unarmed and drably dressed British "bobbies" reflected the early-nineteenth-century Englishman's concerns for individual liberties along with his distaste for continental militarism. Italy's highly politicized and militarized carabinieri resulted from the realities of that nation's unification. The French gendarmerie was a logical extension of France's strong centralist traditions and the immediate need to reinforce state power, whereas the Prussian police were naturally military-like but decentralized, attesting to the ability of the Prussian aristocracy to retain accustomed police functions.[28]

The notoriously romanticized Texas Rangers reflected the largely lawless and politically corrupt society in which they operated, along with the intentions and prejudices of the dominant group they came from and represented. Canada's Mounties hardly fired a shot on duty in the Northwest, but that was because they were relatively well educated, were skilled horsemen, and were reared in an atmosphere of widely respected law and order—and, perhaps more important, because they policed sparsely populated regions where they were frequently welcomed by the inhabitants (Indians) and faced no real opposition to the westward expansion they were to secure. It was a great deal easier to be an exemplary police force in Canada than in most other places.[29]

Mexico's Rurales mirrored their own national development with its uneven and incomplete political centralization and the jarring effects of uncontrollable economic change. Modernization put many individuals at odds with themselves. Even when they wanted to be modern they had no way to accomplish the task, and so much that was new contradicted what had for so long been right. Imagine telling a Rural to police a fiesta without taking a drink, or not to abuse his newly acquired authority for personal gain. People accustomed to informal and somewhat flexible relations with superiors do not take well to a long list of formal written regulations. Most corpsmen could not even read them. Mexicans did not suddenly shed their attitudes toward authority, self-discipline, and duty with the advent of Porfirio Díaz. Campesinos and artisans had their own familiar ways of doing things, and becoming Rurales did not change that. In fact, much in the new order made no sense to them. So guards unaccustomed to bedchecks scaled the walls of their enclosed barracks at night to get out on the town. Or they slipped women and alcoholic drinks into their quarters. Given some authority, they used it. Guards regularly extorted food and pesos from the third-class train passengers they were supposed to police—that is, when they were not lolling around in first-class accommodations.[30] Peasants had always complained about their hard lives, so corpsmen unashamedly told off their superiors and got punished for insubordination, which is one reason they drank a lot and deserted. Rural policemen did what came naturally, behavior no doubt exaggerated by the pressures and exhilaration of change. But regardless of their other shortcomings, the Rurales were obviously doing a good political job for Porfirio Díaz, and that had always been their main assignment.

Chapter 10
The President's Police

Police forces are primarily political, and the Rurales were more political than most. The persistent challenge to the legitimacy of Porfirian rule, and substantial resistance to the dictator's program of national development, required it. Political centralization bred the force, but political centralization really meant only state penetration. Díaz never intended to be totalitarian. He wanted only to survive as president. So the Rurales all along served the needs of international capitalism, the cornerstone of the Porfirian dictatorship. The corpsmen were first used to break down major regional resistance to central interference. Then, as modernization manufactured new challenges to the political order, they switched assignments. The turn of the century found the corpsmen countering proletarian protest, which was demanding an entirely new relationship between government and society, one that the president could not see or did not care to recognize. Díaz was no Bismarck.

The Rurales did not try to integrate and to police all of Mexico; that was never the Díaz plan. The president's flag-waving nationalism did not mean nationhood. The corpsmen went where economic development ordered them. Contingents rode the trains and manned railroad depots both to ensure order and security and to convince travelers and businessmen that Mexico was well-policed and safe. They also protected payrolls in transit, hustled factory hands to their machines, kept campesinos slashing cane, drove natives from productive land wanted for commercial development, and escorted dignitaries anywhere on request. They also made sure that recruits got to their army garrisons and that Díaz choices won their elections—these last two assignments to meet specific needs of the dictator. All in all, Rurales appeared to be everywhere, but in fact Díaz concentrated them in central Mexico, where most of the new enterprises emerged and where modernization most disrupted population and encouraged migration. Although there were only two thousand to twenty-four hundred Rurales in all, they maintained an astounding visibility and made an extraordinary public impact, even though police everywhere are much more ubiquitous than numerous.[1]

Government strategy placed the police corps in cities around the capital in the early 1880s, when the guards were politically less dependable and had to be watched by loyal superiors. Daily patrols rode out from places like Querétaro and Morelia to check on rural conditions around their command positions. Hacendados, merchants, and local officials along the routes signed certificates of vigilance carried by the guards just to assure the administration that both they and the guards were doing their jobs: checking on each other. Three corps protected the railroad from Veracruz to the capital, and a large contingent remained in the Federal District within easy hailing distance of the presidency.[2]

As the dictatorship steadily gained the support or compliance of rural interests that had formerly favored separation, it became safer to factionalize the Rural Police Force. The administration stationed detachments of five to fifteen men each in communities scattered mostly throughout seven central states, putting the majority within short distances of roads and rail lines. Their placement, intended to insure the free flow of commerce, brought them into contact with bandits. In terms of Rurales versus bandits, the result was a standoff. The Porfirian press exaggerated the successes of the corpsmen, but the opposition never let Díaz forget the persistence of brigandage, some of it just outside of the capital. Expanding railroads attracted more Rurales to the lines; as the economy diversified geographically, contingents spread out from the ore mines in Guerrero and Michoacán to textile factories in Tlaxcala and Puebla and to tobacco and sugar plantations in Veracruz. A substantial nucleus always remained at the dictator's elbow in the capital and in federally administered Tepic, where Lozada's successors continued to agitate against the intrusions of commercial enterprise.[3]

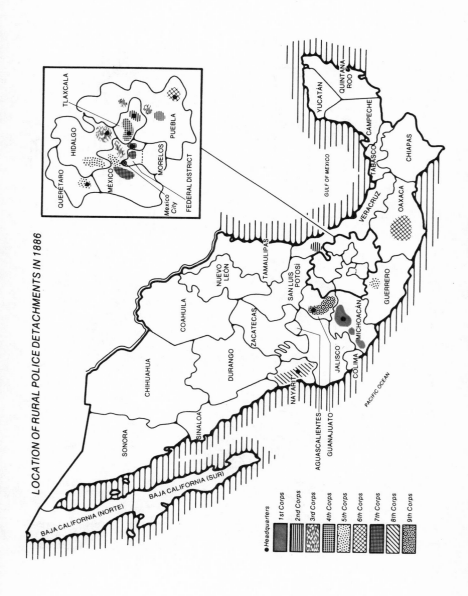

LOCATION OF RURAL POLICE DETACHMENTS IN 1886

BAJA CALIFORNIA (NORTE)
BAJA CALIFORNIA (SUR)
SONORA
SINALOA
CHIHUAHUA
DURANGO
COAHUILA
NUEVO LEÓN
TAMAULIPAS
ZACATECAS
SAN LUIS POTOSI
NAYARIT
AGUASCALIENTES
GUANAJUATO
JALISCO
COLIMA
MICHOACAN
QUERETARO
HIDALGO
TLAXCALA
PUEBLA
MEXICO
MORELOS
FEDERAL DISTRICT
Mexico City
GUERRERO
VERACRUZ
OAXACA
CHIAPAS
TABASCO
CAMPECHE
YUCATÁN
QUINTANA ROO
GULF OF MEXICO
PACIFIC OCEAN

● Headquarters
1st Corps
2nd Corps
3rd Corps
4th Corps
5th Corps
6th Corps
7th Corps
8th Corps
9th Corps

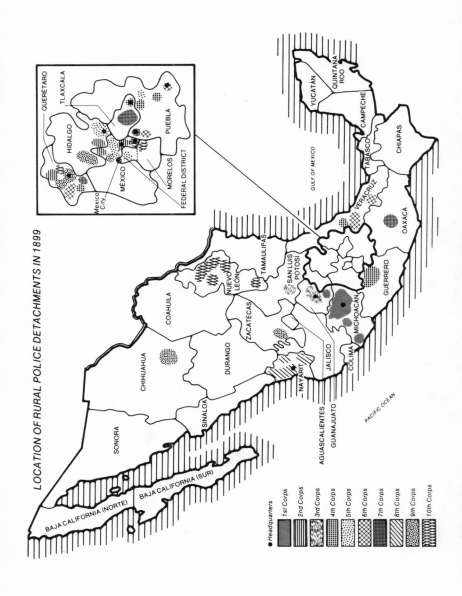

LOCATION OF RURAL POLICE DETACHMENTS IN 1899

● Headquarters
1st Corps
2nd Corps
3rd Corps
4th Corps
5th Corps
6th Corps
7th Corps
8th Corps
9th Corps
10th Corps

BAJA CALIFORNIA (NORTE)
BAJA CALIFORNIA (SUR)
SONORA
CHIHUAHUA
SINALOA
DURANGO
COAHUILA
NUEVO LEÓN
TAMAULIPAS
ZACATECAS
SAN LUIS POTOSÍ
NAYARIT
AGUASCALIENTES
GUANAJUATO
JALISCO
COLIMA
MICHOACÁN
GUERRERO
OAXACA
VERACRUZ
CHIAPAS
TABASCO
CAMPECHE
QUINTANA ROO
YUCATÁN
GULF OF MEXICO
PACIFIC OCEAN

QUERÉTARO
TLAXCALA
HIDALGO
PUEBLA
MÉXICO
MORELOS
FEDERAL DISTRICT
Mexico City

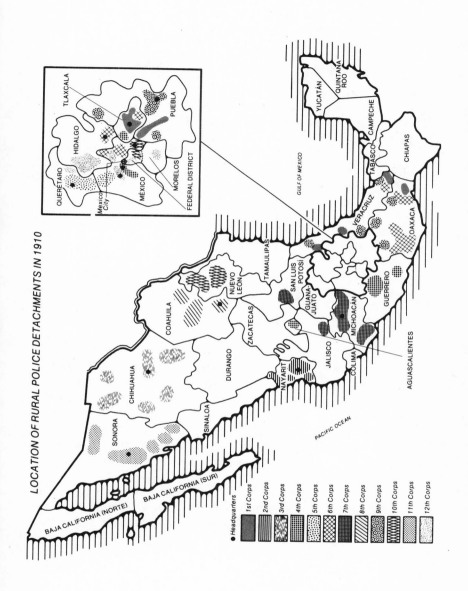

LOCATION OF RURAL POLICE DETACHMENTS IN 1910

- Headquarters
- 1st Corps
- 2nd Corps
- 3rd Corps
- 4th Corps
- 5th Corps
- 6th Corps
- 7th Corps
- 8th Corps
- 9th Corps
- 10th Corps
- 11th Corps
- 12th Corps

BAJA CALIFORNIA (NORTE)
BAJA CALIFORNIA (SUR)
SONORA
CHIHUAHUA
SINALOA
DURANGO
COAHUILA
NUEVO LEON
ZACATECAS
TAMAULIPAS
NAYARIT
JALISCO
COLIMA
AGUASCALIENTES
SAN LUIS POTOSI
GUANA-JUATO
MICHOACAN
GUERRERO
VERACRUZ
OAXACA
CHIAPAS
TABASCO
CAMPECHE
YUCATAN
QUINTANA ROO

PACIFIC OCEAN
GULF OF MEXICO

TLAXCALA
PUEBLA
HIDALGO
QUERETARO
MÉXICO
Mexico City
MORELOS
FEDERAL DISTRICT

Although such concentration becomes evident in overview, the fewer than twenty-five hundred Rurales were in reality rather thinly scattered over a large, territorially truncated area that found individual detachments widely separated if not isolated. Corps commanders had units in as many as six different states, and at one point Rurales from three different corps patrolled the same railroad, causing confusion, overlap, and rancor. No one ever knew who commanded them. Competent supervision was one of the organization's shortest suits.[4]

Proletarian strife after 1900 redistributed the corpsmen, clustering them even more tightly around the capital. By 1905 perhaps 80 percent of the Rurales were stationed in contingents of fifteen to twenty-five men at factories just to keep the workers in line, and others continued to man the railroads. National emergencies also occasioned a few shifts. Headquarters developed a new unit in 1905 to deal with the latest outburst of Yaqui hostilities in Sonora, and it moved the Fifth Corps to the Guatemala border in 1907 when hostilities with that neighbor threatened war. And Madero's call to revolution, of course, caused the transfer of several corps to the north. Fundamentally, however, Mexico's Rural Police organization manned the central states, its tentacles stretching along the major export-import routes.[5]

Just as the government exercised its authority in an arbitrary but limited way, so did the Rurales. They were not professionals concerned with law enforcement; there was only marginal reliance on the law for social control. But the Rurales tried to insure that things went the dictator's way, and their payment included peculations of money and matériel, gifts and concessions from local business, political posts, and permission to carouse, bully, and show off their machismo where they worked. Rurales, everywhere, were big men around town.

The true stories about them are legion. Lieutenant Alfredo Sánchez Pérez was a terror at his post in Dinamita, Durango. Drunk and armed to the teeth, he rode on horseback right into a local restaurant and demanded service; outside, a picket line of his men prevented interruptions. Pérez once also locked up the town tailor in the unit's barracks until the tailor made him a jacket. But, most alarming, he habitually galloped through the explosives factory under his police supervision, bowling over peons toting dynamite while the hoofs of his horse kicked up sparks all about the munitions. The plant manager complained, but Pérez apparently stayed at his post.[6]

The corpsmen bought heavily on credit and then deserted the constabulary or, for a fee, had themselves transferred to another station. Or they took what they wanted and challenged their victims to do something about it, like the second lieutenant at Molino de Guadalupe who threatened tavern owners with mayhem if they did not satisfy his drinking habits, and on credit. Factory managers loaned money for fear corpsmen would mistreat them and their workers if they refused. Guards took twenty pesos worth of fish from a Veracruz vendor without paying him and went unpunished, although two guards who, in 1907, punched a drunken peon and stole two and a half pesos from him, ended up before a municipal judge. And the constabulary discharged a Rural who stole a bottle of brandy from a grocer. "It is a disgrace that those in charge of public security are the first to disrupt it," complained *El Monitor Republicano.* "For what purpose serve the Rurales?" asked *El Hijo del Ahuizote,* reporting that one of them had stolen the municipal treasury where he worked.[7] A good many Mexicans learned the answer to that question the hard way.

Officers frequently took advantage of their position to gain personal profit. One lieutenant established a veterinarian's service across the street from his post, and another forced his men and nearby factory workers to patronize his cantina at Atotonilco, Tlaxcala. An official farmed at his duty station, using his men to cut hay he then sold as horsefeed to the corps for an exorbitant price. Others entered politics. The governor of Veracruz in 1904 named a Rural officer the jefe político of the region he policed, but when corps headquarters made him choose between politics and patrol work he remained a Rural. A lieutenant faced with a similar choice in Guanajuato became a jefe. The official at Santiago, Nuevo León, was all at the same time that community's judge, municipal president, and deputy to the state congress, and the officer at Lampazos, in the same state, was also his town's president and received pay for both jobs. Why were some Rurales allowed to retain political positions and others not? It was up to Díaz, and each case merited a separate decision.[8]

Not all Rural Police activities were self-indulgent. According to their charter, the corpsmen were to serve local public security needs as dictated by the jefe político or the ranking municipal official. In fact, however, orders to the detachments came from Díaz through the Inspector General of Rurales. Public order to Díaz meant the maintenance of his political control, so he withheld the services of the constabulary from those he distrusted or desired to punish, and gave them to subordinates of whose loyalty he remained certain. So the relationship between the corpsmen and the jefe and other local authorities ranged from blind obedience to bitter conflict, and offered further proof of discord within the dictatorship.

Most often, the Rurales cooperated with local authorities. Little jobs: they arrested thirteen individuals who trespassed on an hacienda in Actompam, Veracruz, to steal the aguamiel from maguey plants in order to make pulque, recovered three youngsters who had run away from an orphan's home in Mexico City, and turned other boys who had put stones on railroad tracks over to municipal authorities. Domestic affairs: they investigated the shooting of a priest at Tiacalco, state of México, and discovered that a girl placed in the priest's protective custody several weeks prior to her marriage, in accordance with custom, had been sexually violated by the prelate, so her fiancé had shot the priest. The Rurales understood, and made no arrest.[9] Bigger assignments: they broke up a smuggling ring at Cuesta de Mamulique in Nuevo León and routed bandits rustling cattle in Morelos and Veracruz. They recovered more than 20,000 pesos worth of bank notes within twenty-four hours of their theft from an hacienda near Apizaco, state of Tlaxcala, and they received substantial bonuses for fast work, well done, in 1903 at Santa Lucrecia in Veracruz, where fifty bandits looted the local train depot. Rurales captured forty-four of the robbers within hours and recovered most of the stolen property.[10] Servile work, too: moving house furnishings for a judge in the Federal District, supervising prisoners sweeping the streets, serving as common city patrolmen in Tepic and as low-level administrators in Zacatecas. Their horses were at times worn out lugging mail and doing other personal services for a jefe, and at Ayotla in the state of México they collected church tithes, rounded up drunks, and enforced cantina closing hours.[11] Like most police work, Rural Police service rarely proved as glamorous as it was purported to be, which is one reason why so many deserted it.

As frequently as Rurales did the bidding of local strongmen, they refused to be handmaidens to such authorities. Díaz wanted, maybe preferred it, that way. Conflict among his subordinates kept them beholden to the president-general-dictator. And the relationship between the Rurales and a jefe político was in this sense natural, for it immediately raised the question, Who is in charge? Accusations and counter-charges flew back and forth. The Inspector General of Rurales gamely defended his men, but the going was difficult because the jefes, along with so many others, had the ear of the president. When the jefe político at Huachinango, Puebla, demanded four Rurales to escort postal funds, the unit commander explained that he could spare only two guards for the job. Determined to set the matter straight, the jefe appealed directly to the minister of Internal Affairs, complaining that the Rurales had disobeyed him. The minister replied that the Rural Policemen were not under the ministry's direct authority (which they were), that they had other primary duties to perform (which they did), and that they could be used by the jefe only in emergencies and for authorized police work. Moreover, the corpsmen were never meant to be postal employees.[12]

In retaliation, the chastized jefe launched a vendetta against the guards. One corpsman, arrested for attempted murder, proved his innocence. The jefe charged others with robbery, insubordination, and morals offenses. The complaints grew so thick that the inspector sent an officer to investigate. One guard had indeed stolen a horse, another had publicly molested a girl, and a third had insulted a municipal official, but all had been punished by the local judge. The detachment stayed—but the dispute continued. Within the next four years the jefe managed to have four guards discharged from service, three of them for misconduct and the fourth because he had been bucked off his horse and was therefore judged to be unfit for Rural Police duty.[13]

Rurales who became politically popular obviously threatened the jefe político. It meant that the populace saw the Rural as more influential with higher-ups than the jefe. Serious conflict had to follow. Lieutenant Carlos Pacheco in 1902 became commander of the Rural Police detachment at the critical Necaxa post, where power facilities generated electricity for parts of central Mexico, including the capital. The place soon split between Pachequistas and anti-Pachequistas. The row began when the jefe ordered Pacheco to chase bandits who had reportedly stolen 5,000 pesos from a nearby farm. But Pacheco was suspicious. The jefe's command came just prior to the scheduled arrival of a 50,000-peso payroll for the electrical workers. Did the jefe plan to leave that payroll unprotected? Maybe. Moreover, the Englishmen who ran the operation paid the Rurales well to protect their interests. So Pacheco split his troop. Half pursued the bandits—and failed to find them. The other half guarded the payroll. The jefe called it insubordination.

A flood of accusations against the corpsmen followed. A guard charged with assaulting a peon was finally released when evidence showed that the peon had been the aggressor. Drunkenness, stealing, immorality, abuse of authority—the jefe unloaded all sorts of charges on the corpsmen. A subsequent government investigation cleared the guards, or at least confirmed that they had been punished for their infractions. And the manager of the power plant assured Mexico City that the policemen had fulfilled their duties in a "correct and honorable" manner. So Pacheco stayed on, despite his differences with the jefe. As "the President's men," Rurales normally enjoyed the better of things in their disputes with other Porfirian officials.[14]

But that did not deter their competitors. Officials in Veracruz protested that Rurales had maliciously meddled in local police matters while bandits in the vicinity continued to harass travelers. The jefe at Calpulalpan, state of México, successfully prevented the assignment of Rurales to his town with the lame excuse that no housing existed for their lodging, although other officials who welcomed Rurales easily compelled homeowners to relinquish space for the corpsmen. In the Federal District, Tacuba's police chief argued that the Rurales were prone to arrive late, usually drunk, when they investigated a crime. Moreover, corpsmen had beaten a local policeman and stashed him in their barracks; an entire contingent of city police had to force his release. Chihuahua City authorities reported that a fugitive sought by both the city police and the Rurales had been found hiding beneath the bed of a Rural lieutenant assigned to the case. The unfounded allegation typified the slander hurled at the force by those anxious to discredit it. Díaz must have enjoyed the furious competition.[15]

The Inspector General of Rurales could be adamant in dealing with complainants. The jefe político of Xochimilco charged in 1908 that the sergeant in charge of Rurales in his town had refused to switch his men from one site to another, to which the inspector responded that only he had the authority to transfer units. Municipal officials at San Angel, for security reasons, wanted common criminals lodged in the barracks occupied by Rurales, but the inspector insisted that his men not be wasted on common guard duty. When the governor of the Federal District demanded daily administrative reports from detachments of Rurales, the inspector replied that only his office handled such matters.[16] Díaz carefully decided which governors got Rurales and how they used them. He allowed the trusted Bernardo Reyes to have a contingent in Monterrey, but when the governor of Puebla petitioned for Rurales to work under his supervision, the president replied in no uncertain terms that although corpsmen might cooperate with state authorities in bandit control, they had no business being directed by a state governor.[17]

The Rurales exerted power over the populace. They were respected not so much for their efficiency or harshness as for the haphazard and unpredictable manner in which they operated. If asked what justice meant in Porfirian Mexico, many citizens would have mentioned the Rurales. Although the police did not participate in formal judicial proceedings, they regularly decided the more important everyday disputes that arose between laborers and bosses, villagers and hacendados. Because the corpsmen might construe public protest in any form as insubordination or even subversion, the mere presence of Rurales helped to maintain order. For example, *The Engineering and Mining Journal* (New York) noted in 1903 that labor difficulties at a San Luis Potosí smelter had been resolved after a ten-day strike and that "the men are now working again to better advantage under the moral suasion of the Rurales."[18] The Rural Policemen were not ordinarily repressive; they depended on locals for their food, entertainment, lodging, sex, and payoffs. But they could be truculent. At the Oaxaqueña plantation in Veracruz they beat the peons with the sex organs of bulls.[19] Or they could be restrained, as they were during the blood-soaked labor strife at Cananea and Río Blanco. At the same time, Rurales could apply the ley fuga, which they did in 1905 in the city of Tlaxcala in order to eliminate political competition for Governor Próspero Cahuantzi, himself a former Rural Police corps commander. But these culprits did not go unpunished. They were discharged from service and referred to civil court for disposition. In other ley fuga cases, the corps also sought systematically to rid itself of public criticism while maintaining a tough image.[20] As the Revolution approached and complaints against the government grew more strident, the administration increasingly endeavored to cleanse the corps of criminal accusations or even charges of un-justified harshness. Díaz was less bothered with such matters in his better times.

Although the Rurales undoubtedly impressed them, common Mexicans were not necessarily cowed by the policemen. They fought the corpsmen, as they had so many others, in defense of their claims. Rurales rode to a small village near Texmelucán, in Puebla, to punish natives who had trespassed on an hacienda in order to dispute their lost water rights. A clanging church bell and a fusillade of rifle fire greeted the police, who retreated. Informed of the incident, the governor referred the water question to the courts and ordered the Rurales to hold their peace. Whether or not the villagers ever got their water is not known, but the Rurales did not decide this particular issue with force.[21]

In another trespassing incident, corpsmen arrested five residents of San Pedro, near Pachuca. On their way to jail with the prisoners, the policemen encountered fifty villagers from San Pedro who were determined to free their compatriots. The cam-pesinos wounded a number of Rurales in the shootout that ensued, but the corpsmen finally managed to get their prisoners to

Pachuca. Then the Rurales returned to San Pedro with reinforcements, where they arrested fifty-four natives and turned them over to the jefe político and an unknown fate.[22]

Corpsmen swooped down on settlements around Tlacolula in Hidalgo in 1899 and arrested thirty-three individuals on the orders of the jefe político there. Friends of the prisoners, hiding in brushy fields behind boulders and trees, contested the policemen guerrilla-style all the way to Tlacolula, where local security guards helped to repulse the natives. And Rural Policemen who arrested six peons in connection with the theft of burlap sacks from an hacienda outside of San Marcos, Puebla, were unexpectedly confronted by perhaps sixty adversaries anxious to liberate their accused friends. Insults and fists flew, and the guards needed their swords to drive off the aggressors.[23]

In another incident, campesinos sought to cross a roadblock manned by corpsmen at a Tepic hacienda. The campesinos pelted the guards with rocks and belted them with poles until the exasperated corpsmen opened fire with their rifles. One peon was killed and another wounded. The offending policemen were subsequently arrested and turned over to judicial authorities. The Rurales may have forced the respect of many Mexicans, but they certainly did not always cow the campesinos.[24]

In general, individual men made the constabulary what it was, and because the corps enlisted the most troubled and troublesome members of that unsettled society, highly mixed results could be expected. Mexico's Rural Police Force exemplified the order and disorder characteristic of its times—and, therefore, reflected the instability of the dictatorship.

Chapter 11
It's the Image That Counts

Reputation, much more than performance, makes police what they are in the public mind. Political authorities carefully craft that reputation through deliberate image-building. Myths surrounding police are at least as powerful as those that envelop bandits. Canada's "Mounties" are free of corruption and, as Sergeant Preston proves, always get their man. Texas Rangers are fearless. Scotland Yard employs the best minds, and the F.B.I. defends democracy. When the reputation of a police force is damaged, so is its power, which is why police are so defensive about their image, and why those involved in social control must continually nourish the myth of their police. Porfirio Díaz understood. Modern mass communications make image-building all the more sophisticated, effective, and insidious. Díaz had to depend on travelers, uniforms, parades, newspapers, foreign expositions, and word of mouth to spread the message. And what a job he did! People constantly read and talked about the thousands and thousands of elite Rurales on duty in the republic. Mexicans hailed them as national heroes and gloried in their reputation as a skilled and tough constabulary. To criticize the Rural Police was to attack the president, even Mexico itself, so the corps became untouchable. By inflating their successes and shielding their failure, the Rurales became invincible.

Foreign commentators found the Rurales among the best-paid, most skilled equestrians in the world. They were picked men of great strength and courage, taller than the average Mexican and tougher, and so "the evildoer may expect little mercy at their hands." Nor did the Rurales waste time or patience on criminals. "Their court dockets are never crowded. The official shooter with his Winchester goes from court and shoots the prisoners as fast as they are condemned."[1] The Rurales had pacified Mexic ɔ—so went the myth, absorbed and enlarged by capitalists who hau ɩo believe that their interests were safe.

The Rurales became Mexico itself. To an Englishmen, they recalled *The Pirates of Penzance.* Former bandits, they had been attracted to the law much as United States frontiersmen had sometimes employed desperados as their sheriffs. "Now for the picture. Imagine stalwart men, whose horsemanship is perfect, clad in leather suits profusely ornamented with silver, wearing gray sombreros; their saddles the most expensive and ornate, the horses of each . . . matched to perfection . . . in perfect line as they gallop by; now black chargers, then chestnut, and the new piebald—and even the horses clothed in leather, as were the steeds of the ancient knights of Spain. This indeed is a marvelously characteristic thing—'This IS Mexico.' "[2]

Mexico's press, anxious to embellish favorable comment about the country, enhanced the myth. *El Tiempo* breathlessly recounted the daring of Rurales who appeared at the 1901 International Exposition in Buffalo, New York:

> About 12,000 or 14,000 spectators were gathered in the stadium at the exposition when a lion escaped. A shot only scared the lion as he prepared to attack the audience. The lion tamer continued to fire his gun but with no effect. People stampeded each other heading for exits. Then an event occurred that stopped them in their tracks. . . . One of the Mexican Rurales without any weapons, only a smile on his lips and a rope used in training colts in his hand, leaped into the arena in front of the lion, and with an imperious look and extraordinary valor proceeded by cracking his rope like a whip to drive the lion into its cage. All, including the lion, were amazed and stunned.
>
> When the crowd realized what had occurred, that the king of beasts had been conquered by the magnetic power of a domineering look, the ovation was louder than the panic. The crowd raised the rural policeman Fernández to its shoulders and carried him to his quarters. As a climax to the drama, the lion tamer went mad and remains so today.[3]

The *Buffalo Express* reported the same incident quite differently. Spectators were listening to a band concert when a half-grown lion escaped its cage. People did not panic because a high, solid fence separated them from the lion. A man with a "peaked hat," probably a Rural, attempted to corral the animal, but the lion evaded him until a spectator reached over the fence and grabbed the lion by the nape of the neck and put it back in its cage. Some fifteen minutes before the incident, the lion and its mate had shared their cage with a little girl as part of the entertainment at the fair.[4] So much for *El Tiempo*'s courageous Rural.

Usually the international press beat the drums for the Rural Police corps. The *Illustrated Buffalo Express* explained that

> these Rurales are somewhat similar to the old Texas Rangers, but if this be possible, they are even tougher than the Rangers. Bred from infancy among the hills and valleys of old Mexico and accustomed not only to the saddle but to living on the most meagre rations and requiring no other bed but the green fields or other covering than a serape, the men recruited for the Rurales make a fierce kind of soldier. They can continue the chase of a criminal for hundreds of miles, sleeping in the forest or on the mountains, sometimes meeting with good fare and other times subsisting entirely on corn moistened in water and eaten raw.
>
> These are the soldiers—a sort of revenue officer and mounted policeman rolled into one—whose name strikes terror into the assassin or robber in Mexico. Well does the robber know that with this troop in pursuit, his game is up. The one idea of a Rural is to capture him dead or alive, it makes no difference to him, but capture he knows he must, and he generally does it too. It is due to Rurales that interior Mexico is so free of crime, that trains are not held up, banks are not robbed and that murderers and assassinations are so very rare. Rurales are all over Mexico. Every town or village has its quota. They are seen from every train. . . .[5]

Little myths also abounded. *El Imparcial*, a Porfirian advocate in the capital, reported that during the May 5th celebration in 1897, exploding firecrackers had caused a corpsman's horse on parade to buck and stumble down. The animal had turned around twice on the pavement but had not unseated the corpsman, who sat firmly in his saddle while he slowly raised his mount and then calmly proceeded in the formation as if nothing unusual had happened.[6] Excuses were ready, too. Considerable embarrassment resulted in 1896 when Inspector Ramírez, riding majestically in his silver-ornamented uniform and on his ornate saddle at the front of his colorful troop, was unceremoniously tossed off his mount directly in front of the presidential reviewing stand. But Ramírez was neither ridiculed nor blamed. The city's press explained that the exceptionally nasty horse had caused the incident.[7]

As the Revolution engulfed the country in 1911, image-building increased: "The Rurales are picked horsemen and sharpshooters selected from among trained cattle-riders of the wild mountain ranges and desert plains of Northern Mexico. . . . The fact that there are many notorious outlaws and bandits among them only enhances their fighting efficiency. . . . They have scout dogs trained to run down fugitives and to hold their masters' horses by the bridle. . . . The horse of a Mexican Rural would make crack U.S. polo ponies look poor."[8]

What matter that one-third of the corpsmen never rode horses? Or that inspectors found a great many of the mounts overworked, underfed, blind, and lame? Or that green recruits could hardly ride the scarcely tamed, untrained colts assigned to them on enlistment? Or that the blacksmith assigned to one unit feared horses? Those expert horsemen sent to represent Mexico at foreign expositions may not have been Rurales. They certainly were not the average Rural, but probably a special troop reserved for show.[9]

President Díaz enthusiastically endorsed and enhanced the exaggerations and misconceptions about his Rural Police Force. If observers thought the corps gigantic, fine. Bandits-turned-policemen, excellent. Let the bourgeoisie delude itself about the security of its holdings. The president systematically created pomp and circumstances to feed imaginations. Units sent their best horsemen to special events in the capital, where clean and handsomely decorated suede leather uniforms replaced the dusty, dilapidated daily wear.

The president presided at an annual banquet honoring the corps, although more diplomats and dignitaries attended than did corpsmen. At nine o'clock on the morning of the feast, a corps commander posted elegantly mounted Rurales for three miles along the beautiful Reforma Boulevard from the wooded hill of Chapultepec Park to the Columbus Circle, memorable for its brilliant flower beds. The presidential carriage arrived about noon. Then Díaz reviewed the troops from a balcony of the Elysian

Tivoli, a magnificent restaurant with sumptuous gardens and a gambling casino, all reserved only for the elite. It was stag night at the banquet: only the highest functionaries of government, such as army generals, and foreign diplomats attended it, along with some newspaper correspondents, poets, and novelists. Any male who was anyone in society craved an invitation.

At the banquet the dictator toasted the Rurales as guarantors of the safe peace of the people. Not only did Rurales protect farmers against bandits, but they guarded the innocence of women and children against evildoers. Next, Inspector Ramírez thanked the president for his personal attentiveness to the corps, and then all the company sat down to dinner at a banquet table shaped like a horseshoe and heavily trimmed with floral emblems of state. The menu was absolutely gourmet, usually French, not Mexican: *poulet à l'anglaise, filets de boeufs Colbert, paté de fois gras aspic,* and *salade cresson.* On occasion it was a real Mexican country meal: *mole, carne asada,* and pulque. Then—off they went to the gambling tables.[10]

Like the brigands they occasionally brought to bay, the Rurales were also remembered in poetry and popular *corridos:*

> Long live, long live the valiant Rural,
> Who has spent his life on campaign. . . .
> Our country does itself proud
> To have such brave sons
> In these Rurales of indominable spirit
> Who are free and are not slaves.
>
> Brave when on rugged campaign,
> Calm and ready to fight,
> No enemy is able to conquer
> The natural bravery of the Rural.
>
> This corps of brilliant *charros*
> Is the pride of modern Mexico.
> In their breasts is sheltered
> The flame of a brave and loyal heart.[11]

United States military leaders were so impressed by what they knew of Mexico's Rural Police Force that in 1898 they tried to recreate the constabulary in Cuba, then under United States military government. For months, United States army personnel studied records of the Rurales in Mexico City so that they could apply the institution's role and organization to post-war Cuba, but the Mexican press doubted Yankee intentions. *El Tiempo* suggested that the Americans were collecting military intelligence about Mexico's crack police force prior to aggression against their southern neighbor. The newspaper urged its government to "imitate the eloquent examples of prudence, cunning and foresight" provided by the Americans in planning their country's future.[12] Data concerning the constabulary undoubtedly went into United States intelligence files, but how much the Mexicans let them see and know about the corps is another question. The exhaustive report on the constabulary prepared by the Americans can be traced to Washington, D.C., but its trail disappears in the United States National Archives.[13]

All this carefully tailored image-building of the Rurales obviously affected those whom the president considered most important to his politics and programs. Capitalists saw their investments safe in a country patrolled by Rurales. The masses in the capital, madly cheering Rurales on parade, indicated the nationalistic fervor the corpsmen could inspire. But what of the ordinary Mexicans among whom the policemen worked? They were by and large untouched by the myths—they knew the guards for real, and seem to have admired or at least respected the corpsmen for their machismo as much as they feared and detested them for their abuses. John Reed, the young American newspaperman, sympathetic to Mexican revolutionaries, noted this tendency—the love-hate relationship—in 1913 when he trailed the rebels across Chihuahua. He came across a dead Rural

> upon his back, twisted sideways from his hips; . . . We could reconstruct this man's last struggle. He had dropped off his horse, wounded—for there was blood on the ground—into a little dry arroyo. We could even see where his horse had stood while he pumped shells into his Mauser with feverish hands, and blazed away, first to the rear where pursuers came running with Indian yells, and then at the hundreds and hundreds of bloodthirsty horsemen pouring down from the north, with the Demon Pancho Villa at their head. He must have fought a long time, perhaps until they ringed him with living

flame—for we found hundreds of empty cartridges. And then, when the last shot was spent, he made a dash eastward, hit at every step; hid for a moment under a little railroad bridge, and ran out upon the open desert, where he fell. There were twenty bullet holes in him. They had stripped him of all save his underclothes. He lay sprawled in an attitude of desperate action, muscles tense, one fist clenched and spread across the dust as if he were dealing a death blow; the fiercest exultant grin on his face. . . . They had shot him through the head three times.[14]

Ordinary Mexicans killed Rurales as Rurales killed bandits; they made doubly sure the enemy did not return, because each adversary credited the other with powers that made him more than mortal.[15] An English traveler encountered an example of the manner in which Mexicans disposed of Rurales:

Rounding a bend in the trail, we came across two corpses laid across the road. A sharp command from the lieutenant halted the troop, and we urged our frightened horses nearer the bodies. From what was left we could see that they had been Rurales, two of the crack mounted police corps, but they had been stripped of everything of value, mutilated in true Indian manner, and the desecrated corpses laid across the trail for all to view.

They lay there in the sunlight, their faces and skin olive-grey in colour, a heavy blue growth of beard on jowl and cheek. Their feet and hands had been severed, the feet lay by the stumps of the arms, while the legs terminated in a grotesque hand turned palm upwards to the sky. The bodies had been ripped up, and the ghastly heads were earless. We could not find the ears, they had probably been kept as mementoes by the rebels.[16]

Mexico's long-defunct Rural Police Force still remains entangled in its gigantic myth. Because the Rurales have been closely associated with a dictatorship that is officially detested in Mexico in order to legitimize a proclaimed Revolution, their reputation has been darkened, although hardly diminished. Even a tinge of fearful admiration remains. Porfirio Díaz, greatly assisted by a national fever to declare Mexico peaceful and secure, fabricated a reputation for his federal policemen—his Rurales—that persists today.

PART IV

DEMONS OF REVOLUTION UNLEASHED

Chapter 12
The Rollercoaster Called
Capitalism

There was a feeling of precariousness everywhere, within the government itself as well as among its benefactors and victims. Common workers and the well-to-do alike sensed the fragility of public order. "There is peace in the country, but not in the hearts and minds of Mexicans who fear what will happen after the death of Díaz. Mexico's peace is mechanical, not organic, and it is transitory."[1] Congressman Francisco Bulnes, an acute national observer, proved right, but the oscillations of world capitalism, not the death of Díaz, fatally cracked the facade of Porfirian order. Although genuine economic expansion and the novelty of change had for a time absorbed a measure of the tension, the economy began to ride a rollercoaster after 1900, which led to disorder that climaxed in revolution. Rurales tried to stem the tide, but the organization itself became captive to mounting disruption. Hence the paradox: the frantic drive for development displaced people who joined the police force and were then used to subdue compatriots reacting to the same forces. Again order and disorder: two sides of the same coin.

The dictatorship of Porfirio Díaz did not steadily slide into the abyss. It descended in fits and starts. Brief recoveries were soon battered and then smothered by reversals beyond the president's control, although he was blamed for worsened conditions. A sharp downturn in the exchange position of its currency and a worldwide depression in 1890–1894 had almost driven Mexico into bankruptcy, but Finance Minister Limantour cut federal spending and raised taxes sufficiently to buoy up the country until the next economic upswing could restimulate confidence and investment. A few years later, Mexico slid backward again. By 1903 a good many

Mexicans had begun to lose faith in the regime. Profit margins had shrunk for the wealthy, and the poor had been sucked further into poverty, hopelessness, and outrage.[2]

After 1900 more advanced industrialized countries basked, if somewhat nervously, in new terms of trade that favored manufactured goods over raw materials. Mexican mines produced more, but their products bought less. Domestic manufacturers modernized their mills, eliminated jobs, and drove out competitors in the process. The rising cost of raw materials like cotton, and the limitations of a consumer market mired in subsistence living, sharply curtailed profits. Annual commercial and industrial growth continued, but at a slower rate as the decade wore on. Recurrent recessions buffeted the wobbly economy, and the deepening silver crisis and the world financial panic of 1907 jarred the country into crisis.[3]

Mexico, until the mid-nineteenth century, led the world's silver producers. Four-fifths of all silver in circulation came from Mexico, but United States silver discoveries after 1860 deeply sliced into Mexico's hegemony and drove down silver prices. The shrinkage of Mexico's income began in earnest after 1870, when one nation after another converted to the gold standard. Silver in relation to gold depreciated steadily from 1873 to 1902, and, worse yet for Mexico, it did so in quirky fluctuations that caused inflation and wrecked budget planning.[4]

Prices changed daily as silver reacted to the cost of gold, and Mexicans at every level suffered the consequences. A 15-percent investment gain on silver in 1890 was, in terms of declining silver values, reduced to only 4 percent by 1905. An import for which a Mexican paid 89 cents in 1877–1878 cost 40 percent more in 1911. Measured against the United States dollar, the peso fell from par to 50 cents over the same time span. Blankets priced at $3.45 each in the United States cost $6 apiece in Mexico. Coffee was three times more costly in Mexico than in the United States and milk twice as much. A gallon of kerosene cost 12 cents in the United States and 40 cents in Mexico. An American laborer earned at least five times the salary of a comparable Mexican worker. Rents and food soared beyond the reach of ordinary Mexicans; a factory hand had to labor six months just to buy a bed. No more butter, sugar, beer, and coffee for the working person, only tortillas, onions, chili peppers, and pulque. Begging, for many, became more profitable than work.[5]

The cost of living for the ordinary Mexican went up slowly and irregularly, but for the better-off it rose quickly and in great strides. Small shops closed in bankruptcy, and the salaries of middle-level people failed to support their accustomed standard of living, much of it imported. Financial cutbacks cost bureaucrats their jobs, and commercial farmers could not afford to mechanize. Capitalists in tropical agriculture, henequen, and cattle, who sold their products for gold and paid their labor in silver, profited. But railroad entrepreneurs, who paid in gold for their rolling stock and received fares and tolls in silver, edged toward failure. Fear that one or another American magnate, like Edward Harriman, might buy out the floundering railroad investors and establish a monopoly over the nation's communications caused Limantour in 1905 to negotiate among various investors for Mexican control of the major lines. It was good for Mexico, but a bad sign of the times. Foreign entrepreneurs had come to recognize the risk of investing in Mexico.[6]

Inflation, a soaring national debt, and frantic looting of national resources to narrow the exchange gap moved Mexico onto the gold standard in 1905, briefly stabilized business, but left the country just that much more vulnerable to international economic storms. In the world financial panic of 1907, banks and investment houses recalled loans and curtailed credit. Limantour ordered Mexican banks to tighten their credit line and to collect outstanding mortgages. Hacendados accustomed to easily renewed loans were caught short with bloated debts, and small businessmen lost their credit source. A depression in world henequen prices ruined growers in Yucatán, The international market for copper and other metals collapsed, and by the fall of 1907 hundreds of miners had been laid off in Hidalgo, Durango, Sonora, and Oaxaca. Pachuca alone witnessed twelve thousand unemployed miners walking its streets in anger and frustration. Closure of the American Smelting and Refining foundry, the Guggenheim

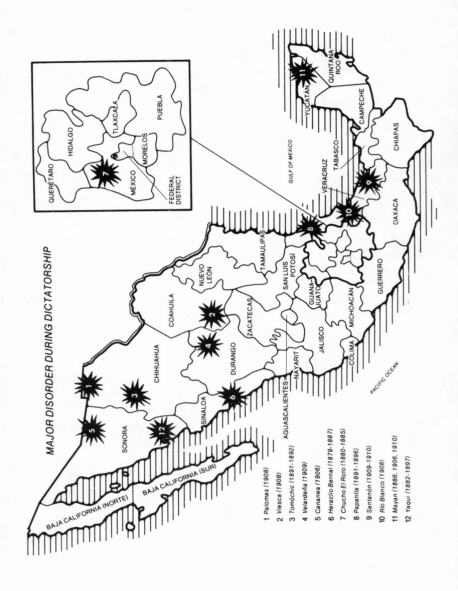

MAJOR DISORDER DURING DICTATORSHIP

1 Palomas (1908)
2 Viesca (1908)
3 Tomóchic (1891-1892)
4 Velardeña (1909)
5 Cananea (1906)
6 Heraclio Bernal (1879-1887)
7 Chucho El Roto (1880-1885)
8 Papantla (1891-1896)
9 Santanón (1909-1910)
10 Río Blanco (1908)
11 Mayan (1886, 1906, 1910)
12 Yaqui (1882-1897)

operation, and the Río Tinto copper works laid off nearly two thousand other workers in Chihuahua. The state's economy reeled under the impact. In 1909, Chihuahua's merchants reported sales off 10 to 30 percent. Silver production there declined 14 percent. Textile mills in other regions merged and collapsed in bankruptcy. Owners tried to stem the tide by trimming wages and slicing the size of the labor force. Such cutbacks cost Mexicans their jobs not only in their own country but in the United States as well.[7]

Díaz was deeply disturbed. An estimated twenty-two thousand Mexicans had migrated to the United States to work in the year 1906–1907; now most had to return empty-handed. North American companies paid the train fare of the Mexicans to El Paso; from there the jobless walked with their bitterness the two hundred miles to Chihuahua City. In the first months of 1907, as many as two thousand laborers were shoved back into Mexico by United States immigration officials at El Paso. Díaz urged hacendados to hire the unemployed migrants. Some did, but drought and unusually heavy snowfalls in 1908 and 1909 made life just that much more miserable for the frustrated returnees. The weak spark of Madero's revolution fell on dry tinder in Chihuahua.[8]

By that time, serious violence had already challenged Porfirian authority: violence by copper miners at Cananea, by the textile workers at Río Blanco, by campesinos around Acayucan, and by radical Liberals at Viesca. The Rurales struggled to hold down the lid; when they could not do so, the army hammered out its ruthless response to the disorder in brutal repression and object lessons written in blood. The dictator's heavy-handed reaction to rising turmoil indicated the narrowness of his national vision. He continued to see conditions as a mid-nineteenth-century military caudillo rather than as a twentieth-century progressive. Modernization may have touched Porifiro Díaz, but it did not change him. All along, the president had played the benevolent patron, professing, even displaying, concern for his ordinary countrymen at the very time that he sacrificed their genuine welfare to the capitalists who maintained his personal dictatorship. The only relief for the people, the only semblance of justice, was to appeal directly to the dictator, who responded with immediate political impulse. Some answers augured well for the common man, most did not. But as conditions worsened and the victims became more organized, the pleas of Mexicans became complaints, then demands, then protest.[9]

Díaz offered sympathy but no betterment, or non-solutions cloaked in sanctimonious trappings. As disorder gained momentum, the dictator responded with force rather than compromise, a change in his mood and style that eventually cost him the presidency. Díaz's obsession with sedition finally caught up with him. Of course, he had previously used his mailed fist. But the tragedies at Tomóchic and Papantla had occurred after long and genuine attempts at compromise. Now it was different: no compromise. Smash the rebels. To most Mexicans, uncompromising force went beyond what people had learned to expect from their government. The ruler was breaking his contract with them. Cruelty rallied the unsophisticated and gave them a battle cry, at a time when organizing factory workers began to emphatically state their grievances.

The ups and downs of the Mexican economy, the people's losing fight against inflation, and the urgings of both Catholic congresses and anarchist propagandists jolted the nation's proletarians into militancy in the first decade of the new century. The workers were disorganized as a class, but plant by plant they had plenty in common: low pay, arbitrary deductions, wretched safety standards, no health or accident benefits, fifteen-hour workdays, overbearing company rules, undeserved punishments, preferred treatment for foreigners, and crass intrusions into their personal lives.[10]

Mutual aid societies and even strikes had to that point earned little relief. For example, wage reductions at Puebla's largest textile mill in 1900 had caused a strike that quickly spread to nearby plants. More than three thousand angry, milling workers quit their jobs. Labor leaders requested the governor to hear their case but he refused, and after two weeks of mumbled discontent the workers wandered back to their looms and spindles with nothing changed. But increasing hardship forged unions, and by 1906 Orizaba's textile workers had formed The Great Circle of Free Workers and were spreading its organization to neighboring states. Far to the north in Sonora, united copper workers at Cananea were already putting management to the test.[11]

The Cananea Consolidated Copper Company was owned by William Greene, an inveterate Yankee gambler who wandered in and out of bankruptcy until he made it big with copper just below Naco, a town split by the international border between Sonora and Arizona. Cananea was a true company town, population twenty-three thousand, about two thousand of them Americans, the rest Mexican, and a private police force to keep the antagonists apart. Greene paid decently enough, 3 pesos daily, but the Mexicans received their wages in silver and the Americans in gold, which gave the latter twice as much purchasing power for the same amount of work. Nor did wages in silver go far in the overpriced company store, which the Mexicans had to patronize for lack of other local business competition.[12]

Management learned in May 1906 that the Mexicans at Cananea were thinking strike. Policemen dressed as peasants mingled with the miners and confirmed that they would demand a 2-peso daily pay increase for an eight-hour working day. Radical Liberals anxious to bring down Díaz fanned the coals. On May 31, rumors of layoffs precipitated a wildcat demonstration by hundreds of miners, then a march on management's quarters. Shots? Who fired first? It only mattered to those who in the aftermath needed to fix blame. Two American foremen died, along with perhaps a dozen strikers. Half the town's policemen refused to confront the rioters, so a call for help went to Governor Rafael Izábal in Hermosillo, the state capital.

Izábal pulled all the levers. All he knew was that he had to keep the peace or answer to the president, so he loaded forty Rurales on a train and headed for Cananea via Naco. He also wired the zone's military commander, General Luis Torres, for reinforcements. He sent "Mad Russian" Kosterlitsky's security troop galloping across the desert from Magdalena to the trouble spot. And he solicited United States assistance—perhaps military but for certain civilian—although he later denied it. They all converged on Cananea.

Some two hundred armed and angry Americans joined the governor at Naco: doctors, lawyers, drunkards, relatives of workers at Cananea, Greene himself, and Tom Rynning, commander of Arizona's Rangers. The arrival of Americans bent on some lesson-teaching only made matters worse at Cananea. There they stood, face to face, hundreds of belligerent strikers and the gringos, spoiling for a fight, their rifles at the ready wait and an occasional bullet zinging overhead. Mounted Rurales formed the only barrier between them. Kosterlitsky had frequently cooperated with Rynning on both sides of the border, but Cananea was strictly Mexican business. Kosterlitsky ordered the Americans home, and, although disgruntled, they reboarded their train and left Mexico. Rurales and the army arrested the miners and confiscated their weapons. Quiet at Cananea.[13]

In Mexico City, Díaz was angry and alarmed. Events at Cananea, complicated by the American intrusion, had left the dictatorship in a bad national and international light. The president had to know the truth so that he could know what to cover up, but the squirming Izábal sent in so many contradictory explanations that he only further entangled the truth. Díaz focused on two problems: 1) what to do with the prisoners, and 2) how to explain away the United States intervention. Izábal and Torres advised political executions. "It's a good time to punish the journalists [who had supported the strike]." Díaz knew better. "It is impossible to shoot the agitators, because it would cause an uproar in the country. Tell the judge to give them the maximum sentence and to send them to San Juan de Ulúa."[14] The old dictator could still think like a fox.

The Mexican newspapers demanded an explanation of the intervention. Díaz had feared the worst and had himself rejected an offer of military support from the United States government, but American soldiers had in fact been moved, as a precautionary measure, from Fort Huachuca in Arizona to Naco. The dictator, through his vice president, had wired Izábal at Naco not to accept foreign assistance of any sort, but the telegram arrived too late. Izábal was by then on his way to Cananea with the trainload of American interventionists. Díaz concocted a smoke screen: "Send me a telegram saying that Americans who came to Cananea were individuals with no military organization. That people on the border always carry guns and that you had no authority to prevent their passage into Mexico. But when you arrived at Cananea, you did not allow them to take part in the events and made them return immediately to the U.S.A." The lie was headlined in the administration's newspaper, *El Imparcial:* "National Territory Has Not Been Invaded."[15]

Only those who had to believe in Porfirio Díaz could have been satisfied by such a transparently false explanation. An Orizaba newspaper, *El Cosmopólita,* stated that although the penetration of national territory was one thing, the fact remained that "Mexicans were villainously assassinated by Yankees during the strike at Cananea."[16] The Americans, of course, saw the fracas as self-defense. But no matter who weighed it and in what proportions, Cananea was a national disgrace and a graphic example of excessive Porfirian authority. Cananea gave a common cause to the nation's disaffected. They had long had common problems but few common goals; now they had a more urgent vision of a Mexico responsive to their needs.

Political radicals did what they could to keep the pot boiling. Mexico's Liberal Party, its leaders exiled in the United States, planned its revolt against the dictatorship for September 16, 1906, in remembrance of national Independence Day. The date passed uneventfully except for its usual patriotic fervor, but ten days later radicals attacked the little village of Jiménez, Coahuila, in an attempt to ignite a general uprising. No support developed, and the army quickly dislodged the rebels, but for the next few days minor outbursts occurred in Veracruz and Tamaulipas, and Rural Police auxiliaries rounded up suspects along the border, in Juárez, for example, and Agua Prieta. Revolutions rarely burst out in full bloom; they bud here and there. Díaz nipped these buds.[17]

But rebellion would not die. The atmosphere of revolt encouraged people to act, to settle old scores, and to choose up sides in new disputes. Some one hundred and fifty Indians from the canton of Acayucan in southern Veracruz, where new sugar development irritated already festering land disputes, raided the community of Soteapa in late September. With rocks, arrows, and machetes they caused widespread mayhem and gave the Rurales stationed there a thorough pelting before being driven off by gunfire. Sensing a constituency, Liberals fueled the turmoil. Two days later the natives returned, this time with rifles, and killed several municipal officials. The rebels were dispersed, but they raised allies in Minatitlán, where the jefe político was hated for his brutal use of the *leva*. Natives robbed the village treasury at Ixhautlán, and disorder erupted at Jaltipan. The rebels got encouragement from merchants who profited by selling them rifles, and they also converted an old ship's cannon into a makeshift fieldpiece. Now they were ready to take on the army—and Díaz obliged. This was no ordinary dispute; it was armed defiance of Porfirian authority, with obvious political overtones to boot.[18]

The combatants, some three hundred and fifty Indians against two hundred soldiers, collided on October 4 at Soteapa. The army sustained the heavier losses but won the day, driving the enemy into guerrilla resistance in the tropical countryside. Díaz ordered the natives pursued with special vigor. He did not want the Indians scattered but arrested and punished so that their "seed" of resistance could no longer sprout. Artillery and machine guns were brought in, but military hardware is not often decisive in the tropics. The federals spent months trying to apprehend the rebels, even though they had the assistance of other Indians anxious for a variety of long-standing reasons to bring their compatriots to bay. In fact, the natives seemed more anxious than the soldiers to capture the bandit-insurgents. Some arrests inevitably occurred, not all of them of individuals associated with the events of Soteapa. Díaz wanted examples. The jefe at Acayucan recommended the execution of the captives, but the president feared repercussions and ordered the prisoners to trial in Veracruz, where the governor switched judges to ensure that the one hearing the cases was "active, intelligent, and loyal to the regime." The convicted disappeared for good, probably into the forced labor camps of Yucatán.[19]

The Soteapa uprising further stretched the already strained seams of the dictatorship. Another serious rupture occurred in January 1907 at Río Blanco, where the textile workers had been increasing their demands and management was ready for a fight. A 50-percent rise in cotton prices had so sharply reduced profit margins that in early 1906 Puebla's industrialists had reduced the wages of their millhands. Strikes followed, countered by a lockout. Díaz upheld the workers' right to strike but warned that the government intended to use "all its resources, all its political organization, all its army, all its authority" to guarantee that individuals who wanted to work got through those picket lines to their machines.[20] As a "willing worker" could always be found or invented to challenge pickets when the government wanted to provoke a confrontation, striking laborers could expect the worst.

The angry dispute escalated into crisis, and by December almost two-thirds of the nation's mills had been closed down, putting thirty-thousand workers in twenty states off the job. Díaz himself had to step in. His arbitration led to a compromise on January 3, 1907, that was accepted by the workers in Puebla and Tlaxcala, but at Orizaba the settlement was challenged in debate. When employees arrived at the Río Blanco plant the morning of January 7 to begin their first day's work in two weeks, they encountered fellow laborers determined to continue the strike. What happened next? Shoving, scuffles, rock-throwing. A worker fell and was trampled. Boisterous shouting at the company store across the street and then shots—probably by panicked employees of the store. Workers mobbed the store and looted and burned it. The police arrived, six mounted Rurales directed by the jefe político, Carlos Herrera, but they did nothing to deter the rioters. Herrera sat on his horse and watched the destruction. The Rurales under Lieutenant Gabriel Arroyo also did not budge.[21]

Army infantrymen from nearby Orizaba soon contained the unrest at Río Blanco, but the rioting proved contagious. Workers burned the company stores at neighboring Nogales and Necoxtla, but soldiers there retaliated with bullets. At day's end, the toll was eighteen laborers dead and eleven wounded, and arrests mounted into the hundreds as the army chased frightened workers and their families into the surrounding hillside. Then Díaz took over: he had heard enough from labor agitators.[22]

General Rosalino Martínez, a subsecretary of War, detrained at Orizaba the morning of January 8 with reinforcements from the capital and orders from the president to severely punish the leaders of the tumult. With him was Colonel Francisco Ruíz, the dictator's henchman, who replaced Herrera as jefe. Brutal suppression was their aim. By evening Martínez held six men identified as strike leaders, and the next day he had them executed without trial on the charred ruins of the company stores they supposedly had helped to destroy. Other workers were forced to watch the executions. As the soldiers vigorously pursued their roundup, the casualties mounted. There were reports of railroad flatcars piled high with bodies to be dumped in Veracruz harbor as shark food. Exaggerations, to be sure, but the enemies of the government meant to discredit the regime as much as possible. Probably fifty to seventy, perhaps more than a hundred, died in the aftermath of Río Blanco. Hundreds more must have been injured, and it cannot even be estimated how many ended up in prisons and work camps.[23] Porfirio Díaz had proved his point, that his power could not be challenged without harsh reprisal. But he made the point at what cost to his dictatorship?

Official investigation into the failures of the jefe Herrera and the Rurales under Arroyo to quell the disturbance at Río Blanco bogged down in the lies and blame-passing of the principals involved. Herrera and Arroyo blamed each other. The jefe charged that the corpsmen had not obeyed his orders to suppress the rioters, but Arroyo contended that Herrera had issued standing orders not to rigorously police the workers. Herrera had a record of such sentiments. The administration would have resolved these contradictions much more forcefully in 1890 than it could afford to do in 1907. The jefe had an ally in the governor, an important friend of the dictatorship. There was, on the other hand, no point in damaging the reputation of the Rurales by emphasizing their reluctance to suppress disorder. So the corpsmen involved returned to duty, and Arroyo was eased out of service. Herrera lost his job as jefe but not political favor in the state.[24]

The government took care of its own but could not erase the bloodstains that Río Blanco had left on society, and Mexicans were starting to keep count of new incidents of violence, such as those at Tepames, Velardeña, and Oaxaqueña. Porfirian officials created sensational scandals with their brutalities and provided more ammunition against the regime. It is hard to know whether these subordinates were following the dictator's obvious lead or whether such events were only receiving more public light in the aftermath of the labor strife. Two campesinos, the Suárez brothers, Marciano, twenty-one, and Bartolo, nineteen, were executed after a minor scuffle with police at Tepames, Colima. Investigation of the murders lagged for a year but finally resulted in death sentences for the former police chief of the village and three of his accomplices in the Suárez slayings. It is doubtful that the penalties were ever assessed, but newspapers did not forget Tepames and what it symbolized. They reported that "Tepames . . . happened again at [such-and-such a place], . . ." and their readers understood.[25]

Velardeña became even more notorious because it involved the army, a notable jefe político, and the peacekeeping Rurales. Velardeña was, like Cananea, a company town, this one the creation of Guggenheim copper investments. Perhaps a thousand miners, led by their popular priest, Ramón Valenzuela, pleasantly paraded through town, that fateful afternoon in April 1909, toward the outskirts, where they intended to burn Judas in effigy. It was actually a social gathering with a thin religious overlay. For some reason the local military commander, José Antonio Fabián, decided to assert his authority. Perhaps he was jealous of the priest's high standing with the townsmen. With four Rurales at his side, Fabián sharply challenged the procession as a violation of the Reform Law that prohibited religious manifestations outside church buildings. It was a tactic frequently used by local officials who wanted to throw their weight around; the Church was an easy mark. In this case, the priest argued back and the crowd's mood turned ugly. Threats and stones followed, The Rurales fired their rifles in the air and caught a barrage of rocks in response. The commander and corpsmen fled for cover in the foreign compound near the smelter, and the miners celebrated their departure in an orgy of looting and burning that gutted the town but did not touch United States interests.[26]

Durango's governor determined to meet the disturbance with force. Porfirian subordinates seemed to learn so little from Cananea, Río Blanco, and the rest. They all wanted to prove to Díaz that they could control disorder. When the state police chief could round up only thirty guards to go to Velardeña, the governor turned to the army for sixty reinforcements. Rurales under Lieutenant Antonio Calvillo joined in. And a jefe político, Jesús

González Garza, volunteered to coordinate the repression. The governor agreed—a fateful decision, for González Garza had a reputation for cruelties to go along with his high political influence. He had, in fact, been transferred to Durango from Puebla because of his abuses. Now he was about to earn the title of "Tiger of Velardeña."

When the security troops arrived, Velardeña was quiet. A good deal of destruction had occurred, but the rioters were subdued— and undoubtedly terrified. González Garza decided he could not return to the state capital "without doing anything." So forty-eight men were arbitrarily designated as instigators of the tumult, and the jefe selected fifteen of them to be shot.

The executions took place over the next two days. First a group of four, then seven, and then the final four. The victims, their hands tied behind their backs, were prodded to the edge of an open trench, and bullets toppled them into their common grave. Hysterical wives and children clung to the men even as the shots were fired. The Rurales made sure the executions came off without interference or resistance.[27]

The governor wired Díaz on April 12 that the Velardeña mission had been successful. González Garza added that his "somewhat energetic procedures" had terminated the disorder, and Díaz replied, "Thanks." But news of the massacre spread fast. *El Tiempo* reported that after the shootings the jefe ordered the burial detail murdered and the families of all victims transported to other states. The *San Francisco Call* claimed thirty dead, many wounded, and much United States property destroyed. Because of the international implications, the administration had to stage a full-blown inquiry into the events.[28]

The bodies of the miners were exhumed to verify the shooting; it was all true. Those minor officials who had directed the firing squads claimed they had done so on orders of the jefe. González Garza's lawyers placed him far from Velardeña on the days of the massacre, but the Rural lieutenant's testimony set matters straight, and he was praised as a "genuine *charro*, intelligent and well-behaved." The priest, Valenzuela, attempted suicide in his jail cell, was released on bond, but still faced charges of sedition, robbery, and arson. The military commander who had sparked the conflagration was thought to be hiding in the mountains of Oaxaca.[29]

Mexico's Supreme Court upheld convictions against the jefe, the Rural officer, and two municipal authorities, and imposed the death penalty on each, but the sentences probably were not carried out. At least González Garza went free. After Díaz had been driven from the presidency, his successor, Madero, appointed the "Tiger of Velardeña" to command army operations at the vital gulf port of Tampico. During the presidential power struggle of February 1913—the Ten Tragic Days—Madero summoned González Garza to Mexico City as superintendent of the penitentiary from which the president's adversaries had escaped. When Madero was murdered and Victoriano Huerta took charge, the "Tiger" was promoted to general and became governor and military commandant of Michoacán. Revolutionaries who drove Huerta into exile in mid-1914 disbanded the federal army and tried González Garza for political outrages in Michoacán. The "Tiger of Velardeña" was then executed by soldiers he had formerly commanded.[30] The convolutions and ironies of Mexican politics may be described but are often difficult to understand.

Velardeña confirmed the worst, known and suspected, about Porfirian moral and social concerns, but those beholden to the regime for their jobs and well-being still applauded the dictator's determination to keep the peace and protect their gains. As long as Díaz proved his ability to do so, he was politically safe. There was criticism but no outrage in 1908 when a few hundred unruly, and thousands of pacific, Yaqui Indians were deported from their homeland in Sonora to labor-hungry Yucatán and southern Mexico. Sonoran entrepreneurs did not take well to the loss of their workers, so Díaz both gained and lost in that transfer.[31] There was also no significant protest against Rurales who literally bent their swords beating peons to their tasks at the sugar-producing plantation Oaxaqueña in Veracruz.[32] Capitalists, embattled by unsettling economic turnabouts, feared the resurgence of early-nineteenth-century turbulence should Díaz, nearing eighty, die in office, and they pressured him to provide for a successor.[33] They meanwhile let the dictator man the floodgates against disorder, not daring to admit how high the national tide had risen against him.

Chapter 13
Unraveling the Old Regime

Porfirio Díaz hastened his own downfall. Amid labor unrest, a seriously weakened economy, increasing charges of brutality, the concerns of investors about his age and health, the strident demands of radical Liberals for political change—with the foundations of his dictatorship cracked and crumbling—he told an American journalist in March 1908 that he considered Mexico ready for democracy and that he was set to retire. He would welcome political competition and campaigning for the presidency of 1910.[1] What a blunder! It is so inconceivable that no one has been able to explain it satisfactorily. Why say it? To solicit the "spontaneous support" of his countrymen? To placate capitalists concerned about the presidential succession? To curry favor with the United States? Did he mean to step down? If so, the idea proved to be short-lived, and Díaz soon announced himself available for the presidency once more, but it was too late to retract his promise of open elections. Personal dictators can afford to be magnanimous only from a position of strength. Díaz either misread or ignored the national roadsigns all around him, and so his feigned political largesse precipitated his downfall.

Mexicans starved for political opportunities enthusiastically accepted the president's offer. They took him at his word, even though Díaz quickly rescinded his announced retirement and declared for another term as president. With the top rung still occupied by the dictator, most of his adversaries concentrated on the second step, the vice-presidency, but with high expectations, for few believed that Díaz would outlive another six-year term. The only genuine presidential challenge came from Francisco Madero and his Anti-Reelectionists, and the dictator demonstrated early-on how he intended to treat such challenges.

Election furor first struck the states: gubernatorial races in Morelos and Sinaloa in 1909. For Morelos, Díaz and the state's sugar planters selected the president's chief of staff in the capital, Pablo Escandón. Their rivals selected a native of Morelos, Patricio Leyva, son of the state's first governor, who had not always seen eye to eye with Porfirian policies. Rurales and soldiers mediated the campaigning to favor Escandón and assured his victory on election day. The official count was never reported, but despite harassment the competition must have polled considerable strength, for reprisals against the Leyvistas continued after the election. Escandón's win was no news in Porfirian Mexico, but the good showing of his challenger certainly was.[2]

In Sinaloa the situation became even more tense. Morelos had taught the administration that even limited tolerance could be dangerous. The official choice, Diego Redo, a merchant with little administrative experience and less political background in Sinaloa, was a friend of the vice-president. His opponent, José Ferrel, was a newspaper editor and ex-congressman who had periodically scolded Díaz for his departure from Liberal ideals and been jailed for his criticism. Students and other young enthusiasts drummed up huge rallies for Ferrel, and the Rurales regularly broke them up with the flats of their swords. Redo spent election day passing out champagne to his constituents in Mazatlán. Even ten-year-olds were rounded up to vote for the official candidate. Meanwhile, Rural Policemen detained Ferrel supporters until the polls had closed. Altered results made Redo's triumph overwhelming. But the word still got out: Díaz was running scared.[3]

It was easy to joke about Madero—his short stature, his high-pitched voice, his idealism, and his penchant for spiritualism—but the thousands attracted to his rallies in the spring of 1910 could not be overlooked by the dictator. Madero received the kind of acclaim to which only the president had become accustomed. Police roughed up and arrested Madero's backers, but the momentum could not be slowed. Díaz had asked for an awakening of the public spirit, and now he was getting it.[4]

To halt the gathering momentum, authorities arrested Madero on June 15 outside Monterrey and charged him with insulting officials and fomenting revolution. With Madero transferred to jail in San Luis Potosí, the electoral process ran its accustomed course. Díaz easily won reelection, along with his vice-president, and now, with that matter settled, Madero was released on bail. Posing as a railroad mechanic, Madero fled Mexico by train to San Antonio, Texas, and issued a clarion call to revolution. The target date: November 20, 1910.[5]

The dictatorship readied for a confrontation. It planned to stamp out the brush fires before they could spread. Simple as that strategy seems, it was critical to a government with an army of only fourteen thousand soldiers, along with twenty-four hundred or fewer Rurales and a few thousand other ill-trained, undependable security forces. Unable to predict who might respond in what sector to Madero's proclamation, Díaz had to be ready everywhere. That spread his military thin. Chihuahua, huge, rugged, and vulnerable to gunrunners from the bordering United States, had only a thousand and sixty-eight soldiers. Veracruz, already restless, had five hundred infantrymen and cavalrymen. The Fourth Military Zone, made up of Zacatecas, Durango, and Querétaro, showed fewer than a thousand regulars, and the Fifth (Michoacán, Guanajuato, and Aguascalientes) counted about twelve hundred troops. Díaz could not hope to crush a serious revolution with that kind of strength, but he tried to stop it before it could earn creditability, and he almost succeeded. Two corps of Rurales were transferred north to Coahuila and Nuevo León to reinforce those vital districts, while Díaz kept thirty-five hundred regulars and most of the federal artillery in the capital poised for rapid train transit to smother sparks wherever they might fall.[6]

Preventive arrests followed. Authorities confiscated documents, weapons, and ammunition linked to an insurrectionary council in Guadalajara. Police banned sales of weapons in the border gateway city of Juárez. A Puebla shoestore owner, Aquiles Serdán, and some associates, all said to be promoters of rebellion, were eliminated in a shoot-out only two days before Madero's scheduled uprising.[7]

November 20, 1910. The Mexican Revolution did not erupt; it barely sputtered to a start. Rurales and other security units quickly subdued a few proletarian outbursts and most minor guerrilla activity, mainly in Chihuahua. Madero himself crossed the Rio Grande forty-five miles south of Eagle Pass on November 21, but the promised Army of Liberation never materialized, and he returned to hiding in the United States.[8] Trouble for the government continued to smolder in western Chihuahua, however, near the little railroad town of Guerrero, population five thousand, garrisoned by sixty-four federal soldiers.

In the mountains around Guerrero, Pascual Orozco, a respected, twenty-eight-year-old muleteer, and Abraham González, an English-speaking beef agent whose economic fortunes had declined in the state's political milieu, rallied several hundred—perhaps a thousand—merchants, dayworkers, ranchers, ne'er-do-wells, the unemployed, the ambitious, and the adventurous, into a substantial guerrilla outfit. Among the recruits was Pancho Villa, the former cattle thief looking for a better way to make a living. Born a peon on an hacienda, Villa started his social climb as a cattle rustler. Later he contracted labor crews for the Kansas City, Mexico, Orient Railroad being built from the United States, through Chihuahua, to the Pacific Ocean. González reasoned that if Villa could recruit a dozen railroad crews, he could as easily recruit revolutionaries. So he offered the former bandit a captaincy in the rebel army, and the opportunity to become a respected citizen once the revolution triumphed, if Villa would induce three hundred men to join the fight against Díaz. Villa seems to have had no trouble locating the manpower, and within a few days the guerrillas took Guerrero. Militarily the victory was insignificant, but politically and psychologically it was vital. It proved to potential rebels that the federals could be challenged and beaten. And it rattled Porfirians who thought the regime impregnable, or at least well able to protect their interests.[9]

Good counter-guerrilla that he was, Díaz knew that such wars are won or lost in the political arena more than on the battlefield. But while maneuvering politically behind the scene, the dictator publicly had to demonstrate his government's will and ability to crush its opponents, so, when an advisor suggested legislative reforms to calm the unrest, the president rebuked him. Soldiers, not reforms, were needed, and Díaz promised to treat the rebels with a *cañonazo*—a cannon blast.[10] Much easier said than done. Reinforcements poured into Chihuahua, but the insurgents battered relief columns headed for Guerrero. Each rebel success raised new recruits and encouraged more violence in the name of Madero's revolution. The state of Guerrero was heard from in January 1911, and Morelos the following month. Sonora reported significant rebel activity in March, then Zacatecas. Thousands of Mexicans vented their indignation and rage, even if only as a cover-up for personal ambitions invigorated by rebellion. Millions of others remained passive and resigned. Mexico's Revolution was no revolt of the masses, but more and more people joined in as the outcome became certain.[11]

Guerrillas cannot risk even a small defeat in a pitched battle, so Mexico's rebels carefully picked their times and places to ensure surprise and numerical superiority. The federals, meanwhile, wallowed in logistical, communication, and tactical problems. Accustomed to the president's personal direction, field commanders would not act without orders from the capital and therefore never developed the aggressive, coordinated strategy needed to successfully combat the rebels. Federal soldiers fought well, even heroically, and so did the Rurales, but, outnumbered two, three, five times, they had little chance to win individual encounters.[12] Solid counter-guerrilla strategy calls for at least a ten-to-one superiority over the insurgents, for objectives taken must be held and sanitized against infectious revolutionary propaganda and personnel.[13] For Porfirio Díaz the manpower ratio was frequently reversed.

The regime was like a gigantic ocean liner rolling over in its death throes. As it listed faster, its former adherents abandoned ship, and many ended up in the rebel camp. Security forces could not be spared to protect rural holdings, so the hacendados made their separate peace with the revolutionaries. The War Ministry's urgent pleas for new recruits floundered in gubernatorial excuses and the deliberate sluggishness of the jefes políticos. The governor of Zacatecas argued in March 1911 that he could raise no reinforcements because municipal officials insisted on keeping their policemen for local use. Besides, newcomers only deserted with their equipment to the enemy. The president's advisors doubted the governor's sincerity, even his loyalty. Since when could a governor not command the assistance of his subordinates!—and revolutionary sentiment was not nearly as widespread in Zacatecas as the governor indicated. And they wondered about the governor's personal goals in the midst of revolution.[14]

There was not much to wonder about, for many who had formerly allied themselves to the regime were by the spring of 1911 plainly worried about their future, their positions, their waning power. They were also rightly concerned about their immediate present, about their personal safety and the security of their possessions, for the revolt had opened, among other opportunities, the chance to settle old political scores, to loot municipal buildings, to seize real estate, and to take revenge. Disorder unchained mighty demons disguised as patriots and do-gooders.

By February 1911 Díaz badly needed an important battlefield victory to demonstrate the vitality of his government, and Madero had to take charge of his factionalized revolution. Their respective needs collided in early March at Casas Grandes in northwestern Chihuahua. Madero, accompanied by his chiefs of staff and some American sympathizers, forded the Rio Grande on February 14 and headed for a rendezvous with supporters in their mountain hideout in central Chihuahua. Federal soldiers tracked but could not catch up with the entourage, which was not always sure of its own direction. But by the first week in March Madero had assembled six hundred armed followers, including a platoon of American mercenaries with demolition skills. Their target: the important railhub of Casas Grandes, which controlled much of northwestern Chihuahua.[15]

The federals braced for the assault. Colonel Agustín A. Valdés defended the town with only three hundred and twenty-three soldiers of the 18th Infantry, thirty Rurales, and fifty local volunteers. Madero's initial assault on March 5 thrust his vanguard into the city, where the dynamiters began to burrow through the lines of adobe homes toward the army's headquarters at the main plaza. But rebel intelligence failed to spot the arrival of five

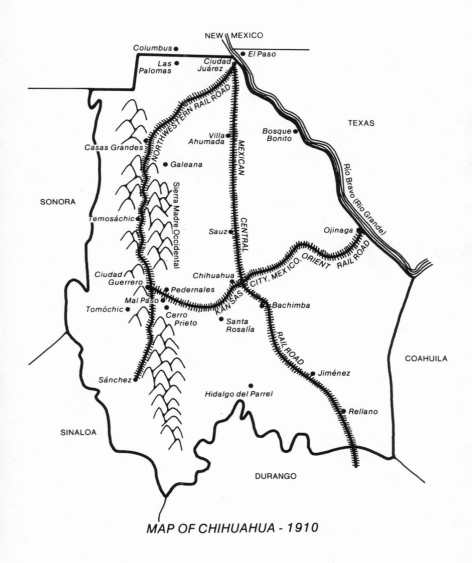

MAP OF CHIHUAHUA - 1910

hundred federal reinforcements with field artillery. The newcomers hit hard and turned the whole fight around. Artillery fire decimated the forward elements of Madero's force, including the Americans, while federal infantrymen smashed the rebel's right flank and drove the enemy into disorganized retreat. It was just what Díaz needed: a big victory, with perhaps a bonus. Madero himself was wounded in the arm and within capture.

The federals overran the rear positions of the insurgents and took their horses, weapons, and supplies. Rebels were captured, but not yet Madero. Then the army stopped just when it might have dismantled the entire insurgent troop. It was later officially explained that the soldiers had to eat, rest, and replenish their ammunition before they could advance. Perhaps so. The soldiers had been train-lifted and forced-marched two hundred miles to reach Casas Grandes and then hurled into a fast-paced, exhausting battle. Luck failed them, too. Their aggressive infantry commander had been seriously wounded in the attack and was forced to relinquish his duties to his artillery chief, who may have known his mortars and cannon but not much about infantry and cavalry field tactics. Under the circumstances, he possibly suffered that fatal military flaw of indecision. Whatever the cause, the moment was lost to the dictatorship. Around such pivotal battles as Casas Grandes entire wars are decided. As it turned out, Díaz was denied the military triumph so critically required to shore up his beleaguered government, and no other opportunity presented itself.[16]

After Casas Grandes the regime's political position steadily deteriorated. Attempts to negotiate a peace, proposed land reforms, and cabinet changes were correctly interpreted by the rebels as signs of weakness. The insurgents knew that they did not need to compromise, that victory was at hand. Conciliation offered by Díaz only encouraged the revolutionaries to up the stakes for peace. With the outcome visible, although not well-defined, the dictator's subordinates and supporters began to defect. It must have been especially painful to Díaz to learn that one of his better field commanders, General Rómulo Cuéllar, had offered to surrender his entire unit to the rebels in exchange for a watered hacienda.[17]

Thousands more joined up for the kill and, not incidentally, the rewards of disorder. While massive, ill-defined armies swept from the south toward the capital, peace talks opened in the north. Even as the negotiations continued, the rebels in the first week of May captured Juárez, across from El Paso. It was insignificant militarily, but to take an important customs post was a diplomatic plum that added to the general euphoria of the moment. In mid-May Porfirio Díaz agreed to go into exile. By then, the rebels held most of the national territory, although strong federal army garrisons remained intact in major cities. Politics presided for a few days while the contending armies stayed put. Then on May 25, amid somewhat tattered pomp, Díaz sailed from Veracruz for European exile. He predicted the country would lapse into anarchy, and disorder did indeed prevail as Mexicans scrambled for the proceeds of the Revolution.[18]

Order and disorder are not opposites but a matter of balance. Substantial disorder had always existed within the Porfirian peace. In fact, Díaz, for political use, had fomented some of his own. The mainstay of his regime, however, had never been his will. Instead, he offered prosperity and protection to earn compliance. Sufficient prosperity was not available by 1910 to bank ambitions that had been fired by development, and Díaz did not intend to redistribute more evenly what had already been accumulated. Nor did he possess the force necessary to protect established gains. So disorder became the order of the day; it was the way to relieve frustrations and fulfill personal satisfactions. In no way could Francisco Madero satisfy those drives, even if he intended to, and he probably did not. Too many of his revolutionaries embraced disorder as the means to substantial change, and many envisioned a new Mexico that in no way matched the plans of their proclaimed leader.

Chapter 14
Disorder in Search of Order

Above all else, Francisco Madero aimed to stop the rebellion, no easy task when so many wanted it to go on. Numerous Mexicans saw disorder as the opportunity for significant change, so when Madero tried to restrain them they fought all the more furiously. What began as middle-class reform drifted toward popular revolution. People snatched for themselves in the name of social justice what they could not get in other ways. Others responded to past exploitation and injustices; it was their time to settle scores. Unions agitated. Political competitors jockeyed for position. Some capitalists aimed to reform the system more in their favor; other capitalists defended their holdings. Foreigners sought special status with whatever administration. Guerrillas demanded profitable work and payoffs. If not, banditry beckoned. Many became brigands anyway; they wanted progress, not peace. Power blocs formed, collided, and crumbled in a deluge of demands that no government could meet, not only Madero's but those of his immediate successors. Only by late 1915 did one faction have the guns necessary to design a shaky truce. Some people felt war-weary; others began to profit substantially from the World War, so peace became worthwhile to them. International capitalism once again became the peacemaker, but genuine domestic order still remained distant.

Even before Díaz departed for exile, the word went out to cease hostilities and to submit to constituted authority. But who constituted authority? That is what the fighting was all about. The old order collapsed so quickly that there had been no time to plan its aftermath. All sorts of hopefuls poured into the vacuum; given the opportunity of their lives, they fought passionately for their share of power. Maderistas attacked the governor's palace in Jalapa, Veracruz, because they did not like the state legislature's choice of governor. Townsmen out front for an evening's concert got caught in the crossfire. Thirteen died and twenty-four were wounded. Prominent citizens in Colima refused to recognize their newly-appointed interim governor. The rebel chief in Campeche demanded the governorship for himself. Early June brought rumors that Díaz had about-faced in mid-Atlantic and would unite with his nephew, Félix, and twenty thousand men at Coatzalcoalcos to march on the capital. Another report had the Porfirian general Bernardo Reyes buying a United States Navy cruiser to attack Veracruz with seven thousand troops. As there was no political consensus to monitor governmental change, positions went to those who had the armed strength to take and to hold them, but they rarely escaped continuing challenge, and so the fighting went on everywhere.[1]

Guerrillas-turned-bandits were also on the loose. These were not the brigands of the post-Independence epoch, who had only a vague notion of the creole world they meant to enter. This new breed was the product of development and had been impressed, even excited, by its possibilities. They had seen progress and they wanted some for themselves. The winners of this struggle, they knew, would set Mexico's future. Some did not want to join the system; they favored change. They had a vision that was frankly political. There were also many like Emiliano Zapata who wanted to turn back the clock to old times that they considered to be better. As the dictatorship unraveled, individuals of varied ambitions grabbed for the loose ends. In lieu of other recompense, plunder suited many. Guerrillas around Durango had been promised the right to loot for two hours the cities they took in the name of the Revolution. Such opportunities were not squandered. An insurgent leader in Sonora threatened to attack the capital at Hermosillo if not paid 20,000 pesos. Bandits who labeled themselves revolutionaries terrorized haciendas in Guanajuato and Chiapas. The state of Guerrero literally dropped out of communication with the rest of the country as bandits cut ties to permit open plunder. Rebels rode into Cholula, looted shops, burned municipal records, freed criminals from jail, and shot residents who tried to protect their money and property. Civilians in Mexico City donned khaki uniforms and pillaged merchants in the name of the rebellion. Mexico's democratic Revolution became a popular orgy, but not necessarily without purpose.[2]

The turmoil also meant open season on foreigners, although the plunderers, by and large, respected American interests. Ex-rebels claiming their fee for revolutionary services stole 800,000 pesos from a mill near Puebla, then raided the nearby compound that housed the plant's managers. Four Germans and three Spaniards died in the melee that ensued. At Torreón, insurgents massacred three hundred Chinese immigrants and tossed their bodies down water wells. Nationalism had gone berserk, but, for many, by design.[3]

Madero and his advisors had anticipated some disorder in the wake of their victory, but not this. Like their predecessors who had seized power by revolution, they had no place for their fighters once they had triumphed, or perhaps numbers of the guerrillas never intended to continue to support Madero's limited revolution. But this time the turbulence was worse than ever, for Madero—with reason—openly distrusted many of the rebel leaders who had paved his road to the Federal District. He therefore decided to retain the Porfirian army (minus some ranking officers) as a bulwark against disorder, to disarm as many revolutionaries as possible, and to put the rest into an expanded Rural Police Force alongside the former regime's Rurales. Madero hoped that the Porfirian army would loyally serve the new administration for the good of the country, that the great majority of insurgents would be content with a few pesos for their guns and services, and that Porfirian Rurales could be mixed with ex-guerrillas without curdling the blend. In other words, he wanted the Porfirian army and police to discipline his revolution.[4]

But here are some examples of what actually happened. An army officer toting a dynamite bomb meant to kill Madero was arrested in Guadalajara. Federal troops continued to resist rebel attacks at Chinipas, because they received no orders to stop fighting. The commander of the Eleventh Rural Police Corps outspokenly endorsed Reyes for president. General Juan G. Cabral refused to march to Baja California to subdue a separatist

movement launched by radical Liberals. Porfirian soldiers and ex-
guerrillas engaged in a furious shoot-out at Puebla's bullring, and
only the hurried presence of Madero himself restored order. Rebels
broke into the Rural Police barracks at Atlixco and murdered the
lieutenant in charge and eight of his men, on the presumption that
the Rurales must on some occasion have abused the factory
workers. Instead of amalgamating themselves with the federal
garrisons in places like Durango City, the ambitious insurgents tore
up the towns they took and then headed elsewhere for more loot.[5]

Rebels urged to surrender their weapons for pesos seldom did
so, and the government could not afford to be insistent or to punish
offenders. These were not Madero's men; they belonged to Pascual
Orozco, Ambrosio Figueroa, Villa, Zapata, and hundreds of now
lesser known but then equally important guerrilla leaders. A word
from any one of the chiefs turned loose his horde. Orozco found the
discharge bonus so small that he advised his troops to sack
Chihuahua City. Zapata would not disarm until his demands for
land reform in Morelos had been met—no more promises for
Emiliano Zapata. Even Madero's brother recognized the im-
possibility of ordering ambitious people who had battled Díaz to
return to their prerevolutionary lives without recompsense.
"Disappointment reigns among disbanded Maderista troops in
Hidalgo," warned the *Mexican Herald*. "They had enlisted with
the understanding that they would receive good positions at the
end of the war. . . . The larger towns of the state are filled with idle
men and disorder is increasing." Not only in Hidalgo but
everywhere. Brigandage boomed like a flashback into the
nineteenth century. Get those malcontents and bandits into the
Rurales.[6]

The delicate work of enlisting ex-rebels, many of them now
brigands, as Rurales fell not to any ranking revolutionary but to a
Porfirian general, Clemente Villaseñor. The rebel chieftains immediately protested. Why not one of their own for such an important job? Because Madero feared they did not intend to halt the
Revolution. He explained rather lamely that although Villaseñor
may have remained dedicated to Díaz during the Revolution, his
sentiments had always been with the insurgents. Angry rebels
already suspicious of their leader's intentions do not accept such

explanations. Many now felt that Madero had broken faith with his own movement, the most serious charge that can be brought against any revolutionary.[7]

Disorder drifting into rebellion accompanied Madero's formal inauguration as president in November 1911. The government claimed that sixteen thousand rebels had voluntarily returned to peaceful civilian life. Among them was Pancho Villa. But the victors had made it worthwhile for Villa to settle down. He received 50,000 pesos in mustering out pay and was encouraged to open a butchering business in Chihuahua City. So Villa imported technicians and refrigeration equipment from the United States and began his new life as a respected businessman. No one questioned where he got the cattle that he slaughtered, but his operation was the first modern meat service in the state capital. Meanwhile, the federal government inducted some three thousand other insurgents into fifteen new Rural Police units and planned to recruit another eight thousand for the corps. But that still left a good third of the rebel troops under arms, or nearly twenty thousand men on the loose, many of them as bandits. And how many more joined them daily? How many of those discharged guerrillas took their bonus and turned to brigandage?[8]

The president, Madero, who had originally endorsed negotiations with bandits, asked his congress in December 1911 to suspend constitutional trial procedures for bandits in the most infested sectors of the republic. It was another stopgap solution applied to an entirely new problem, but the legislators concurred, and military and civil authorities could try and execute brigands on the spot. Rural Police commanders received the same extraordinary powers, but not the regular corpsmen, for it was feared that they would only make "tons of deviled ham from the meat of their victims." That did not prevent the guards from using the *ley fuga* to the same end. Not only did such a stern decree do little to deter banditry, it undercut Madero's political stance. It just did not seem right for the "Apostle of Democracy" to be curbing individual liberties barely a month after taking office.[9]

Disillusionment with the president turned to disgust and then revolution. The reaction was not all the result of Madero's policies; some of his top-level people had not really been with him from the start. Francisco León de la Barra, accepted as interim president pending Madero's official election, was by no means an impartial stand-in. He probably favored Reyes for president and had heavy patronage commitments to fulfill. The acting Interior minister, Emilio Vásquez Gómez, even more openly dedicated himself to building his own political base. When Sonora's governor wrote to him that he intended to replace an untrustworthy military commander, Vásquez Gómez replied, "Do it, but not with a Maderista." The minister also shoveled out army promotions like a nineteenth-century caudillo and refused to name Madero's recommendation to important posts.[10] Madero finally fired him, and by early 1912 Vásquez Gómez had rebelled in the north, where he was soon joined by Orozco, who wanted to be War minister but only got to be Rural Police commander of Chihuahua. Orozco's decision was the culmination of a long-standing quarrel with Madero's leadership that had begun in the fighting days against Díaz. With such defections in the north, and with Zapata rampaging in the south, Madero had no chance to guide the Revolution.[11]

By the fall of 1911, negotiations with Emiliano Zapata had deteriorated into rebellion, limited mainly to Morelos but ferociously destructive and threatening to expand. Zapata demanded property relief for the state's campesinos, but Madero had set rigid priorities: peace first (surrender your arms), then land reform. Zapata saw things the other way around. The debate ended when federal troops under Victoriano Huerta ignored Madero's orders to stay put near Cuernavaca and advanced toward Zapatista strongpoints. A crafty, dangerous man, this Huerta. Madero ordered Huerta cashiered for this disobedience, but Zapata had already lost confidence in Madero's Revolution. Now he would fight his own battles.[12]

The government floundered into 1912 with disorder gnawing away at its underpinnings. It was only a matter of time. Moments of exhilaration occurred among peace-seekers when the long-expected uprising of Bernardo Reyes fizzled at Linares in Nuevo León, along with that of Félix Díaz in Veracruz, and both were imprisoned. The army under Huerta, who had been resurrected by the national emergency, drove Orozco and Vásquez Gómez into exile. These revolutionary movements naturally had to be dealt with, but their suppression further drained the government of the vitality needed to combat the brigands and other purveyors of disorder who had left the administration mired in chaos. The Rurales proved no help. The wholesale induction of bandit types into their ranks simply legitimized brigandage as police work. Police have to be paid off, and handsomely, either by public subscription, corruption, or both, but no government can let them run wild.[13]

The administration did not even know how many Rural Police units it had. Individuals who claimed to be ex-revolutionaries assembled bands of armed men and petitioned (demanded) to join the corps. Madero took them all, even recently released criminals who volunteered for police duty. The president told congress in April 1912 that seventy-three Rural Police units had been organized, although few had their full complement of men. The 67th Corps, for example, had only a commander and four policemen. The 53rd had a hundred and seventy men, but fifty of them were officers. The Internal Affairs minister in June talked about reducing the force to sixteen corps of five hundred men each, and two months later the Inspector General was mentioning three-hundred-man units, or forty-eight hundred Rurales in all. They both hoped to reorganize the force for better control. But Madero had other needs; he still aimed to convert more of those troublesome brigands into policemen, to give them profitable work in the service of his government. He apparently never considered that people on the rampage might not want to serve his government. The president told the new legislative session in September that the country needed sixty-seven Rural Police units, and by 1913 the government was talking about over eighteen thousand Rurales—five times the size of the Díaz corps and bigger than the Porfirian army. Perhaps it all looked good on paper, but in the field it was another story.[14]

Madero could not pay his police enough to tame them. Some may have wanted more out of government than pay. For both types, disorder offered more possibilities, which is why the president's Rurales served disorder more than order. A unit deserted at Tehuantepec to join bandits operating in the district.

Others in Tlacolula, Veracruz, got drunk, revolted, and ravaged the town. The detachment at Cuyutlán, Colima, opted for banditry under José Pérez Castro y Oropeza, whom Maderistas had released earlier from a Zacatecas jail to join their rebellion. Twenty-five Rurales of the 15th Corps shouted "Viva Zapata" and sacked the national pawnshop and other businesses in Guadalajara before heading for the mountains. When the jefe político at Tixtla, Guerrero, accused the Rurales stationed there of working with bandits, they killed him and joined their brigand friends in depredations. One paymaster stole his unit's treasury, 2,200 pesos, and headed for the United States. People got what they could out of the police force and then left.[15]

Nor was it very secure being a Rural in a country torn by revolution. Rurales refused to fight against Orozco in Sonora because they respected him as a leader of the fight against the dictatorship, but they feared the Zapatistas—with reason. The 52nd Corps left Mexico City with three hundred men to battle Zapata and returned with ninety, most of them wounded. When the Inspector General tried to reorganize the unit, none of the ninety would reenlist. More than a thousand Zapatistas caught the 16th Corps at Ixtapan, Michoacán, and killed a third of the force. Rurales in the company of their families were watering their horses at Sultepec de Pedro in the state of México when the Zapatistas surprised them. The corpsmen holed up in a farmhouse, so the rebels burned it, suffocating two hundred men, women and children. Corpsmen caught in an ambush at Santa Lucía in Guerrero galloped for freedom into an unfamiliar countryside, where they ran out of ammunition fending off rebels, who then let campesinos hack the guards to death with their machetes.[16]

A favorite tactic of the Zapatistas was to masquerade as Rurales to gain entrance to an hacienda or a train station, which they then plundered. Rurales traveling by train from Córdoba to Mexico City suddenly found themselves under rifle fire from several members of their own escort, Zapatistas in disguise. The rebels demanded that the corpsmen join the Zapatistas, which they did—but only temporarily. When the rebels fell asleep, the Rurales murdered them. It was that kind of disorder all over Mexico, with no holds barred.[17]

Porfirio Díaz, for more than two decades the president and dictator of Mexico. *Amon Carter Museum, Fort Worth, Texas*

Rurales desperately defended the nation's vital railroad network when the Revolution erupted in 1910. *Amon Carter Museum, Fort Worth, Texas*

In a Posada print a Rural Policeman rounds up Yaqui Indians from their homeland in Sonora for deportation to far-off Yucatán. *Fondo Editorial de la Plástica Mexicana*

Francisco Madero (front center), leader of the Revolution, prepares for battle in the spring of 1910 in the crucial northern state of Chihuahua. *Photography Collection, Humanities Research Center, University of Texas at Austin*

Using a commandeered train, Pancho Villa, in one of the Revolution's most brilliant tactical maneuvers, captured the unsuspecting federal garrison at Ciudad Juárez (across the border from El Paso, Texas) in November 1913. The feat made Villa famous and earned him a cache of money and supplies, such as the hand grenades he proudly displays. *Aultman Collection, El Paso Public Library*

Rurales ensure that their mounts are properly entrained as the police prepare to embark for a trouble spot. *Amon Carter Museum, Fort Worth, Texas.*

Yaqui Indians, promised land and autonomy, fought doggedly for Alvaro Obregón and his Constitutionalist forces from 1913 to 1916. Although Obregón eventually triumphed, the Yaquis received few rewards. *Aultman Collection, El Paso Public Library*

Villista-turned-bandit José Ynéz Chávez García profited from the disorder of the Revolution. *Ernest Otto Schuster*, Pancho Villa's Shadow: The True Story of Mexico's Robin Hood as Told by His Interpreter *(New York: Exposition Press, 1947)*

Complaints about abusive Rurales flooded the Inspector General's office, but he could not discipline them because they would only ride into brigandage. Such realities cost the government more prestige. One case proved lethal. Residents of Tererio, Michoacán, charged that the former Porfirian lieutenant in charge there regularly robbed and mistreated them. They named Francisco Cárdenas as the culprit—the same man who had oversold the role of the Rurales in the Santanón affair. Investigation confirmed the accusations and found Cárdenas harshly embittered toward the new regime, but no discipline, no punishment followed: Madero did not want Cárdenas in rebellion.[18] The Rural Police officer and the president met face to face the following February, at night outside a penitentiary in the Federal District, where Cárdenas executed the president on behalf of persons not yet positively identified.

When Madero could not guarantee the peace, the search began for someone who might. A virulent conservative reaction, a truculent press, a sneering United States ambassador, and a kaleidoscope of unfulfilled aspirations and expectations among campesinos, laborers, and bourgeois capitalists all bedeviled an administration born in the highest hopes, even though many of those hopes were selfish. What began on February 9, 1913, as an old-fashioned barracks uprising against the government evolved into all-out civil war. Assisted by military cadets who freed them from prison, Félix Díaz and Bernardo Reyes launched the revolt in the heart of the capital. Reyes was killed in the initial assault on the presidential palace, but Díaz found protection in a sturdy downtown arms factory and military barracks called the Ciudadela. The crisis again placed Huerta in charge of the major federal operations, and the Decena Trágica—the Ten Tragic Days—began. The key was the Ciudadela. Perhaps, after heavy bombardment, Rurales could take it by storm.[19]

An artillery barrage softened up the target, and on the evening of February 20, the 18th Corps, among the best in service, three hundred strong, began its somewhat majestic (if ill-advised) advance down Balderas Street toward the Ciudadela. Row on row of Rurales, pinched together by the buildings along their flanks, approached at a slow trot. Then the charge, sabres held high, the clamor of hoofbeats mingled with those wonderful *charro* yelps. But pageantry is no match for machine guns and artillery. All the rebel gunners had to do was to point and shoot. In less than two minutes, sixty-seven Rurales, dead and wounded, stained the pavement with their blood. Side streets offered escape for a few, but the corps lay decimated on Balderas. Whose fault? Huerta's? Was it a tactical blunder or deliberate design?[20]

The turning point in hostilities came on February 18, when Huerta publicly turned traitor and pronounced against his president. He had hated Madero personally for a long time and had often disputed his policies, but the general had never leaned toward a coup d'etat. But now came the pact with Félix Díaz and connivance with foreign ministers, among the most important, United States Ambassador Henry Lane Wilson, himself no admirer of Madero. The president and his vice-president were forcibly removed from office, and the congress ensured that Huerta became interim president. Many understood Madero's life to be in jeopardy, but those who could do so declined to shield him. Then it was done: Madero and his vice-president were dead. Who ordered the murders? Suspicion abounds, but no proof exists. If Huerta had ordered the deed—and he denied it—how stupid. The martyrdom of Madero focused the forces of disorder on Huerta, drove him from the presidency, and hurled the country into unrestrained fratricide.[21]

Within a week of the assassinations Mexicans started to choose sides. The governors of Jalisco, San Luis Potosí, Puebla, Tabasco, and Colima sided with Huerta. Venustiano Carranza of Coahuila, a patronizing conservative who had first supported Díaz and then Madero, saw an opportunity to move up in politics and declared war on the usurper. Sonora and Chihuahua followed Carranza, who became First Chief of the Constitutionalists. Concessions lured Orozco into Huerta's camp, but Zapata rejected similar overtures as a betrayal of the Revolution. He did not side with the Northerners but stepped up hostilities in Morelos. The federal army by and large supported Huerta, although its loyalties were uncertain. The Rurales splintered in all political directions, switching allegiance at will, and most seemed to have remained bandits at heart. At least, none of the available political options suited their tastes.[22]

Police often vacillate when faced by genuine revolution, because of the nature of their work. Unlike soldiers, they are not outsiders suddenly thrust into a community to suppress disorder— they are in daily contact with a populace, and they hesitate to confront acquaintances on whom they are in many ways dependent. Police are also more personally ambitious than soldiers. They may watchdog society, or at least the segments they are ordered to police, but they also watch out for themselves, something unchanged by professionalization. When enmeshed in serious social disorder, police aim to end up on the winning side. The Paris police disappeared during France's great revolution, as did the Berlin police at the end of World War I. The German police first joined the Liberal rebellion of 1848 and then helped the German army to suppress it. Italy's carbinieri proved malleable when challenged in the 1920s by rising fascist violence. Some of Mexico's Rurales displayed similar opportunism. Others expressed or feigned interest in more far-reaching political goals.[23]

Mexico's Rural Police Force was such a hybrid of allegiances and self-interest in 1913 that it fell apart under the new stress. The 21st Corps, stationed by Huerta in Tlalnepantla, just outside the Federal District, veered toward the Constitutionalists in late March and attacked government troops in Veracruz before joining Carranza in Tamaulipas. The 28th and 41st Rurales stopped fighting Zapatistas in Michoacán and turned into Constitutionalists; so did the 18th, or the remnant left after the charge on the Ciudadela. Rural Police commander Lauro Fernández swore allegiance to Huerta in Mexico City, returned to his Hidalgo assignment, and promptly revolted against the president. Commander Alfonso Zaragoza rebelled against the federals, was captured, promised to fight for Huerta, was released, and a few days later was again at war with the government. The War minister commissioned Ramón Romero, 15th Corps commander, to organize a new unit and then detained him for preaching sedition. Rurales under Francisco Cárdenas and many others supported the regime, but allegiances remained insecure because the police gravitated more toward material reward than political commitment.[24]

By the summer of 1913, disparate guerrilla activities had broken out in Guerrero, Tepic, Zacatecas, and Michoacán. Pancho Villa built up enormous strength in Chihuahua. Bandits assumed the political stance that best suited their moment and looted at will. Noncombatants, called *pacíficos*, as well as the better-off, caught the brunt of the whirlwind. The wealthy had the means to make deals with the rebels, or they could hide their assets—cows, horses, grain, pesos, rifles, clothing, and pulque—or flee the country. Every possession was up for grabs, and guns decided the owner. A foreign observer wrote, "It must have puzzled the devil to know which side to favor, their ethics being undistinguishable."[25]

Of course, the fighting did not sweep the country evenly and thoroughly. Some regions were much more affected than others, and when violence arrived it came in waves and degrees. Most Mexicans stayed at productive work throughout it all, although they changed jobs as some businesses boomed and others went bankrupt. In short, the nation's economy remained quite durable— and thoroughly capitalistic—during the strife, although it experienced various occupational and structural shifts. Oil and henequen returned tremendous profits. The railroads were devastated, but mules, donkeys, trucks, and planes moved the commerce. Foreign involvement in the economy remained strong. Small mining ventures collapsed, but large ones, like Cananea, expanded. Distribution was cut off from some districts but grew rapidly in others. And arrayed against the forces of disorder were powerful interests that craved peace and were willing to pay for it.[26]

Santa Anna, Maximilian, Juárez, Díaz, Madero—and now Huerta as head of government—inherited the job of pacification on behalf of their constituents. In the midst of the holocaust Huerta tried to reorganize and reform his army and Rural Police Force. The army was assembled into ten divisions, each under a general officer, and the president authorized the recruitment of up to two hundred thousand soldiers. So the *leva* got to work, desperately. It hardly achieved Huerta's goals, and it must have created many more enemies for him.[27]

As dissatisfied ordinary people, the bulk of the Rurales

presented a special problem. Huerta first placed the corpsmen under military supervision as "Explorers," which meant that they functioned as Rurales but under army control. The corpsmen, nonetheless, proved so undependable (more than 50 percent deserted) that the exasperated president in August 1913 consigned them all to the regular army and ordered his Inspector General of Rurales to rebuild an entirely new police corps along the Porfirian pattern. Plans called for twenty units of four hundred and fifty men each, and by July 1914, the inspector reported six thousand men on duty.[28]

The administration tried to shape up the constabulary with a long list of regulations: in-service infractions would draw fines, horses taken from civilians had to be returned, officers required a passport to leave their duty stations, medals and a bonus awaited outstanding performance. Music professors from the national university formed a Rural Police band to raise morale, and, to curb the panicky expenditures of ammunition in combat, unassembled cartridges were mixed in with the regular issue. This made the corpsmen think about how fast they used their bullets, since trying to assemble new ones while under fire could prove fatal. The mettle of these new Rurales was never really tested, for they had only a few brushes with the enemy before Huerta's regime collapsed. But the attention paid them by Huerta indicated the kind of government he meant to establish: a personal dictatorship supported by a strong central police force. Many Mexicans would not have it.[29]

As a three-pronged Constitutionalist attack rolled toward Mexico City, Zapatismo became more virulent in the south. At the same time, financial paralysis gripped the country, and foreign bankers refused to honor contracted loans. New taxes only increased disaffection. Personality differences wrecked Huerta's cabinet just as the ministers were developing socially concerned agrarian, labor, and educational programs, and the national congress was dominated by contemptuous, carping Maderistas. Finally, election returns showed that Huerta was not very popular. So he settled into a personal dictatorship, not precisely neo-Porfirian, but nonetheless a dictatorship with its censorship, arbitrariness, assassinations, conspiracies, and capitalistic bent.[30]

Crucial recognition of the administration was denied by the

didactic moralization of United States President Woodrow Wilson, who averred that his country "can have no sympathy for those who seize the power of government to advance their own personal interests or ambitions." It was a kind of "Democracy or bust" pronouncement, followed by an affair of substantial dishonor when in April 1914 United States sailors seized Veracruz and its revenue-producing customshouse, effectively quarantining the Huerta regime so that internal disorder could eat it away.[31]

When he first took office, Huerta had promised the congress to reestablish peace, "cost what it may," but most knew by 1914 that it was a vow he could not keep, and the scramble for new patronage commenced. But whom to turn to? No one could predict how this directionless power struggle would be resolved. In late June, Villa rampaged into Zacatecas, and the race for the capital was on. The rebel who took it would probably rule. Then in July came a negotiated peace. Huerta resigned on July 15 and headed for exile. Carrancistas nervously manned the capital with an eye on Pancho Villa in the north and with its troops dispersed to prevent Zapata's advance from the south. The federal army and the Rurales in August lined up along the railroad tracks north of the capital to be disarmed and discharged. Was it to be peace or only a momentary lull in the struggle?[32]

The issue was vigorously debated at a boisterous national convention at Aguascalientes in October. The decision was to fight, basically Villa and Zapata against Carranza, but with many other interchangeable factions. Ex-soldiers and former Rurales aligned themselves with the variety of contenders in search of a winner. Carranza got most of the army officers.[33] For the next couple of years, disorder reigned while Mexicans killed each other for the right to set the national pace and direction, to mold a new order from the disorder at hand. There were, of course, conflicting ideas about the shape and composition of any new order. To recruit for his cause. Carranza, like Díaz at Tuxtepec, promised much more than he could (or ever intended to) deliver, including substantial land and labor reforms. When Carranza triumphed, people wanted to collect on those promises. In response, the Constitutionalists ignored their commitment to the campesinos and workers who had manned their battalions, and rewarded the capitalists with a new constitution that ensured their future in a somewhat reformed, but hardly changed, economic atmosphere. Then came the mop-up. Villa and Zapata, still active in the field, needed to be eliminated. Brigands such as José Inés Chávez García terrorized the Bajío like those bloody bandit-patriots of the French Intervention, and Chávez García may have been the worst of the lot. He called himself a Villista, although Villa disowned him, and from mid-1915 to 1918 Chávez García ruled Michoacán and bordering districts of Guanajuato and Jalisco. He and his troop celebrated their victories by raping virgins in the villages they pillaged. Rape became the gang's trademark. In Tacámbaro they came across several young girls hiding in the gallery of a motion picture theater. Rather than submit to the bandits, the girls tossed themselves to their deaths off the high balcony, and are still remembered as the "Virgins of Tacámbaro." At Villa Morelos a mother protested to Chávez García that her daughter, desired by the bandit, was only a child of thirteen years, to which Chávez García purportedly replied, "A child, you say? Well, that's what we're going to determine."[34]

Chávez García was by no means the only brigand on the rampage. As Villa's massive army disintegrated in defeat, many of his officers took their men into banditry. Disorder also increased the threat of foreign intervention. The United States, worried about its business stake in Mexico, had to be placated. Carranza himself was only a coalition leader, and others sought the presidency. These difficult matters invited discord, but as peace, for a variety of reasons, became more attractive to increasing numbers of Mexicans, the civil war simmered down. Order slowly and uncertainly began to redress its imbalance with disorder.

Làzaro Cárdenas, Benigno Serrano, and Anacleto López led columns against Chávez García. The bandit eluded them with clever guerrilla tactics, but the Spanish flu that swept large portions of Mexico in 1918 finally caught and killed him. Serrano and López became important army generals in the 1920s, and Cárdenas became president of the republic in the 1930s. Federal army strategists tricked Zapata into an ambush at the Chinameca hacienda in Morelos in April 1919 and killed him—but not his ideal of land reform, which proved to be a handy tool for future governments to defuse unrest.[35] Two years later, 1921, the government won over Villa with the gift of a 25,000-acre hacienda near the Chihuahua-Durango border. Assassins shot him to death in 1923 for motives not yet well explained.[36]

The Constitutional of 1917 confirmed the new order, which did not differ fundamentally from the old one. The victors proved to be reformist, not revolutionary, and they remained true to the broad patterns of national direction established by the mid-nineteenth-century Reform and re-enforced by the Porfiriato. Mexico remained capitalist, and perhaps even more firmly tied to foreign investment. Loudly-proclaimed nationalism did not deter thousands of Mexicans from seeking betterment in the United States. The revolt may have rearranged and redistributed some components of Mexican development, but it did not discard or replace the mainstays of the structure.[37] But that does not mean that nothing happened in Mexico's Revolution, or that there was no direction to the movement—no sense of order within the disorder. In the country's past turbulence, a definite order can be discerned, and also with the Revolution a tentative outline has begun to emerge. The bourgeois thrust of the movement is reasonably well-understood, but perhaps the challenge of campesinos and workers to that direction has been underestimated.[38] On observation, it seems that most ordinary people who rebelled sought betterment within an established society; but the impulse for significant change, even if not well-articulated, may have been quite strong. Nor has the temper of that immense majority of Mexicans who did not rebel been carefully analyzed. It is not necessarily true that people who do not join rebellions do not care about the outcome. Much also needs to be learned about the nature of the bourgeoisie that made and eventually captured the Revolution. Where were its schisms? And where did the bourgeois rebels find allies? The blend between the old regime and the new one remains largely unexamined—although a mixture of the two obviously occurred.

So order once more restored its predominance over disorder in Mexico, with new chiefs in charge, and to date it has displayed a remarkable capacity for parrying and absorbing the thrusts of disorder. Order did not gain ascendancy all at once. Three decades of dispute, discussion, rebellion, experimentation, and drift followed the Revolution until the economic proceeds of World War II finally cemented the new order, again grounded in the world capitalism that supports authoritarian government. More than a few Mexicans have profited substantially through economic development, which has financed a social mobility previously unavailable to so many aspirants, but the great majority of ordinary people have enjoyed few benefits from the national progress as orchestrated by the power brokers. Official rhetoric, a modicum of land redistribution (but hardly agrarian reform), and limited labor gains have glazed over the vast social disparities along with the unfulfilled promises and expectations that steadily grind away at domestic tranquility. National planners are not unmindful of the fragility of the peace that they administer, but international considerations necessarily mold their thinking and control their choices. And for any number of Mexicans, disorder still equals progress.

Disorder, as always, has been impatient, and repression has been harsh. A nationwide railroad strike was suppressed in blood in 1959. Thirteen people were killed and thirty-seven wounded in the following year while protesting governmental corruption in Guerrero. Bitterly remembered are the 1962 murder by federal troops of the controversial farm labor leader Rubén Jaramillo and his family and that Night of Sorrow six years later at the Tlatelolco housing project in the capital, when soldiers fired on a largely student rally: perhaps a hundred killed, five hundred wounded, a thousand jailed. Radical Leftist terrorist attacks marked the 1970s, as did reprisals from the Right. There was brigandage too: Jenaro Vásquez Rojas, a school teacher, demanded betterment for ordinary Mexicans from his mountain hideouts in Guerrero. Troops killed him in 1972. But even more strident outrage came from another teacher, Lucio Cabañas, who for seven years fended off federal pursuit until 1974, when he was killed in Michoacán. The government called it a car crash, but others talked of political murder. It does not matter. What does is that the name of Lucio

Cabañas is still being painted on adobe walls in many parts of
Mexico and that police are still trying to track down members of
his band.

The old Rural Police Force has disappeared, but the government has substituted regular militia units of campesinos called
fuerzas rurales, which receive continual political indoctrination
from army officers stationed among them. Díaz could never trust
his army in such work, but a system of payoffs still makes army
and police work attractive to quite a few Mexicans, and the
nation's forces of repression are more formidable than ever.

In terms of its present balance between order and disorder,
Mexico's future is still tied to, and is the same as, that of the rest of
the world. That mighty ally of disorder—the unpredictable and
uncontrollable gyrations of international capitalism—remains
ominous, perhaps more so today than ever before, and especially so
for a country that has experienced appreciable economic growth,
but where the gap between the well-off and others has widened.
The drive for self-betterment among numbers of Mexicans may be
stronger, and more frustrated, than ever. Assuredly, a good many
have struggled a few rungs up the social ladder, but it will not take
much disruption to tumble them back down. And rebels are at
work. Banditry that recalls those great Mexican brigands of the
past has been reinforced by a new strain of urban terrorism.
Disorder is asleep with one eye open.

Order and disorder remain in opposition, all the time,
everywhere. The tilt between the two is eternally precarious and
temporary, and is manipulated by conditions that cannot always
be contained. Countries will always experience the relentless
competition between the two; it cannot be escaped. Order breeds
disorder and there is an order to disorder. The state and the individual use each at will to further their ends. Sooner or later
disorder will more actively renew its challenge to the existing
system of order, and the shape of society to emerge from that
turbulence remains to be seen.

Notes

ABBREVIATIONS IN ARCHIVAL CITATIONS

AGN
  Mexico City, Archivo General de la Nación, Ramo de Gobernación.
  Cited AGN, Leg. (legajo no.), Exp. (expediente title). Titles of some expedientes are given in shortened form.

AHDN
  Mexico City, Secretaría de la Defensa Nacional, Departamento de Archivo de Correspondencia e Historia, Archivo Histórico. Cited AHDN, document no., folio no., page no. if pagination exists.

APD
  Cholula, Puebla, University of the Americas, Archivo de Porfirio Díaz. Cited APD, Leg. (legajo no. in roman numerals, No. (document no. in arabic numerals), date.

CEHM
  Mexico City, Centro de Estudios de Historia de México, Condumex, S.A., Archivo de Francisco León de la Barra. Cited CEHM, document, date.

MRP
  Austin, Texas, University of Texas at Austin, Nettie Lee Benson Latin American Collection, Mariano Riva Palacio Papers. Cited MRP, No. (document no.), correspondents, date.

RDS
  Washington, D.C., National Archives, Department of State, Records of the Department of State Relating to the Internal Affairs of Mexico, 1910–1929, Record Group 59. Cited RDS, file no., correspondents, date.

1 / AMBITIOUS BANDITS: DISORDER EQUALS PROGRESS

1. Francisco López Cámara, *La estructura económica y social de México en la época de la Reforma*, pp. 233–34.
2. Edward Dunbar, *The Mexican Papers*, pp. 105–14.

184 Notes (p. 3-7)

3. Dunbar, *Mexican Papers*, p. 105; John Lewis Geiger, A *Peep at Mexico: Narrative of a Journey across the Republic from the Pacific to the Gulf in December 1873 and January 1874*, p. 95; Charles Lempriere, *Notes in Mexico in 1861 and 1862: Politically and Socially Considered*, p. 281; [Wise, Henry Augustus], *Through the Land of the Aztecs, or, Life and Travel in Mexico*, p. 70; Brantz Mayer, *Mexico As It Was and Is*, pp. 9, 14.

4. Geiger, *Peep at Mexico*, pp. 105-11; López Cámara, *Estructura económica*, p. 231. For colorful accounts of stagecoach travel in Mexico plus technical details on the coaches themselves see: Antonio García Cubas, *El libro de mis recuerdos*, pp. 197-200; [Wise], *Land of the Aztecs*, pp. 148-53; J. H. Bates, *Notes of a Tour in Mexico and California*, p. 29; Dunbar, *Mexican Papers*, pp. 105-14; Ralph Moody, *Stagecoach West*, pp. 13-14; Mayer, *Mexico*, pp. 9-14, 284-85.

5. Laurens B. Perry, "The Dynamics of the Insurrection of Tuxtepec: Mexico in 1876," p. 654; MRP, No. 5402, Mariano Arista to Mariano Riva Palacio, September 10, 1851. MRP, No. 6783, Manuel Zerón to Francisco Iturbe, 7 August 1857; MRP, No. 8021, Vincent Oritgosa to Mariano Riva Palacio, 8 August 1869; MRP, No. 8550, José María Verdiguel y Fernández to Mariano Riva Palacio, 21 February 1870; [Wise], *Land of the Aztecs*, p. 85; Lempriere, *Notes in Mexico*, pp. 273-74.

6. Dunbar, *Mexican Papers*, pp. 109-11.

7. Ibid., pp. 112-13.

8. Frances E. Calderón de la Barca, *Life in Mexico during a Residence of Two Years in That Country*, p. 343; Niceto de Zamacois, *Historia de Méjico, desde sus tiempos mas remotos hasta nuestros días*, 15:632; García Cubas, *Recuerdos*, p. 200; Albert S. Evans, *Our Sister Republic: A Gala Trip through Tropical Mexico in 1869-70*, pp. 203-24; C. A. Stephens, *The Knockabout Club in the Tropics. The Adventures of a Party of Young Men in New Mexico, Mexico, and Central America*, pp. 185-86.

9. Dunbar, *Mexican Papers*, pp. 111-14.

10. Julio Guerrero, *La génesis del crimen en México, estudio de psiquiatría social*, p. 213; Salvador Ortiz Vidales, *Los bandidos en la literatura mexicana*, p. 21; Lamberto Popoca y Palacios, *Historia de la bandalismo en el estado de Morelos, ¡ayer como ahora! 1860 (Plateados) 1911 (Zapatistas)*, pp. 62, 65, 73; Moisés Ochoa Campos, *La revolución mexicana*, 2:87; Felipe Buenrostro, *Historia del primero y segundo congresos constitucionales de la república mexicana*, 4:373-75, 5:415-16; Nicole Giron, *Heraclio Bernal: ¿Bandolero, cacique o precursor de la Revolución?*, p. 35, quoting José Bravo Ugarte, *Historia sucinta de Michoacán*, 3:242.

11. Ireneo Paz, *Algunas campañas, 1863-1876*, pp. 33-34, 41-42; José María Vigil, "La Reforma," in Vicente Riva Palacio, ed., *México a través de los siglos*, 5:678-81; Angelica Peregrina, "Documentos: Antonio

Rojas, un bandido jalisciense," *Boletín del Archivo Histórico de Jalisco* 2, no. 2 (May–August 1978): 10–11.

12. Vigil, "La Reforma," 5:678–81; Paz, *Algunas campañas*, pp. 33–34, 41–42.

13. Eduardo Ruiz, *Historia de la Guerra de Intervención en Michoacán*, pp. 708–09; Billy Joe Chandler, *The Bandit King, Lampião of Brazil*, p. 176.

14. Ochoa Campos, *Revolucíon mexicana*, 2:87; Ma. Guadalupe Flores and Angelica Peregrina, "Historiografía: Las gavillas en Jalisco de 1856 a 1863," *Boletín del Archivo Histórica de Jalisco* 2, no. 2 (May–August 1978): 2–8.

15. S. S. Hill, *Travels in Peru and Mexico*, 2:223, 270–71; Evans, *Our Sister Republic*, p. 203; Geiger, *Peep at Mexico*, pp. 96–97; Robert A. Wilson, *Mexico: Its Peasants and Its Priests; or, Adventures and Historical Researches in Mexico and Its Silver Mines during Parts of the Years 1851–52–53–54*, p. 123; José López-Portillo y Rojas, *Elevación y caída de Porfirio Díaz*, p. 77; Mayer, *Mexico*, p. 10.

16. Enrique Martínez Ruiz, "La crisis del orden público en España y la creación de la Guardia Civil," *Revista de Estudios Históricos de la Guardia Civil* 5 (1970): 58; Constancio Bernaldo de Quirós, *El bandolerismo en España y México*, p. 231.

17. Margo Glantz, ed., *Viajes en México: Crónicas extranjeras*, p. 44; Stephens, *Knockabout*, p. 181; Dunbar, *Mexican Papers*, p. 114; Henry C. Becher, *A Trip to Mexico, Being Notes of a Journey from Lake Erie to Lake Tezcuco and Back*, p. 137; García Cubas, *Mis recuerdos*, p. 201; López Cámara, *Estructura económica*, p. 234; Thomas W. Knox, *The Boy Travellers in Mexico: Adventures of Two Youths in a Journey to Northern and Central Mexico*, p. 75.

18. Glantz, *Viajes en México*, p. 44; Lempriere, *Notes in Mexico*, p. 284; López Cámara, *Estructura económica*, p. 234.

19. Eric J. Hobsbawm, *Bandits*, p. 29; López Cámara, *Estructura económica*, p. 233; Popoca y Palacios, *Bandalismo*, p. 13.

20. Popoca y Palacios, *Bandalismo*, pp. 5–7, 92; Vigil, "La Reforma," 5:444; Bravo Ugarte, *Historia sucinta*, 3:242; Giron, *Heraclio Bernal*, p. 35; Geiger, *Peep at Mexico*, pp. 308–09.

21. Anton Blok, "The Peasant and the Brigand: Social Banditry Reconsidered," *Comparative Studies in Society and History* 14, no. 4 (September 1972): 497; Hobsbawm, *Bandits*, p. 77; Dunbar, *Mexican Papers*, p. 113; MRP, No. 3513, Lorenzo Calderón to Mariano Riva Palacio, 30 November 1849; MRP, No. 8172, José María Verdiguel y Fernández to Mariano Riva Palacio, 21 October 1869; MRP, No. 9104, Francisco Limón to Mariano Riva Palacio, 9 February 1871; Dennis E. Berge, trans. and ed., *Considerations on the Political and Social Situations of the Mexican Republic, 1847*, pp. 19–20; Giron, *Heraclio Bernal*, p. 56; Popoca y Palacios, *Bandalismo*, pp. 36, 40–41, 76–77; Ochoa Campos,

Revolución mexicana, 2:87; Ortiz Vidales, *Bandidos*, p. 18; García Cubas, *Recuerdos*, p. 200; Edith B. Couturier, "Hacienda of Hueyapan: The History of a Mexican Social and Economic Institution," p. 114.

22. Peter Singelmann, "Political Structure and Social Banditry in Northeast Brazil," *Journal of Latin American Studies* 7, no. 1 (May 1975): 62; Chandler, *Bandit King*, pp. 60, 86–89, 116–17, 164–65, 182–83.

23. Popoca y Palacios, *Bandalismo*, pp. 33–35; Ortiz Vidales, *Bandidos*, pp. 15–19, 33–36.

24. Popoca y Palacios, *Bandalismo*, pp. 7, 43–49, 86; Hobsbawm, *Bandits*, pp. 73–74; for last of the Plateados, José de la Cruz Domínguez, see *El Heraldo* (Mexico City), 14 September 1966, p. 31.

25. AGN, Leg. 1384, Exp. Plateados.

26. *La Independencia* (Mexico City), 7 March 1861, p. 4; 13 March 1861, p. 4.

27. *La Independencia*, 3 April 1861, p. 3; *Archivo mexicano: Colección de leyes, decretos, circulares y otros documentos* 5:616–18; Zamacois, *Historia de Méjico*, 15:588–89, 628–31.

28. AGN, Leg. 1384, Exp. Plateados; Guerrero, *Génesis del crimen*, p. 217; Paz, *Algunas campañas*, p. 61; MRP, No. 7445, [Cuaderno] Miguel Cardena Asunción [unsigned], 2 February 1862 to 20 April 1863; MRP, No. 7533, Miguel Cardena Asunción to Mariano Riva Palacio, 11 March 1863.

29. Enrique Lopéz Albújar, *Los caballeros del delito: Estudio criminológico del bandolerismo en algunos departamentos del Perú*, pp. 40, 75–76, 93, 121–24, 225, 268–75; Eul-Soo Pang, "Agrarian Crisis, Social Banditry and Messianism in Brazil, 1870–1940," pp. 2–10.

30. Quirós, *Bandolerismo*, pp. 321, 328; Hobsbawm, *Bandits*, pp. 15, 17, 25, 58, 61–62; Guerrero, *Génesis del crimen*, pp. 202–04; López Cámara, *Estructura ecónomica*, pp. 232–36; Zamacois, *Historia de Méjico*, 12:125–27; Giron, *Heraclio Bernal*, p. 37; Hans F. Gadow, *Through Southern Mexico: Being an Account of the Travels of a Naturalist*, p. 337; Mario Gill, "Heraclio Bernal, caudillo frustrado," *Historia Mexicana* 4, no. 1 (July–September 1954), p. 147; Lempriere, *Notes in Mexico*, pp. 274–75; Chandler, *Bandit King*, pp. 216–17.

31. Torcuato S. DiTella, "The Dangerous Classes of Early Nineteenth-Century Mexico," *Journal of Latin America Studies* 5, no. 1 (May 1973): 84, 102–05.

32. Singelmann, "Social Banditry," pp. 72–73; Hobsbawm, *Bandits*, pp. 81–82; Gill, "Heraclio Bernal," pp. 141–47; Calderón de la Barca, *Life in Mexico*, pp. 463, 485–86; Chandler, *Bandit King*, pp. 17–35.

33. Calderón de la Barca, *Life in Mexico*, p. 463. Other examples: García Cubas, *Recuerdos*, pp. 201–02; Zamacois, *Historia de Méjico*, 15:654–55; MRP, No. 9528, Francisco Limón to Mariano Riva Palacio, 26 September 1871.

34. Singelmann, "Social Banditry," p. 81; Hobsbawm, *Bandits*, p. 37; [Wise], *Land of the Aztecs*, p. 150; Chandler, *Bandit King*, p. 213.

35. Singelmann, "Social Banditry," p. 81; Hobsbawm, *Bandits*, pp. 13, 39; Blok, "Peasant and Brigand," pp. 494–503; Chandler, *Bandit King*, pp. 47, 169.
36. Albert Stagg, *The Almadas and Alamos, 1783–1867*, p. 36; *El Dictamen* (Veracruz), 22 June 1910, p. 1: Giron, *Heraclio Bernal*, pp. 50–51, 83–84; Robert M. Alexius, "The Army and Politics in Porfirian Mexico," pp. 291–94; Chandler, *Bandit King*, pp. 47, 169–72.
37. Hobsbawm, *Bandits*, pp. 21–22.

2 / AURA OF THE KING

1. Lucas Alamán, *Historia de Méjico*, 1:41; Letter from William B. Taylor, University of Colorado at Boulder, to Vanderwood, 11 March 1978; Letter from Christon I. Archer, University of Calgary, to Vanderwood, 22 March 1978; López Cámara, *Estructura económica*, p. 232; J. Eric S. Thompson, ed., *Thomas Gage's Travels in the New World*, passim; William B. Taylor, *Drinking, Homicide and Rebellion in Colonial Mexican Villages*, p. 98.
2. James Lockhart, introduction, *Provinces of Early Mexico: Variants of Spanish American Regional Evolution*, Ida Altman and James Lockhart, eds., pp. 14–22; Marta Espejo-Ponce Hunt, "The Processes of the Development of Yucatán, 1600–1700," in Altman and Lockhart, eds., *Provinces*, pp. 38–42; Eric R. Wolf, *The Mexican Bajío in the Eighteenth Century: An Analysis of Cultural Integration*, pp. 182–84; P. J. Bakewell, *Silver Mining and Society in Colonial Mexico: Zacatecas, 1546–1700*, pp. 225, 235; Richard Boyer, "Mexico in the Seventeenth Century: Transition of a Colonial Society," *Hispanic American Historical Review* 57, no. 3 (August 1977): 455–78; Taylor, *Drinking*, pp. 22, 25, 27.
3. Justo Sierra, *The Political Evolution of the Mexican People*, p. 252; Enrique Florescano and Isabel Gil Sánchez, eds., *Descripciones económicas regionales de Nueva España. Provincias del norte, 1790–1814*, p. 339; Philip Wayne Powell, "The Chichimecas: Scourge of the Silver Frontier in Sixteenth-Century Mexico," *Hispanic American Historical Review* 57, no. 2 (August 1945): 92–93.
4. Powell, "Chichimecas," p. 94; Robert C. West, *The Mining Community in Northern New Spain: The Parral Mining District*, p. 85.
5. West, *Parral*, pp. 74, 81, 85–84, 130; John H. Coatsworth, "The Impact of Railroads on the Economic Development of Mexico, 1877–1910," pp. 34-35; letter from Philip Wayne Powell, University of California, Santa Barbara, to Vanderwood, 9 January, 1978.
6. Powell, "Chichimecas," pp. 315–338; West, *Parral*, pp. 88–89; Boyer, "Colonial Society," p. 472; Powell letter, 9 January, 1978.
7. Francisco Bulnes, *La Guerra de Independencia: Hidalgo–Iturbide* pp. 206–7; Wolfe, *Bajío*, p. 189.
8. Wolf. *Bajío*, pp. 187–89; Taylor letter, 11 March 1978; Christon I. Archer, *The Army in Bourbon Mexico, 1760–1810*, pp. 94–98; William B.

Taylor, "Town and Country in the Valley of Oaxaca," in Altman and Lockhart, eds., *Provinces*, pp. 77–78; William B. Taylor, *Landlord and Peasant in Colonial Mexico*, pp. 53, 82–84; Taylor letters, 11 March 1978 and 22 April 1978; John M. Hart, *Anarchism and the Mexican Working Class, 1860–1931*, p. 60; Taylor, *Drinking*, pp. 124–44.

9. John Leddy Phelan, *The People and the King: The Comunero Revolution in Colombia, 1781*, pp. 10, 17; West, *Parral*, pp. 83–84.

10. Archer, *Army*, pp. 91–92; Enrique Florescano and Isabel Gil Sánchez, *Descripciones ecónomicas regionales de Nueva España. Provincias del centro, sureste y sur, 1766–1827*, pp. 55–56; Taylor letter, 11 March 1978.

11. Colin M. MacLachlan, *Criminal Justice in Eighteenth-Century Mexico: A Study of the Tribunal of the Acordada*, pp. 11, 32–36, 53–54, 65–68, 71, 89; Florescano and Gil Sánchez, *Provincias del centro*, pp. 55–56; Enrique Florescano and Isabel Gil Sánchez, *Descripciones económicas generales de Nueva España, 1784–1817*, pp. 81–82.

12. MacLachlan, *Acordada*, p. 51.

13. Wolf, *Bajío*, pp. 192–93; MacLachlan, *Acordada*, p. 125; Glantz, *Viajes en México*, p. 29; Powell, "Chichimecas," pp. 95–96.

14. François Chevalier, "The North Mexican Hacienda: Eighteenth and Nineteenth Centuries," in Archibald R. Lewis and Thomas F. McGann, eds., *The New World Looks at its History*, pp. 103–06; Father Norman F. Martin, who is working on vagabonds in New Spain, telephone conversation with Vanderwood, 10 May 1978; Wolf, *Bajío*, pp. 192–93; Archer, *Army*, pp. 10–37.

15. Archer, *Army*, pp. 91–92.

16. Ibid., p. 301; West, *Parral*, p. 49.

17. Archer, *Army*, pp. 5–6, 93–94; Taylor, "Town and Country," p. 93.

18. Raymond Vernon, *The Dilemma of Mexico's Development: The Roles of the Private and Public Sectors*, pp. 93–94; Taylor letter, 11 March 1978; Archer letter, 22 March 1978; Taylor, *Landlord*, p. 93; Guerrero, *Génesis del crimen*, pp. 103, 110–11; Taylor letter, 11 March 1978; Taylor, *Drinking*, pp. 113–15, 164–70; Phelan, *People and King*, pp. xiii, 17.

3 / THE SPOILS OF INDEPENDENCE

1. Enrique Florescano and María del Rosario Lanzagorta, "Política económica, antecedentes y consecuencias," in Luis González, Enrique Florescano, et al., *La economía mexicana en la epóca de Juárez*, pp. 75–77; David A. Brading, "A Creole Nationalism and Mexican Liberalism," *Journal of Inter-American Studies and World Affairs* 15, no. 2 (May 1973): 186–87; Guerrero, *Génesis del crimen*, pp. 184, 194; Wolf, *Bajío*, p. 189; Glantz, *Viajes en México*, p. 256; Josefina Zoraida Vázquez, "Los primeros tropiezos," in *Historia general de México*, 3:12–15; MacLachlan, *Acordada*, p. 105.

2. Calderón de la Barca, *Life in Mexico*, p. 342; Archer letters, 22 March and 4 January 1979; H. G. Ward, *Mexico*, 1:231.

3. Capt. G. F. Lyon, *Journal of a Residence and Tour in the Republic of Mexico in the Year 1826, with some Account of the Mines in that Country*, 2:171–72; Guerrero, *Génesis del crimen*, p. 204; Vázquez, "Primeros tropienzos," p. 46; Lieut. R. W. H. Hardy, *Travels in the Interior of Mexico in 1825, 1826, 1827, and 1828*, pp. 164–65; Hobsbawm, *Bandits*, p. 18; Ward, *Mexico*, 1:231; Eric R. Wolf and Edward C. Hansen, "Caudillo Politics: A Structural Analysis," *Comparative Studies in Society and History* 9, no. 1 (January 1967): 170–72; DiTella, "Dangerous Classes," pp. 104–05; Edward Thornton Tayloe, *Mexico, 1825–1827: The Journal and Correspondence of Edward Thornton Tayloe*, C. Harvey Gardiner, ed., p. 35; Wolf, *Bajío*, p. 189; Archer letter, 4 January 1979; Luis Villoro, "La Revolución de Independencia," in *Historia general de México*, 2:348–49; Luis González y González, "The Revolution of Independence," in Daniel Cosío Villegas, et al., *A Compact History of México*, p. 85.

4. Guerrero, *Génesis del crimen*, p. 213; Richard N. Sinkin, "Modernization and Reform in Mexico, 1855–1876," pp. 22, 184.

5. Enrique Florescano, "México: Ensayo de interpretación," in Roberto Cortés Conde and Stanley J. Stein, eds., *Latin America: A Guide to Economic History, 1830–1930*, pp. 447–50; Alejandra Moreno Toscano and Enrique Florescano, "El sector externo y la organización espacial y regional de México (1521–1910)," in James W. Wilkie, Michael C. Meyer, and Edna Monzón de Wilkie, eds., *Contemporary Mexico: Papers of the IV International Congress of Mexican History*, pp. 80, 84; Florescano and Lanzagorta, "Política económica," pp. 77–85; Stagg, *Almadas*, p. 33; Sinkin, "Modernization" pp. 179–80; Captain Basil Hall, *Extracts from a Journal Written on the Coasts of Chile, Peru, and Mexico in the Years 1820, 1821, 1822*, 1:185, 190.

6. Romeo Flores Caballero, "Comercio interior," in González, Florescano, et al., *Epoca de Juárez*, pp. 167, 182–83; Florescano and Gil Sánchez, *Provincias del norte*, p. 146; Moreno Toscano and Florescano, "Sector externo," p. 83; Mayer, *Mexico*, p. 13.

7. Wistano Luis Orozco, *Legislación y jurisprudencia sobre terrenos baldíos*, pp. 181–82, 191–92; Jean Meyer, *Problemas campesinos y revueltas agrarias (1821–1910)*, pp. 116–18; Ochoa Campos, *Revolución mexicana*, 2:243; Charles A. Hale, *Mexican Liberalism in the Age of Mora, 1821–1853*, p. 225; Donald J. Fraser, "La política de desamortización en las communidades indígenas," *Historia Mexicana* 21, no. 4 (April-June 1972): 618–25; Peter Gerhard, "La evolución del pueblo rural mexicano, 1519–1975," *Historia Mexicana* 24, no. 4 (April-June 1975): 575–76; Robert Wasserstrom, "A Caste War That Never Was: The Tzeltal Conspiracy of 1848," *Peasant Studies* 7, no. 2 (Spring 1978): 74.

8. Stagg, *Almadas*, pp. 34, 36, 40; Hardy, *Interior of Mexico*, pp. 91–92.

9. Moisés González Navarro, "Las guerras de castas," *Historia Mexicana* 26, no. 1 (July-September 1976), pp. 79–87; López Cámara, *Estructuras económicas*, pp. 218–21; Francisco de Paula de Arrangoiz, *México desde 1808 hasta 1867*, p. 401; Zamacois, *Historia de Méjico*, 13:31–33, 300–01; Hale, *Mora*, pp. 236–37.

10. González Navarro, "Guerra de castas," pp. 87–90; Elena Galaviz de Capdevielle, "Descripción y pacificación de la Sierra Gorda," *Estudios de Historia Novohispana* 4 (1971): 144–48; MRP, No. 2686, José María Godoy to Mariano Riva Palacio, 8 June 1848.

11. González Navarro, "Guerra de castas," p. 90; Galaviz de Capdevielle, "Sierra Gorda," pp. 144–48.

12. González Navarro, "Guerra de castas," pp. 90–91; Arrangoiz, *México desde 1808*, p. 406; Galaviz de Capdevielle, "Sierra Gorda," pp. 144–48.

13. González Navarro, "Guerra de castas," pp. 91–93; Galaviz de Capdevielle, "Sierra Gorda," pp. 144–48.

14. López Cámara, *Estructura económica*, p. 233; Nevin O. Winter, *Mexico and Her People To-Day. An Account of the Customs, Characteristics, Amusements, History and Advancement of the Mexicans*, p. 330; Vázquez, "Primeros tropiezos," 3:60; Guerrero, *Génesis del crimen*, pp. 213–14; John H. Coatsworth, "The Mobility of Labor in Nineteenth-Century Mexican Agriculture," pp. 10–11.

15. Moreno Toscano and Florescano, "Sector externo," p. 83; Wolf and Hansen, "Caudillos," pp. 170–73; Sinkin, "Modernization," pp. 181–82, 187–88; Hobsbawm, *Bandits*, pp. 13, 32, 79–82; Glantz, *Viajes en México*, pp. 44–45, 237–39; Vázquez, "Primeros tropiezos," 3:48; Brantz Mayer, *Mexico; Aztec, Spanish and Republican: A Historical, Geographical, Political, Statistical and Social Account of that Country*, 2:149. For Brazil see Singelmann, "Social Banditry," p. 60; Chandler, *Bandit King*, pp. 177–96.

16. López Cámara, *Estructura económica*, pp. 235–36; Guerrero, *Génesis del crimen*, pp. 213–14; Taylor, *Journal*, pp. 67–68; *Archivo Mexicano*, 2:677.

17. Alamán, *Historia de México*, 5:564; Guerrero, *Génesis del crimen*, pp. 110–11, 200–07, 227; Frank Samponaro, "The Political Role of the Army in Mexico, 1821–1848," pp. 12, 62, 85–148; Mayer, *Mexico; Aztec*, 2:117; Sierra, *Political Evolution*, p. 253; Vázquez, "Primeros tropiezos," 3:23, 55; Mariano Otero, "Ensayo sobre el verdadero estado de la cuestión social y política que se agita en la república mexicana," in Jesús Reyes Heroles, *Mariano Otero, Obras: Recopilación, selección, comentarios y estudio preliminar*, 1:52; T. G. Powell, "Los liberales, el campesinado indígena y los problemas agrarios durante la Reforma," *Historia Mexicana* 21, no. 4 (April-June 1972): 653; Stanislav Andreski, *Parasitism and Subversion: The Case of Latin America*, pp. 127, 178, 211; Jaime E. Rodríguez O., *The Emergence of Spanish America: Vicente Rocafuerte and Spanish Americanism*, pp. 217, 227–28, 285n.

18. Samponaro, "Army," pp. 28–30, 65, 74–75; Taylor, *Journal*, p. 72; Ward, *Mexico*, 1:230; Sinkin, "Modernization," p. 188; Berge, *Considerations*, pp. 32–33; Coatsworth, "Autoritarismo," p. 212; Otero, "Ensayo," pp. 53, 117; Fernando Díaz Díaz, *Santa Anna y Juan Alvarez frente a frente*, p. 26.
19. Otero, "Ensayo," p. 118; Guerrero, *Génesis del crimen*, p. 111; Díaz Díaz, *Santa Anna*, pp. 27, 30.
20. Guerrero, *Génesis del crimen*, p. 162; Mayer, *Mexico; Aztec*, 2:119; Mayer, *Mexico*, p. 286.
21. Zamacois, *História de Méjico*, 14:29–33, 112–18; Otero, "Ensayo," pp. 116–17.
22. Vázquez, "Primeros tropiezos," 3:43; Sinkin, "Modernization," p. 188; Díaz Díaz, *Santa Anna*, pp. 23–24, 27, 30.
23. Guerrero, *Génesis del crimen*, pp. 214–15; José María Luis Mora, *El clero, la milicia y las revoluciones*, pp. 16–17; Lempriere, *Notes in Mexico*, p. 282; DiTella, "Dangerous Classes," p. 87; Samponaro, "Army," pp. 216, 228–29; Mexico, State of Puebla, Juan Múgica y Osorio [governor], *Memoria sobre la administración del Estado de Puebla en 1849, bajo el gobierno del ESCMO. Sr. D. Juan Múgica y Osorio*, pp. 18–24.
24. México (state), Archivo de la Cámara de Diputados de 1822–1823, de México MSS, Actas de la Diputación Provincial de México, 1822–1823, V, Session 49 (November 13, 1823), p. 144; AGN, Leg. 1351, Exp. Guía de Hacienda [1825]; Leg. 1020, Exp. 160 [1842]; Leg. 1054, Exp. 12 [1846]; Leg. 1048, Exp. Sección 1° [1855]; MRP, No. 3597, Alejandro Villaseñor to Mariano Riva Palacio, 16 December 1849; MRP, No. 3760, Agustín Escudero to Mariano Riva Palacio, 22 January 1850; México, Secretario de Estado y del Despacho de Relaciones Esteriores y Gobernación de la República Mexicana, *Memoria . . . correspondiente a la administración provisional en los años de 1841, 42, 43*, p. 55; Arrangoiz, *México desde 1808*, p. 350; Mayer, *Mexico; Aztec*, 2:149–50; Charles H. Harris, *A Mexican Family Empire: The Latifundio of the Sánchez Navarros, 1765–1867*, pp. 192, 196; Sinkin, "Modernization," pp. 201–02.
25. Alberto María Carreño, ed., *Archivo del General Porfirio Díaz, memorias y documentos*, 1:51–52.
26. Zamacois, *Historia de Méjico*, 12:50–52; Samponaro, "Army," pp. 217, 234–37, 303; Arrangoiz, *México desde 1808*, p. 369; Chevalier, "North Mexican Hacienda," p. 105; Hale, *Mora*, p. 144; Harry E. Cross, "The Mining Economy of Zacatecas, Mexico in the Nineteenth Century," pp. 13–14, 24, 155, 221–28, 234.
27. Maurice Brungardt, "The Civic Militia in Mexico: 1820–1835," passim; Hale, *Mora*, pp. 16–17, 143; Samponaro, "Army," pp. 194–95; Jorge Alberto Lozoya, "Un guión para el estudio de los ejércitos mexicanos del siglo diecinueve," *Historia Mexicana* 27, no. 1 (April–June 1968): 555.
28. Brungardt, "Civic Militia," pp. 27, 41; AGN, Leg. 1020, Exps.

20-1/2 and 35; Díaz Díaz, *Santa Anna*, p. 24; Mayer, *Mexico; Aztec*, 2:149–50.
 29. Lilia Díaz, "El liberalismo militante," in *Historia general de México*, 3:87–89.
 30. Zamacois, *Historia de Méjico*, 13:168–69; Guerrero, *Génesis del crimen*, pp. 215–18.
 31. López Cámara, *Estructura económica*, p. 219; Vernon, *Mexican Development*, p. 31; Guerrero, *Génesis del crimen*, p. 217.

4 / BENT ON BEING MODERN

 1. Fraser, "Política de desamortización," p. 627; Luis González, "El liberalismo triunfante," in *Historia General de México*, 3:174–79; Ochoa Campos, *Revolución mexicana*, 4:54; Hale, *Mora*, pp. 156, 246; Brading, "Creole," pp. 148–52, 175, 178, 183; Powell, "Campesinado indígena," p. 673.
 2. Sinkin, "Modernization," pp. 49–55; Zamacois, *Historia de Méjico*, 14:135–36.
 3. Stephen R. Niblo, "The Political Economy of the Early Porfiriato: Politics and Economics in Mexico, 1876 to 1880," p. 276; Laurens B. Perry, "El modelo liberal y la política práctica en la república restaurada, 1867–1876," *Historia Mexicana* 23, no. 4 (April–June 1974): 674–99; Brading, "Creole," p. 153; Vernon, *Mexican Development*, pp. 33–35; Florescano and Lanzagorta, "Politica económica," p. 100; Hale, *Mora*, p. 182; Sinkin, "Modernization," p. 176.
 4. Moisés González Navarro, "La venganza del sur," *Historia Mexicana* 21, no. 4 (April–June 1972): 685–90; Powell, "Campesinado indígena," pp. 661–63, 655, 688; Vigil, "La Reforma," p. 92; Meyer, "Problemas campesinos," pp. 15–16; Sinkin, "Modernization," pp. 191–92; Zamacois, *Historia de Méjico*, 14:127, 299, 390–92.
 5. Zamacois, *Historia de Méjico*, 14:195–97, 231.
 6. Powell, "Campesinado indígena," p. 673; Florescano and Lanzagorta, "Política económica," p. 99; Hale, *Mora*, pp. 95, 233, 238–39, 246; Castillo Velasco, "Adiciones," pp. 215–17.
 7. Moisés González Navarro, "Tenencia de la tierra y población agrícola," *Historia Mexicana* 19, no. 1 (July–September 1969): 63; José Miranda, "La propiedad communal de la tierra y la cohesión social de los pueblos indígenas mexicanos," *Cuadernos Americanos* 149, no. 6 (November–December 1966): 179–81; Powell, "Campesinado indígena," p. 656.
 8. Robert J. Knowlton, *Church Property and the Mexican Reform, 1856–1910*, p. 26; Richard N. Sinkin, "The Mexican Constitutional Congress, 1856–1857: A Statistical Analysis," *Hispanic American Historical Review* 53, no. 1 (February 1973): 7–11.
 9. González, "El liberalismo triunfante," pp. 174–79.

10. *El Siglo XIX* (Mexico City), 17 April 1858, p. 2; 4 May 1858, p. 3; 30 May 1858, p. 1; 19 July 1858, p. 4; AGN, Leg. 1429, Exp. Organización de fuerzas rurales; Leg. 988, Exp. Guardia Civil; Guerrero, *Génesis del crimen*, p. 213; Vigil, "La Reforma," 5:376–81; Powell, "Campesinado indígena," pp. 664–65.

11. *Colección de leyes, decretos y reglamentos que interinamente forman el sistema político, administrativo, y judicial del imperio: Ministerio de Guerra*, 4:135–48; The Bazaine Archive in the Genaro García Collection in the Benson Latin American Collection at the University of Texas at Austin contains abundant correspondence concerning the efforts of the Interventionists to deal with Mexican banditry. For examples see: Napoleon Bonaparte III to Achille François Bazaine, July 20, 1863, volume 1, folleto 63; Bazaine to Leonardo Márquez, November 29, 1863, vol. 2, fol. 365; Bazaine to Minister of War, 27 September 1863, vol. 1, fol. 92; Napoleon to Bazaine, 30 July 1863, vol. 1, fol. 63; Bazaine to political prefect at Apam, 16 October 1863, vol. 1, fol. 141; Bazaine to Minister of War, 9 January 1865, vol. 9, fols. 2101–02. Also, AGN, Leg. 1350, Exp. A consecuencia de los robos; Leg. 988, Exp. Estados de fuerza; Exp. Consulta sobre various puntos; Exp. Córdoba disfruten el haber; Exp. Bases para la formación; Percy F. Martin, *Maximilian in Mexico: The Story of the French Intervention*, pp. 447–50; Jack A. Dabbs, *The French Army in Mexico, 1861–1867*, pp. 145–48, 268–70.

12. AGN, Leg. 1333, Exp. Projecto de organización.

13. José María Lafragua, *Ley orgánica de la Guardia de Seguridad de la República Mexicana.* . . . Lafragua's comments concerning origins of the police force are handwritten on this printed copy of the law, Mexico City, Biblioteca Nacional, Archivo de Lafragua.

14. Gerald Brenan, *The Spanish Labyrinth: An Account of the Social and Political Background of the Civil War*, pp. 106–09; Galaviz de Capdevielle, "Sierra Gorda," p. 147; Raymond Carr, *Spain, 1808–1939*, pp. 159, 160–62, 180–82, 232–34; José María Lafragua, *Miscelánea de política*, 1:120; Enrique Martínez Ruiz, *Creación de la Guardia Civil*, pp. 25–32; Sinkin, "Modernization," p. 186.

15. David H. Bayley, "The Police and Political Development in Europe," in Charles Tilly, ed., *The Formation of National States in Western Europe*, pp. 334, 355, 360, 363; David H. Bayley, "The Police and Political Change in Comparative Perspective," *Law and Society Review* 6, no. 1 (August 1971): 91–112.

16. Lafragua, *Ley orgánica*, passim; Paul Vanderwood, "Genesis of the Rurales: Mexico's Early Struggle for Domestic Security," *Hispanic American Historical Review* 50, no. 2 (May 1970): 324–25.

17. *Archivo mexicano: Colección de leyes, decretos, circulares y otros documentos*, 1:196–97; 2:641–77.

18. Vigil, "La Reforma," 5:208; MRP, No. 6544, Mateo Salazar to

Mariano Riva Palacio, 11 May 1857; MRP, No. 7016, José B. Espejo to Mariano Riva Palacio, 25 September 1857; Lafragua, *Miscelánea*, p. 115; Enrique M. de los Ríos, et al., *Liberales ilustres mexicanos de la Reforma y la Intervención*, p. 86; Zamacois, *Historia de Méjico*, 1:439–49.

19. Manuel Dublán and José María Lozano, *Legislación mexicana, o colección completa de las disposiciones legislativas expedidas desde la independencia de la República*, 7:364; AGN, Leg. 1079, Exps. 6, 7, 67.

20. Zamacois, *Historia de Méjico*, 14:105 and passim.

21. *El Siglo XIX*, 5 January 1870, pp. 1–2; Geiger, *Peep at Mexico*, pp. 308–09; Evans, *Sister Republic*, p. 205; Vigil, "La Reforma," 5:325; Gadow, *Southern Mexico*, p. 337.

22. *Diario Oficial del Gobierno Supremo de la República* (Mexico City), 22 March 1868, pp. 1–2.

23. Mexico, Secretaria de Gobernación, *Memoria que el oficial Mayor encargado de la Secretaría de Estado y del Despacho de Gobernación presenta el Séptimo Congreso Constitucional*, pp. 37–38. The *Memorias* are divided into two sections, Minister's report and supporting documents. In some Memorias each section has its own pagination.

24. *El Siglo XIX*, 5 January 1870, pp. 1–2; López-Portillo y Rojas, *Elevación y caída*, p. 77.

25. Sierra, *Political Evolution*, pp. 345, 348; Ochoa Campos, *Revolución mexicana*, 3:53–56; David Lynn Miller, "Porfirio Díaz and the Army of the East," pp. 280–81; Walter V. Scholes, *Mexican Politics during the Juárez Regime*, p. 137; Charles A. Smart, *Viva Juárez! A Biography*, p. 395; Frank A. Knapp, *The Life of Sebastián Lerdo de Tejada, 1823–1889: A Study of Influence and Obscurity*, p. 118; Lopez-Portillo y Rojas, *Elevación y caída*, pp. 68–71; Daniel Cosío Villegas, *Historia moderna de México: La Republica Restaurada: La vida política* 1:229; *El Mundo* (Mexico City), 3 June 1889, p. 1; *Memoria de Gobernación*, 1880–1884, p. 34; AGN, Leg. 2178, Exp. Circulares; *Colección de decretos, reglamentos y circulares referentes a los Cuerpos Rurales de la Federación desde su fundación hasta la fecha*, p. 5; AHDN, D/481.4/8.55.

26. AGN, Leg. 1436, Exp. Policía Rural, and Exp. Creación de cuatro cuerpos; AHDN, D/481.4/8.234; Dublán and Lozano, *Legislación* 9:206–07.

27. AGN, Leg. 1436, Exp. Policía Rural.

28. AGN, Leg. 1436, Exp. Policía Rural; Leg. 324, Exp. Historia de los cuerpos rurales; Leg. 343, Exp. Contiene varios extractos and Exp. 5, Cuerpo; *Memoria de Gobernación*, 1873, Document No. 15, pp. 53, 61–64.

5 / Bandits into Police—and Vice Versa

1. Hobsbawm, *Bandits*, pp. 74, 78; Singelmann, "Social Banditry," pp. 61–63, 81; Guerrero, *Génesis del crimen*, pp. 119–21; Bolk, "Peasant

and Brigand," p. 501; Sinkin, "Modernization," p. 45; Neill Macaulay, *The Prestes Column: Revolution in Brazil*, p. 191: Pang, "Agrarian Crisis," p. 14.

2. Frank R. Prassel, *The Western Peace Officers*, pp. 49, 106–07, 109, 134; W. Eugene Hollon, *Frontier Violence: Another Look*, pp. 147, 175; James D. Horan, *The Authentic West: The Gunfighters*, pp. 3–4, 11, 125–29; Dane Coolidge, *Fighting Men of the West*, pp. 167–70.

3. [Michel] Élie Reclus, *Primitive Folk: Studies in Comparative Ethnology*, pp. 245, 269–73.

4. Hobsbawm, *Bandits*, p. 44; Wolf, *Peasant Wars*, pp. 113–14.

5. R. H. Hilton, "The Origins of Robin Hood," *Past and Present* (November 1958): 31–44; J. C. Holt, "The Origins and Audience of the Ballads of Robin Hood," *Past and Present* no. 18 (November 1960): 89–110.

6. Reclus, *Primitive Folk*, pp. 273–74.

7. MRP, No. 8088, Ignacio Mejía to Mariano Riva Palacio, 6 October 1869, and No. 8687, Francisco Limón to Mariano Riva Palacio, 2 February 1870.

8. For descriptions of uniforms, see *El Siglo XIX*, 17 September 1877, p. 3; *El Mundo* (Mexico City), 5 May 1885, p. 7; *El Tiempo* (Mexico City), 6 May 1908, p. 2; Hudson Strode, *Timeless Mexico*, p. 205; Carleton Beals, *Porfirio Díaz, Dictator of Mexico*, pp. 225–26; Anita Brenner, *The Wind That Swept Mexico*, p. 11; José C. Valadés, *El Porfirismo: Historia de un régimen, el crecimiento*, 1:68; Manuel Conrotte, *Notas mejicanas*, pp. 131–32; Dublán and Lozano, *Legislación*, 9:206–07; AGN, Leg. 1436, Exp. Policía Rural and Exp. Creación de cuatro Cuerpos. . . .

9. *El Heraldo* (Pachuca), 31 May 1908, p. 5; for image-building of Rurales, see chap. 11, "It's the Image That Counts." For other examples of police uniforms as symbols, such as those of the British and Germans, see Bayley, "Police and Political Development," pp. 373–74.

10. Zamacois, *Historia de Méjico*, 15:629–31.

11. *El Siglo XIX*, 5 April 1861, p. 2, 26 August 1861, p. 3; Guerrero, *Génesis del crimen*, p. 213; Zamacois, *Historia de Méjico*, 15:629–31; *Archivo mexicano*, 5:616–18; AGN, Leg. 1436, Exp. Ladrones; José Basilio Arriaga, ed., *Recopilación de leyes, decretos, bandos, reglamentos, circulares y providencias de los poderes y otras authoridades de la república mexicana . . .* , 5:42–43; Dublán and Lozano, *Legislación*, 9:21; Zamacois, *Historia de Méjico*, 13:628–31; Hart, *Mexican Working Class*, pp. 33–35.

12. *El Siglo XIX*, 9 June 1861, p. 3; 3 October 1861, p. 1; 11 October 1861, p. 2; *Unión Federal* (Mexico City), 16 July 1861, p. 1.

13. *El Siglo XIX*, 9 September 1861, p. 3; 30 October 1861, p. 2; *Victoria: Periódico del Gobierno de Oaxaca* (Oaxaca), 4 November 1861, p. 2; Daniel Muñoz y Pérez, *General Don Ignacio Zaragoza*, p. 33.

14. Giron, *Heraclio Bernal*, p. 35, quoting Bravo Ugarte, *Historia sucinta*, 3:242.

15. Ruiz, *Michoacán*, pp. 466–69; Vigil, "La Reforma," 5:678–81; Ireneo Paz, *Algunas campañas*, pp. 58, 61.

16. AGN, Leg. 204, Exp. 13; Leg. 271, Exp. Faltas cometidas; Leg. 324, Exp. Contiene varios extractos; Leg. 1180, Exp. Jiménez, Vicente; Leg. 1180, Exp. Sobre la baja; Leg. 1189, Sublevación; Leg. 1260, Exp. Ramón Sottil; Leg. 1270, Exp. Compañía de Tampico; Leg. 1270, Exp. Compañía de Tepic; Leg. 1612, Exp. Agustín Reyes; Leg. 1612, Exp. Mayer del 7° batallón; *Decretos de Rurales*, pp. 28–29; *Memoria de Gobernación*, 1873, p. 85.

17. Ruiz, *Michoacán*, pp. 324–25, 390–91, 454, 536–37.

18. AGN, Leg. 1524, Exp. León Ugalde; *El Monitor Republicano* (Mexico City), 1 October 1874, p. 3; 6 October 1874, p. 3.

19. *Boletín de Noticias* (Mexico City), 13 March 1861, p. 1; AHDN, D/481.4/8.555; *Archivo Mexicano*, 5:40–41; *Memoria de Gobernación*, 1873, Document No. 15, p. 58; AGN, Leg. 324, Exp. Historia de los Cuerpos Rurales.

20. AGN, Leg. 324, Exp. Historia de los Cuerpos Rurales; Leg. 343, Exp. Contiene varios extractos; Leg. 343, Exp. 5° Cuerpo; *Memoria de Gobernación*, 1873, Document No. 15, p. 53, Guerrero, *Génesis del crimen*, p. 213; *El Siglo XIX*, 5 April 1861, p.2; 26 August 1861, p. 3.

21. Mexico, Ministerio de Guerra y Marina, *Memoria del Secretario de Estado y del Despacho de Guerra y Marina, leída a la cámara del Congreso Nacional de la República Mexicana*, pp. 6–24 (hereafter cited as *Memoria de Guerra.*); John M. Hart, "Miguel Negrete: La epopeye de un revolucionario," *Historia Mexicana* (July–September 1974), pp. 79–93; Smart, *Viva Juárez!*, pp. 395–96; MRP, No. 8198, Sebastián Lerdo de Tejada to Mariano Riva Palacio, 29 October 1869; No. 9658, T. Tuñón Canedo to Mariano Riva Palacio, 2 November 1871; No. 9675, same to same, 11 November 1871; No. 9688, same to same, 17 November 1871, and No. 9770, same to same, 6 December 1971.

22. *El Monitor Republicano*, 6 October 1875, p. 4; 9 October 1875, p. 3; 14 October 1875, p. 3; 15 October 1875, p. 4; 16 October 1875, p. 3; 2 November 1875, p. 4; AGN, Leg. 324, Exp. Que tiene varios extractos; *Boletín de la Policía Rural*, 15 October 1875, p. 4; 15 November 1875, p. 2.

23. AGN, Leg. 1524, Exp. Persecución de gavillas.

24. AGN, Leg. 1291, Exp. Huehuetoca; Leg. 1306, Exp. Quejas del Gob° de Puebla; Leg. 1306, Exp. El Gobierno del Estado de Méjico.

25. *El Monitor Republicano*, 8 January 1869, p. 3; 1 October 1874, p. 3; 6 October 1874, p. 3; 22 October 1874, p. 3; 25 October 1874, p. 3; *El Siglo XIX*, 26 October 1874, p. 3; AGN, Leg. 204, Exp. 13; Leg. 1180, Exp. Gobierno del distrito; Leg. 1260, Exp. Sobre mal comportamiento; Leg. 1270, Exp. Aprensión de un contrabandista.

6 / ORDER, DISORDER, AND DEVELOPMENT

1. Florescano and Zanzagorta, "Política económica," pp. 89–92; González, "El liberalismo triunfante," 3:187–90; Scholes, *Mexican Politics*, p. 145; Vernon, *Mexican Development*, p. 56; Robert L. Delorme, "The Political Basis of Economic Development: Mexico, 1884–1911, a Case Study," pp. 40–44; Knowlton, *Church Property*, pp. 169–71; Walter F. McCaleb, *The Public Finances of Mexico*, p. 136; Coatsworth, "Railroads," pp. 35–36; David L. Miller, "Porfirio Díaz and the Army of the East," pp. 269–70, 284; Laura Randall, *A Comparative Economic History of Latin America, 1500–1914: Volume 1: Mexico*, pp. 157–58.

2. Ochoa Campos, *Revolución mexicana*, 3:93–94; Knapp, *Lerdo de Tejada*, p. 191; John W. Foster, *Diplomatic Memoirs*, 1:71–72, 115.

3. Ochoa Campos, *Revolución mexicana*, 3:93–94; López-Portillo y Rojas, *Elevación y caída*, p. 99; Powell, "Campesinado indígena," pp. 670–72; González, "El liberalismo triunfante," 3:199; Knapp, *Lerdo de Tejada*, pp. 188–90, 212–15; Meyer, *Problemas campesinos*, p. 6; Vanderwood, "Genesis of Rurales," pp. 332–33, 338.

4. Sinkin, "Modernization," pp. 223–31; Jean Meyer, "El ocaso de Manuel Lozada," *Historia Mexicana* 18, no. 4 (April–June 1969): 536, 559–61, 565; Knapp, *Lerdo de Tejada*, pp. 184–85.

5. Sinkin, "Modernization," pp. 224–30; Guerrero, *Génesis del crimen*, p. 219; Quirós, *Bandolerismo*, p. 320; Meyer, "Lozada," pp. 536–55.

6. Meyer, "Lozada," p. 558; Sinkin, "Modernization," pp. 229–30.

7. MRP, No. 9821, T. Tuñón Canedo to Mariano Riva Palacio, 19 December 1871.

8. Perry, "Insurrection," pp. 79, 321, 328–29; B. W. Aston, "The Public Career of Don José Ives Limantour," p. 20; Niblo, "Political Economy," pp. 4–7, 192–206; Ochoa Campos, *Revolución mexicana*, 3:97, 243–46; Carreño, *Archivo de Díaz*, 12:96–99; Valadés, *Porfirismo*, 1:249–52; Alberto Bremauntz, *Panorama social de las revoluciones de México*, p. 129; Hart, *Mexican Working Class*, pp. 66–67.

9. Niblo, "Political Economy," pp. 199–202; Valadés, *Porfirismo*, 1:253–54.

10. Valadés, *Porfirismo*, 1:252–54 and 398–99; González, "El liberalismo triunfante," 3:202–03; Niblo, "Political Economy," pp. 145–48; John M. Hart, "Anarchist Thought in Nineteenth-Century Mexico," pp. 150–52, 164–65; Hart, *Mexican Working Class*, pp. 69–70, 77.

11. Niblo, "Political Economy," pp. 191–92; Valadés, *Porfirismo*, 1:129–34, 347–48; Foster, *Diplomatic Memoirs*, p. 28; *Memoria de Gobernación*, 1879–1880, p. 45; *El Monitor Republicano*, 8 January 1878, p. 1; 2 September 1881, p. 2; *El Siglo XIX*, 12 March 1877, p. 1; 5 November 1879, p. 4; *La Libertad* (Mexico City) 17 October 1878, p. 3; 11

June 1879, p. 3: 30 September 1879, p. 2; *El Hijo del Trabajo* (Mexico City), 9 May 1880, p. 3.

12. *Memoria de Gobernación*, 1877–1878, Document No. 24, pp. 115–24; *El Socialista* (Mexico City), 4 March 1878, p. 3; 9 June 1878, p. 3; *El Hijo del Trabajo*, 23 February 1879, p. 3; *El Monitor Republicano*, 1 January 1878, p. 3; 8 January 1878, p. 1; 13 January 1878, p. 3; 26 February 1878, p. 3; *El Siglo XIX*, 30 May 1878, p. 3; Valadés, *Porfirismo*, 1:128–29.

13. *El Monitor Republicano*, 30 June 1877, p. 3; 29 July 1879, p. 2; 27 September 1879, p. 4; 17 January 1880, p. 3; 13 February 1881, p. 3; *La Libertad*, 19 October 1880, p. 3; *El Siglo XIX*, 5 November 1879, p. 4; *Memoria de Gobernación*, 1879–1880, pp. 51–53; Michoacán, Gobernador, *Memoria presentada por el ciudadano General de División Manuel González al ejecutivo de la unión, al del Estado de Michoacán y a la legislatura del mismo sobre el uso de las facultades discrecionales que la fueron concedidas para reorganizar politicamente y administrativamente dicho estado*, pp. 18, 166–68.

14. González, "El liberalismo triunfante," 3:202–06; Niblo, "Political Economy," pp. 188–89, 194–95; Daniel Cosío Villegas, *The United States versus Porfirio Díaz*, pp. 10–11, 28–29, 37, 42, 46–47, 52, 152, 166, 179, 207; Foster, *Diplomatic Memoirs*, 1:89–95; López-Portillo y Rojas, *Evolución y caída*, p. 155; Daniel Cosío Villegas, *Historia moderna de México: El Porfiriato: Vida politica interior*, 1:291, 294, 345, 655, 688–70; Valadés, *Porfirismo*, 1:29–30, 291–95, 316, 330–37; Delmar Leon Beene, "Sonora in the Age of Ramón Corral," pp. 32–64; Leopoldo Solís, *La realidad económica mexicana: Retrovisión y perspectivas*, p. 61.

15. Niblo, "Political Economy," pp. 49–73; David M. Pletcher, "Inter-American Trade in the Early 1870s—A State Department Survey," *The Americas* 33, no. 4 (April 1977): 593.

16. *Mexican Herald* (Mexico City), 15 January 1911, p. 5; *La Libertad*, 3 March 1880, p. 3; Valadés, *Porfirismo*, 1:316.

17. *Mexican Herald*, 15 January 1911, p. 5; *Memoria de Gobernación*, 1877, p. 15; *El Monitor Republicano*, 29 November 1876, p. 3; *Memoria de Gobernación*, 1879–1880, p. 209; *Decretos de Rurales*, p. 52; *El Hijo del Trabajo*, 8 August 1880, p. 2.

18. Carreño, *Archivo de Díaz*, 23:230–32; AGN, Leg. 490, Exp. Novedades.

19. *El Monitor Republicano*, 2 February 1878, p. 2; 5 February 1878, p. 1; 19 April 1878, p. 3; 23 April 1878, pp. 1–2; 7 May 1878, p. 3; 8 May 1878, p. 1; 16 January 1880, p. 3; 22 January 1880, p. 2; 14 February 1880, p. 3; 13 July 1880, p. 2; 15 July 1880, p. 3; 20 July 1880, pp. 2–3; *El Combate* (Mexico City), 11 July 1880, p. 3; *La Patria* (Mexico City) 11 July 1880, p. 3; 14 July 1880, p. 3; *La República* (Mexico City) 4

July 1880, p. 3; 16 July 1880, p. 3; 17 July 1880, p. 3; *La Voz de México* (Mexico City) 11 July 1880, p. 2; *La Tribuna* (Mexico City), 22 July 1880, p. 2; *El Siglo XIX*, 25 October 1879, p. 3; AGN, Leg. 2178, Exp. Circulares; Mexico, Congreso, Cámara de Diputados, *Diario de los debates de la Cámara de Diputados, 1871–1910*, Legislatura VIII (April 1878), 3:177–79, 185.

20. *Memoria de Gobernación*, 1877–1878, pp. 19–20; Document No. 23, pp. 95–96; AGN, Leg. 1647, Exp. Circulares (No. 97); *El Monitor Republicano*, 3 September 1878, p. 2; 4 September 1878, pp. 2–3; 12 September 1878, p. 2; 15 September 1878, p. 3.

21. *Memoria de Gobernación*, 1879–1880, Document No. 116, p. 264; *La Patria*, 21 July 1880, p. 2; 12 August 1880, p. 1; *El Combate*, 22 June 1880, p. 2; 25 July 1880, p. 2; AGN, Leg. 324, Exp. 5° cuerpo, Relación histórica; Leg. 1837, Exp. Sublevados.

22. *El Monitor Republicano*, 5 August 1880, p. 3; 10 August 1880, p. 3; 13 August 1880, p. 2; 14 August 1880, p. 3; *La Patria*, 8 August 1880, p. 3; *El Hijo del Trabajo*, 8 August 1880, p. 3; *La Tribuna* 31 July 1880, p. 2; *El Combate*, 15 August 1880, p. 1.

23. *El Monitor Republicano*, 5 August 1880, p. 3; 8 August 1880, p. 3; 10 August 1880, p. 3; 13 August 1880, p. 2; 14 August 1880, p. 3; *La Patria*, 8 August 1880, p. 3; *El Hijo del Trabajo*, 8 August 1880, p. 3; *El Combate*, 15 August 1880, p. 1.

24. *El Republicano* (Mexico City), 13 August 1880, p. 3; *La República*, 18 August 1880, p. 1; *La Patria*, 25 August 1880, p. 1; *La Tribuna*, 22 July 1880, p. 3; 10 August 1880, p. 3; *El Monitor Republicano*, 8 August 1880, p. 3.

25. Cosío Villegas, *Porfiriato: Vida política*, 1:xxii, 207, 588–89, 591, 615, 623, 645, 648–49; González, "El liberalismo triunfante," 3:217; Lozoya, "Ejércitos mexicanos," p. 558; Cosío Villegas, *United States versus Díaz*, pp. 216–19; AGN, Leg. 2178, Exp. Circulares; *Memoria de Gobernación*, 1880–84, p. 34; John H. Coatsworth, "Obstacles to Economic Growth in Nineteenth-Century Mexico," *American Historical Review* 83, no. 1 (February 1978): 99; Solis, *Realidad económica*, pp. 76, 79; Don M. Coerver, *The Porfirian Interregnum: The Presidency of Manuel Gonzáles of Mexico, 1880–1884*, chaps. 3, 5.

26. Aston, "Public Career," pp. 76–82, 99–102, 108–09, 117–18, 204–05; Coatsworth, "Railroads," pp. 47–48, 57–59, 196; Ochoa Campos, *Revolución mexicana*, 1:168; Valadés, *Porfirismo*, 1:377; Randall, *Comparative Economic*, pp. 162–64; Coerver, *Interregnum*, pp. 202–10, 266–67.

27. Florescano and Lanzagorta, "Política económica," p. 101; Moreno Toscano and Florescano, "Sector externo," pp. 93–95; Vernon, *Mexican Development*, p. 30; Coerver, *Interregnum*, pp. 205–10.

28. Coerver, *Interregnum*, p. 297.

7 / THE LIMITS TO DICTATORSHIP

1. Clark W. Reynolds, *The Mexican Economy: Twentieth-Century Structure and Growth*, pp. 25, 137: Luis Nicolau d'Olwer, et al., *Historia moderna de México: El Porfiriato: La vida económica*, 2:639–40, 657, 672; Fredrich Katz, "Labor Conditions on Haciendas in Porfirian Mexico: Some Trends and Tendencies," *Hispanic American Historical Review* 54, no. 1 (February 1974): 35; Clifton B. Kroeber, "La cuestión del Nazas hasta 1913," *Historia Mexicana* 20, no. 3 (January–March 1971): 428–29; Meyer, *Problemas campesinos*, p. 223; David S. Landes, *The Unbound Prometheus: Technological Change and Industrial Development in Western Europe from 1750 to the Present*, pp. 3–5, 11–12; W. Arthur Lewis, *Economic Survey, 1919–1939*, pp. 140–48; Luis González y González, *San José de Gracia: Mexican Village in Transition*, pp. 74–75.

2. Vernon, *Mexican Development*, pp. 38–39; D'Olwer, et al., *Porfiriato: Vida económica*, 2:637–39; John H. Coatsworth, "Los orígines del autoritarismo moderno en México," *Foro Internacional* 16, no. 2 (October–December 1975): 222–23; Lewis, *Economic Survey*, pp. 74–75, 194–95; Wolfe and Hansen, "Caudillo Politics," p. 178; Ochoa Campos, *Revolución mexicana*, 1:210–12; Delorme, "Political Basis," pp. 105–07.

3. Vernon, *Mexican Development*, p. 43.

4. D'Olwer, et al., *Porfiriato: Vida económica*, 2:658, 665, 673–78, 682–86; Francisco Bulnes, *El verdadero Díaz y la Revolución*, pp. 224–29; Valadés, *Porfirismo*, 1:86; Percy F. Martin, *Mexico of the XXth Century*, 2:151–52; Ochoa Campos, *Revolución mexicana*, 1:153–54.

5. D'Olwer, et al., *Porfiriato: Vida económica*, 2:670–72.

6. Reynolds, *Mexican Economy*, pp. 25, 137; D'Olwer, et al., *Porfiriato: Vida económica*, 2:639–43; Lewis, *Economic Survey*, pp. 194–95.

7. Merrill W. Gaines, "Effects of the Silver Standard in Mexico," *Yale Review* 12 (May 1903–February 1904): 276–85; Delorme, "Political Basis," pp. 185–91 ff; David M. Pletcher, "The Fall of Silver in Mexico, 1870–1910, and its Effect on American Investments," *Journal of Economic History* 18, no. 1 (March 1958): 34–52; Aston, "Limantour," pp. 119–30; Edwin W. Kemmerer, *Modern Currency Reforms: A History of Recent Currency Reforms in India, Porto Rico, Philippine Islands, Straits Settlements and Mexico*, pp. 467–73, 477, 484, 488; D'Olwer, et al., *Porfiriato: Vida económica*, 2:657, 699; Valadés, *Porfirismo*, 1:109–10; Archibald W. Butt, "Where Silver Rules: Wages, Prices and Conditions in the Most Prosperous Silver Using Country of the World," pp. 6–13; Marvin D. Bernstein, *The Mexican Mining Industry, 1890–1950: A Study of the Interaction of Politics, Economics, and Technology*, p. 29; McCaleb, *Public Finances*, pp. 177, 182; Ochoa Campos, *Revolución mexicana*, 1:240; A. Piatt Andrew, "The End of the Mexican Dollar," *Quarterly Journal of Economics* 18 (May 1904): 321–22.

8. Meyer, *Problemas campesinos*; D'Olwer, et al., *Porfiriato: Vida económica*, 2:642; Charles C. Cumberland, *Mexican Revolution: Genesis under Madero*, pp. 14–15; *New York Times*, 1 September 1896, p. 4; Fernando Rosenzweig, "El desarrollo económico de México de 1877 a 1911," *El Trimestre Económico* 32 (3), No. 127 (July–September 1965): 447; Ochoa Campos, *Revolución mexicana*, 1:265; E. A. H. Tays, "Present Labor Conditions in Mexico," *The Engineering and Mining Journal* 84, no. 14 (5 October 1907): 622; Rodney D. Anderson, *Outcasts in Their Own Land: Mexican Industrial Workers, 1906–1911*, p. 30; Walter E. Weyl, "Labor Conditions in Mexico," *Bulletin of the* [*U.S.*] *Department of Labor* 38 (January 1902): 34–38.

9. Everett S. Lee, "The Turner Thesis Reexamined," *American Quarterly* 13, no. 1 (Spring 1961): 81; Donald B. Keesing, "Structural Change Early in Development: Mexico's Changing Industrial and Occupational Structure from 1895–1950," *Journal of Economic History* 29, no. 4 (December 1969), pp. 22, 30–31, 35–36; Coatsworth, "Mobility of Labor," pp. 2–11; Eric J. Hobsbawm, "Economic Fluctuations and Some Social Movements," *Economic Historical Review* 5, no. 1 (1952): 21.

10. William K. Meyers, "Politics, Vested Rights, and Economic Growth in Porfirian Mexico: The Company Tlahualilo in the Comarca Lagunera, 1855–1911," *Hispanic American Historical Review* 57, no. 3 (August 1977): 437; Katz, "Labor Condition," pp. 28–29; Victor S. Clark, "Mexican Labor in the United States," *Bulletin of the Bureau of Labor* (Department of Commerce and Labor) 17 (1908): 514–15; Robert Sandels, "Antecedentes de la Revolución en Chihuahua," *Historia Mexicana* 24, no. 3 (January–May 1975): 396–97.

11. Clark, "Mexican Labor," 17 (1908): 466–70; John Martínez, *Mexican Emigration to the United States, 1910–1930*, pp. 2–5; Sandels, "Chihuahua," pp. 396–97; Moisés González Navarro, "Los braceros y el Porfiriato," *Estudios Sociológicos* 5 (1954): 263–78; Martin, *Mexico of XXth Century*, 2:214–15; Paul Friedrich, *Agrarian Revolt in a Mexican Village*, p. 46.

12. Anderson, *Workers and Politics*, pp. 28, 48; Carlos Aguirre Anaya, "The Geographic Displacement of Population, 1895–1910: Perspectives in the Study of Urban Systems," *Latin American Research Review* 10, no. 2 (Summer 1975): 123–24; Rosenzweig, "Desarrollo económico," pp. 419–21; Barry Carr, "Las peculiaridades del norte mexicano, 1880–1920: Ensayo de interpretación," *Historia Mexicana* 22, no. 3 (January–March 1973): 328–30; Mexico, Secretaría de Agricultura y Fomento, Direción de Estadística, *Tercer censo de población de los Estados Unidos Mexicanos verificado el 27 de octubre de 1910*, 1:8, 10–11, 14–23; Solís, *Realidad económica*, pp. 71–72.

13. Friedrich, *Agrarian Revolt*, p. 46; Martin, *Mexico of XXth Century*, 2:215.

14. Katz, "Labor Conditions," pp. 1–47, passim; Friedrich, *Agrarian*

Revolt, pp. 44–46; Ochoa Campos, *Revolución mexicana*, 1:94; Evelyn Hu-DeHart, "Development and Rural Rebellion: Pacification of the Yaquis in the Late Porfiriato," *Hispanic American Historical Review* 54, no. 1 (February 1974): 81–89; Weyl, "Labor Conditions," pp. 42, 47–49.

15. John H. Coatsworth, "Anotaciones sobre la producción de alimentos durante el profiriato," *Historia Mexicana* 26, no. 2 (October–December) 1976): 168, 183–86. Aston, "Limantour," p. 192.

16. Moisés González Navarro, "Tenencia de la tierra y población agricola," *Historia Mexicana* 19, no. 1 (July–September 1969): 67–70; Miranda, "Propriedad comunal," p. 181; Ochoa Campos, *Revolución mexicana*, 1:50–62, 2:71–78, 131; Katz, "Labor Conditions," p. 41; Wistano Luis Orozco, *Legislación y jurisprudencia sobre terrenos baldíos*, pp. 905–13, 918, 943–45, 1091–92, 1097; Valadés, *Porfirismo*, 1:258–59; Cumberland, *Genesis under Madero*, pp. 22–23; Jan Bazant, "The Division of Some Mexican Haciendas during the Liberal Revolution, 1856–1862," *Journal of Latin American Studies* 3, no. 1 (May 1971): 27–37; Meyer, *Problemas campesinos*, pp. 225–30.

17. Cosío Villegas, *Porfiriato: Vida política*, 24:25–426; Alexius, "Army," chapters III–V.

18. Cosío Villegas, *Porfiriato, Vida política*, 2:494; Bulnes, *Verdadero Díaz*, p. 191.

19. Alexius, "Army," pp. 39–40, 113–15, 137–38, 171–75; Anderson, *Workers and Politics*, p. 128; Beene, "Ramón Corral," pp. 154, 159–66; APD, LV, No. 003972, 18 July 1896; Ochoa Campos, *Revolución mexicana*, 4:89–92; Cosío Villegas, *Porfiriato: Vida política*, 2:491; Peter Henderson, "Counterrevolution in Mexico: Félix Díaz and the Struggle for National Supremacy, pp. 5–7.

20. Henderson, "Félix Díaz," pp. 6–7, 13, 19–21, 54; Cosío Villegas, *Porfiriato: Vida política*, 2:23–25.

21. Cosío Villegas, *Porfiriato: Vida política*, 2:426, 491–93; Ochoa Campos, *Revolucíon mexicana*, 2:110–11, 4:190; Alexius, "Army," 155–57, 176, 199; Harold D. Sims, "Espejo de caciques: Los Terrazas de Chihuahua," *Historia Mexicana* 18, no. 3 (January–March 1969): 381–87; Enrique Cordero y Torres, *Primera obra completa sobre la historia general del Estado de Puebla (1531–1963) con el rubro de historia compendida del Estado de Puebla*, pp. 354–55.

22. Ochoa Campos, *Revolución mexicana*, 4:215–23; Hale, *Mora*, pp. 79–80; AGN, Leg. 1906, Exp. Sarrelangue; Leg. 1906, Exp. Ministros de policía; Jorge Vera Estañol, *Historia de la revolución mexicana: Orígenes y resultados*, pp. 44.

23. Alexius, "Army," p. 47–67.

24. Vera Estañol, *Revolución mexicana*, p. 46; Tays, "Present Labor," p. 622; APD, LXVI, No. 000880, [n.d.], and LXVII, No. 001604, 21 April 1909; Alexius, "Army," pp. 41–44.

25. Cosío Villegas, *Porfiriato: Vida política,* 2:167, 186–208; 313–14, 629, 648–76; Ochoa Campos, *Revolución mexicana,* 4:71–80, 89–92, 202, 217–20; Ricardo García Granados, *Historia de México desde la restauración de la república en 1867, hasta la caída de Huerta,* 1:296; López-Portillo y Rojas, *Elevación y caída,* pp. 217, 226–29; Aston, "Limantour," pp. 55–56; Walter N. Breyman, "The Científicos: Critics of the Díaz Regime, 1892–1903," *Proceedings of the Arkansas Academy of Science* 7 (1955): 91–97; Charles A. Hale, " 'Scientific Politics' and the Continuity of Liberalism in Mexico, 1867–1910," in *Dos revoluciones: México y los Estados Unidos,* pp. 141–50.

26. Jorge Fernando Iturribarría, *Porfirio Díaz ante la historia,* p. 13; Rafael Zayas Enríquez, *Porfirio Díaz,* pp. 34–35; Albert Leonard Mills (1st Lieutenant, US Cavalry), "The Military Geography of Mexico," *Military Geography* 15, no. 72 (1894): pp. 66–89.

8 / A Kind of Peace

1. *Memoria de Gobernación,* 1900, parte expositiva, pp. 3–4

2. Paz, *Algunas campañas,* p. xi.

3. *El Monitor Republicano,* 12 September 1885, pp. 2–3; 15 September 1885, p. 4; 23 September 1885, p. 3; 26 September 1885, p. 3; 1 October 1885, p. 3; 10 October 1885, p. 4; *El Diario del Hogar* (Mexico City), 13 September 1885, p. 2; *El Siglo XIX,* 22 September 1885, p. 2; 28 September 1885, p. 2; *La Voz de México* (Mexico City), 24 September 1885, p. 3; *La Patria,* 26 September 1885, p. 3; *La República,* 12 September 1885, pp. 1–2; 13 September 1885, p. 2; *El Tiempo,* 13 November 1885, p. 2; Alexius, "Army," pp. 273–75; *Memoria presentada a la honorable legislatura del Estado de Veracruz—leída por el governador constitucional, General Juan Enríquez, en la sesión del 17 de septiembre de 1886 y que corresponde al período de su administración comprendido entre el 1 °de enero de 1885 y el 30 de junio de 1886, pp. 29–30.*

4. *El Monitor Republicano,* 4 July 1891, p. 3; 11 July 1891, p. 2; 6 August 1891, p. 3; *Historia de la Revolución* (anonymous typescript, n.d., located in Biblioteca del Instituto de Antropología e Historia and Los Angeles Public Library), pp. 7–8 (chap. 3); *La Patria,* 21 June 1891, p. 3.

5. *El Monitor Republicano,* 25 June 1891, p. 3; 11 July 1891, p. 2; 23 July 1891, p. 2; 24 July 1891, p. 3; 6 August 1891, p. 3; 10 September 1891, p. 3; 9 October 1891, p. 3; 6 November 1891, p. 3; 25 November 1891, p. 3; 2 December 1891, p. 3; 24 December 1891, p. 2.

6. APD, Leg. LV, Nos. 003396–003398, 25 June 1896; Leg. LV, Nos. 003605–003608, 1 July 1890; Leg. LV, Nos. 003691–003692, 3 July 1896; Leg. LV, Nos. 003834–003835, 13 July 1896; Leg. LV, No. 003972, 18 July 1896; *La Nacional* (Mexico City), 7 July 1896, p. 4; 13 July 1896, p. 1; *La Patria,* 11 July 1896, p. 3; *El Día* (Mexico City), 16 July 1896, p. 1;

El Diario del Hogar, 10 July 1896, pp. 1–2; 11 July 1896, p. 3; 17 July 1896, p. 2; 21 July 1896, p. 1; Alexius, "Army," pp. 276–78; Cosío Villegas, *Porfiriato: Vida política* 2:680; Manuel B. Trens, *Historia de Veracruz*, 6:349–53; Lázaro Gutiérrez de Lara and Edgcumb Pinchon, *The Mexican People: Their Struggle for Freedom*, pp. 317–18.

7. *El Diario del Hogar*, 14 October 1892, p. 2; 18 October 1892, p. 3; Jesús González Monroy, "El lapso más tormentoso de la dictadura porfirista: El Porfirismo y la oposición," p. 53.

8. *La Patria*, 29 October 1892, p. 3; 30 October 1892, p. 2; *El Monitor Republicano*, 2 November 1892, p. 1; 3 November 1892, p. 4; 9 November 1892, p. 1; *El Diario del Hogar*, 14 October 1892, p. 2; 18 October 1892, p. 3; 22 October 1892, p. 1; 1 November 1892, p. 1; 2 November 1892, p. 1; 3 November 1892, p. 3; 9 November 1892, pp. 1–2; *La Voz de México*, 13 November 1892, p. 3; *La Patria*, 29 October 1892, p. 3; García Granados, *Historia de México*, 2:635–37; Cosío Villegas, *Porfiriato: Vida política*, 2:635–37; William Curry Holden, *Teresita*, passim.

9. *La Patria*, 29 October 1892, p. 3; 30 October 1892, p. 2; 1 November 1892, p. 2; *El Diario del Hogar*, 14 October 1892, p. 2; 18 October 1892, p. 3; 22 October 1892, p. 1; 25 October 1892, pp. 2–3; *La Voz de México*, 13 November 1892, p. 3; *El Monitor Republicano*, 2 November 1892, p. 1; 3 November 1892, p. 4; 9 November 1892, p. 1; 15 November 1892, p. 3.

10. *La Patria*, 29 October 1892, p. 3; 1 November 1892, p. 2; 13 November 1892, pp. 2–3; *La Voz de México*, 13 November 1892, p. 3; *El Siglo XIX*, 3 November 1892, p. 3; *El Diario del Hogar*, 3 November 1892, p. 3; *El Monitor Republicano*, 29 October 1892, p. 3; 1 November 1892, p. 1; 15 November 1892, p. 3.

11. *La Patria*, 29 October 1892, p. 3; 1 November 1892, p. 2; 12 November 1892, pp. 1–2; *El Diario del Hogar*, 28 October 1892, p. 2; *La Voz de Mexico*, 13 November 1892, p. 3; 23 November 1892, p. 3; *Memoria de la administración pública del Estado de Chihuahua presentada a la legislatura del mismo por el gobernador constitucional, Coronel Miguel Ahumada* (1896), p. 138; *El Monitor Republicano*, 19 November 1892, p. 3; 22 November 1892, p. 2.

12. David A. Wells, *A Study of Mexico*, pp. 17–18; AGN, Leg. 718, Exp. Descarrilamento; Valadés, *Porfirismo*, 1:61; Thomas A. Rickard, *Journeys of Observation*, pp. 95–96; Arthur P. Schmidt, Jr., "The Social and Economic Effect of the Railroad in Puebla and Veracruz, Mexico, 1867–1911," pp. 174–75; *El Monitor Republicano*, 2 February 1888, p. 3; Frank W. Green, *Notes on New York, San Francisco, and Old Mexico by Frank W. Green*, p. 163; Cosío Villegas, *Porfiriato: Vida política*, 2:679; Peter Rees, *Transportes y comercio entre México y Veracruz, 1519–1910*, p. 123.

13. *Memoria de Gobernación*, 1900, documents section, pp.

289–303; Bernard Moses, *The Railway Revolution in Mexico*, pp. 18–19; Cosío Villegas, *Porfiriato: Vida política*, 2:679; Hans F. Gadow, *Through Southern Mexico: Being an Account of the Travels of a Naturalist*, p. 341.

14. For lack of roads and the consequences see: Thompson, *People of Mexico*, pp. 163–64; Ochoa Campos, *Revolución mexicana*, 1:176; Valadés, *Porfirismo*, 1:364; Bulnes, *Verdadero Díaz*, pp. 293–94.

15. Hobsbawm, *Bandits*, pp. 13–33.

16. Quirós, *Bandolerismo*, pp. 343–49.

17. Ibid., pp. 349–355; Ortiz Vidales, *Los Bandidos*, p. 66; *El Siglo XIX*, 2 June 1884, p. 3.

18. *El Correo del Lunes* (Mexico City), 9 June 1884, pp. 2–3; *El Cable Transatlántico* (Mexico City), 23 August 1881, p. 3.

19. *El Monitor Republicano*, 1 June 1884, p. 3; 21 June 1884, p. 3; 31 October 1885, p. 3; *El Tiempo*, 3 June 1884, p. 4.

20. Moisés González Navarro, *Historia moderna de México: El Porfiriato: La vida social*, p. 433.

21. *El Tiempo*, 3 June 1884, p. 4; *El Monitor Republicano*, 3 October 1885, p. 3; González Navarro, *Porfiriato: Vida social*, p. 433.

22. González, "Liberalismo triunfante," 2:203; *El Tiempo*, 5 November 1885, p. 1; 13 November 1885, p. 3; 8 November 1885, p. 3; *El Monitor Republicano*, 31 October 1885, p. 3.

23. Quirós, *Bandolerismo*, p. 366; Owen W. Gillpatrick, *Wanderings in Mexico: The Spirited Chronicle of Adventure in Mexican Highways and By-Ways by Wallace Gillpatrick*, p. 329; Gill, "Heraclio Bernal," pp. 141–47; Giron, *Heraclio Bernal*, p. 29; Antonio Nakayama A., *Sinaloa: El drama y sus actores*, p. 210.

24. Gill, "Caudillo frustrado," pp. 141–47; *La República*, 5 November 1885, p. 1.

25. Wells, *Study of Mexico*, pp. 19–20; Alfred O. Coffin, *Land without Chimneys, or, The Byways of Mexico*, pp. 199–200.

26. Giron, *Heraclio Bernal*, pp. 50, 57–58, 61, 65; *El Tiempo*, 12 November 1885, p. 3; Chandler, *Bandit King*, pp. 45, 185.

27. Gill, "Caudillo frustrado," p. 147.

28. Giron, *Heraclio Bernal*, pp. 19–20; Gill, "Caudillo frustrado," p. 139; *El Monitor Republicano*, 1 February 1887, p. 2; González, "Liberalismo triunfante," 3:29; Quirós, *Bandolerismo*, pp. 368–69; J. Ascensión Reyes, *Heraclio Bernal (El Rayo de Sinaloa)*, p. 245.

29. *La Evolución* (Durango), 1 July 1910, p. 1; my examination of Rural Police targets preserved in Mexico's National Archive proves the corpsmen to have been mediocre marksmen.

30. Quirós, *Bandolerismo*, pp. 370–73; *Periódico Oficial* (Veracruz), 27 October 1910, pp. 2–3; *El Nacional*, 15 February 1959, pp. 3 and 9; *El Imparcial* (Mexico City) 19 October 1910, pp. 1 and 5; 20 October 1910, pp. 1 and 5; *El País*, 17 October 1910, p. 2; *El Dictamen* (Veracruz), 26 June 1910, p. 4.

31. *Periódico Oficial* (Veracruz), 27 October 1910, p. 3; Quirós, *Bandolerismo*, pp. 273–74; *El País*, 18 October 1910, p. 1; *El Dictamen*, 14 June 1910, p. 1; 15 June 1910, p. 1; 16 June 1910, p. 1; 18 June 1910, p. 1; 25 June 1910, p. 4; 2 July 1910, p. 1; 14 July 1910, pp. 1–2; 27 July 1910, p. 1; 28 September 1910, p. 1; 3 November 1910, p. 1.

32. *El Dictamen*, 18 June 1910, p. 1; *El Nacional*, 15 February 1959, pp. 3 and 9; APD, Leg. XIX, No. 004020, 18 October 1910; *El Tiempo*, 19 October 1910, p. 1; Gustavo Casasola, *Historia gráfica de la revolución mexicana*, 1:215; *El Imparcial*, 22 January 1911, p. 1; José C. Valadés, *Historia general de la revolución mexicana*, 1:193; AHDN, XI/481.5/310, fs. 1–3.

33. C. D. Padua, *Movimiento revolucionaria—1906 en Veracruz . . .*, pp. 46–48, 65–67, 75, 81; RD5, No. 812.00/450, Wilson to Knox, 15 December 1910; *El Nacional*, 15 February 1959, pp. 3, 9; *El Dictamen*, 22 June 1910, p. 1; James D. Cockcroft, *Intellectual Precursors of the Mexican Revolution, 1900–1913*, pp. 154–55, 180.

34. Quirós, *Bandolerismo*, pp. 374–76; Padua, *Movimiento*, p. 64; *El Nacional*, 15 February 1959, pp. 3, 9; *La Evolución*, 1 July 1910, p. 1; *El Dictamen*, 22 June 1910, p. 1; 22 July 1910, p. 1.

35. *Mexican Herald*, 25 October 1910, p. 3; *El Dictamen*, 19 October 1910, pp. 1, 4; 20 October 1910, p. 1; 22 November 1910, p. 1; APD, Leg. LXIX, No. 004021, 18 October 1910; Leg. LXIX, No. 004025, 19 October 1910; *Periódico Oficial* (Veracruz), 27 October 1910, pp. 1–2; Hermosillo, Sonora, Archivo General del Estado de Sonora, Ramo de Gobernacíon, Vol. 54, Nos. 182–83; Padua, *Movimiento*, pp. 78–81; *El Imparcial*, 19 October 1910, pp. 1, 5; 20 October 1910, pp. 1, 5; 22 January 1911, p. 1; *El País*, 20 October 1910, p. 3; 22 October 1910, p. 2; 1 February 1911, p. 3.

36. RDS, 812.00/355, Wilson to Taft, 31 October 1910; Quirós, *Bandolerismo*, pp. 376–78; *El Dictamen*, 16 November 1910, p. 14.

37. Harold J. Sullivan, "The Indian Policy of Porfirio Díaz," p. 74; Dane Coolidge, *Fighting Men of the West*, pp. 223–24; Cornelius Smith, *Emilio Kosterlitsky, the Eagle of Sonora*, pp. 96–101, 168; Bulnes, *Verdadero Díaz*, p. 296; Ochoa Campos, *Revolución mexicana*, 1:186, 4:144; Paul Vanderwood, "The Counter-Guerrilla Strategy of Porfirio Díaz," *Hispanic American Historial Review* 56, no. 4 (November 1976): 558–59; Beene, "Ramón Corral," p. 113; Ildefonso Villarello Vélez, *Historia de la revolución mexicana en Coahuila*, pp. 39–40; Jalisco (state), *Memoria presentada por el ejecutivo del Estado a la XII Legislatura Constitucional en la sesión del 2 de febrero de 1890*, p. 4. These *Memorias*, which were the official reports of governors to their respective state congresses, normally included statements on the size and preparedness of the state security forces. For further examples, see the *Memorias* from: Sinaloa, 1886; Tamaulipas, 1889; Veracruz, 1891; Tlaxcala, 1894; Michoacán,

1894; Nuevo León, 1895; Guerrero, 1896; México, 1900; Oaxaca, 1903; and Zacatecas, 1909.
38. *El Siglo XIX*, 7 May 1888, p. 1. Trans. by Vanderwood.

9 / CONSTABULARY OF CAMPESINOS

1. Vanderwood, "Computer Study." Statistics concerning the composition and performance of the Rurales are the result of a computerized study of the force. Thirty-four pieces of data, such as age at enlistment, job prior to enlistment, length of service, reason for discharge, punishments, promotions, home district, and marital status were taken from the personnel records of 1,930 rural policemen, The records are now preserved at Mexico's National Archive. The number 1,930 was selected because it represents the size of the corps in any average year. The period analyzed is 1885 to 1910, broken into three time segments: 1885–1890, 1891–1900, and 1901–1910. The initial computer run yielded a frequency distribution for all periods and the second a series of cross tabulations. It then became evident that a significant aspect of the constabulary concerned its changes over the 25-year period. So a third computer run measured the cross tabulations against time segments. (Hereafter cited as "Computer Study.") I am beholden to my friend, Thomas H. Gillooly, a mathematics teacher with substantial university training in Mexican history, for his labor in reducing and weighting the raw computerized data into meaningful form for this book, and for assisting me to focus on the most important questions raised by the statistics.

For budget data see *Ley de presupuesto del erario federal para el año fiscal que comienza el 1° de julio de 1910 y termina el 30 de junio de 1911*, pp. 46, 267; *Ley de ingresos y presupuesto de egresos del tesoro federal para el año fiscal que comienza en 1 de julio de 1884 y termina en 30 de junio de 1884*, pp. 32, 238; *Ley de ingresos . . . 1904*, p. 35; *Decretos de Rurales*, pp. 151–52; AGN, Leg. 312, Exp. Carlos Acota y Porfirio Ortiz; Leg. 700, Exp. El Gobernador. For reenlisted deserters see: AGN, Leg. 497, Díaz, Cornelio; Leg. 544, Exp. Rebollo, Agustín; Leg. 575, Gómez, Isidro; Leg. 719, Exps. Martínez, Filomeno, and Hernández, Telesforo. A few enlisted men were, over time, promoted through the ranks. For such examples see: AGN, Leg. 690, Exp. Miguel Cuéllar; Leg. 908, Exp. Juan J. Jiménez; Leg. 968, Exp. Oficiales inútiles; AHDN, Archivo de los Candelados, Exps. Rangel, Desiderio; Hernández, Luis; and Ramos, Liborio.

2. "Computer Study"; AGN, Leg. 599, Exp. Visita. For specific discipline problems see: AGN, Leg. 305, Exp. García, Miguel; Leg. 324, Exp. Historia reseña del 6° cuerpo; Leg. 582, Exp. Jefe político de Acámbaro; Leg. 668, Exp. 6° cuerpo; Leg. 690, Exp. 5° cuerpo; Leg. 980, Exp. Juan J. Jiménez.

3. "Computer Study." For examples of "typical" enlistees see: Leg. 490, Exp. Novedades; Leg. 825, Circulares; Leg. 908, Exp. Juan J. Jiménez; Leg. 2175, Exp. Fiadores; Legs. 668, 688, 690, 850, 1535, 2191, all Exps. passim.

4. "Computer Study." Also see documentation for "typical" enlistees in note no. 3 above.

5. "Computer Study." Also see documentation for "typical" enlistees in note no. 3 above.

6. AGN, Leg. 312, Exp. Alcalde penal; Leg. 582, Exps. *Progreso Industrial* and Pueblo de Mexpam; Leg. 598, Exp. Ordenanado al Cabo 1° Espinoza; Leg. 670, Exp. Correspondencia oficial; Leg. 824, Exp. Juan Martínez; Leg. 1647, Exp. Olvera, Fortunato; *Memoria de Gobernación*, 1884–1886, p. 26; *La Libertad*, 25 January 1879, p. 2; *El Monitor Republicano*, 24 January 1879, p. 3; *Decretos de Rurales*, pp. 204–05.

7. "Computer Study"; *Tercer censo*, 1:77–86; Cross, "Mining Economy," pp. 360–63; Donald A. Brading, "Estructura de la producción agrícola en el Bajío, 1700–1850," in Enrique Florescano, ed., *Haciendas, latifundios, y plantaciones en América Latina*, p. 131: Donald A. Brading and Celia Wu, "Population Growth and Crisis: León, 1720–1860," *Journal of Latin American Studies* 5, no. 1 (May 1973): 6–10; Cockcroft, *Intellectual Precursors*, pp. 18–19, 20–26.

8. "Computer Study"; Bailey Millard, "The Shame of Our Army; Why Fifty Thousand Enlisted American Soldiers Have Deserted," *Cosmopolitan Magazine* 49 (September 1910): 412–13. R. C. MacLeod, *The North-West Mounted Police and Law Enforcement 1873–1905*, p. 83; for details on desertions see: *Decretos de Rurales*, pp. 89–90, 151–52; *El Monitor Republicano*, 14 February 1879, p. 3; *El Tiempo*, 24 August 1907, p. 3; *Memoria de Gobernación*, 1906–1908, Document No. 26, p. 47; AGN, Leg. 203, Exp. No. 2; Leg. 305, Exp. 6° cuerpo; Leg. 316, Exp. Ramírez, Teodoro; Leg. 1207, Exp. Informe; Leg. 1777, Exp. Circulares (No. 63); Leg. 2079, Exp. 1° cuerpo, 1ª compañía.

9. "Computer Study."

10. Ibid.; AGN, Leg. 908, Exp. Juan J. Jiménez.

11. "Computer Study." For regulations concerning qualifications for enlistment see: *Memoria de Gobernación*, 1879–1880, Document No. 114, p. 210; *Memoria de Gobernación*, 1860–1900, pp. 35–36.

12. AGN, Exp. Certificados; Leg. 582, Exp. Visitador; Leg. 679, Exp., Conceptos; Ignacio T. Carro, Francisco Alvarez, Francisco A. Caballero, Crispín Ugalde, Adolfo Peña; Leg. 824, Exp. Moncada, Luis; Leg. 825, Exp. Circulares de mil novecientos tres y cuatro; Leg. 908, Exp. Juan J. Jiménez; Leg. 968, Exp. Documentos que archivo recibió; Leg. 1850, Exp. Solicitudes; Leg. 2191, Exp. Cervantes, Daniel; Mexico, Presidente, *Informes y manifiestos de los poderes ejecutivo y legislativo de 1821 a 1904*, 2:136; APD, Leg. 5, Nos. 002126 and 002132, 15 July 1880.

13. *Ley de ingresos*, 1885, pp. 32, 238; *Ley de presupuesto*, 1910–1911, pp. 46–47. For peculations and forced contributions see *Decretos de Rurales*, pp. 81–82, 162, 166, 195, 209–10, 212–16; *La Federación*, 12 September 1887, p. 1: *El Hijo de Trabajo*, 16 March 1879, p. 3; *El Monitor Republicano*, 14 May 1878, p. 2; 18 February 1883, p. 3; *El Siglo XIX*, 27 November 1877, p. 3; AGN, Leg. 312, Exp. viuda del mayor; Leg. 512, Exps. Circular (No. 70) and No. 69; Leg. 554, Exp. Monumento; Leg. 582, Exp. Visitador; Leg, 587, Exp. Junta de beneficencia; Leg. 825, Exp. Circulares de mil novecientos tres y cuatro; Leg. 908, Exp. Juan J. Jiménez; Leg. 1027, Exp., Informe; Leg. 1438, Exp. Víctimas de Tehuantepec.

14. "Computer Study"; AGN, Leg. 718, Exp. Presupuesto de egresos, 1907 à 1908.

15. AGN, Leg. 1500, Exp. Tepic.

16. *Decretos de Rurales*, p. 197; AGN, Leg. 825, Circulares de mil novecientos tres y cuatro; Leg. 908, Exp. Juan J. Jiménez. Also "peculations and forced contributions" in note no. 13 above.

17. *El Monitor Republicano*, 13 April 1892, p. 3; *Memoria de Gobernación*, 1880–1884, pp. 35–36; *Decretos de Rurales*, pp. 213–14; AGN, Leg. 535, Exp. Documentos del informe; Leg. 582, Exp. Visitas; Leg. 718, Exp. 10,000 cartuchos; Leg. 727, Exp. Armamento; Leg. 888, Exp. Documentos varios mandados; Leg. 908, Exp. Juan J. Jiménez; Leg. 968, Exp. Reconocimiento del armanento; Leg. 1207, Exp. Informe.

18. AGN, Leg. 512, Exps. Circular (No. 70) and No. 69; Leg. 888, Exp. Documentos varios mandados; Leg. 824, Exp. Se le piden al Inspector; Leg. 908, Exp. Juan J. Jiménez; Leg. 1207, Exp. Informe; Leg. 1436, Exp. Policia Rural; Leg. 1777, Exp. Circulares (No. 55); Leg. 2178, Exp. Circular (1880); *Memoria de Gobernación*, 1879–1880, Document No. 114, pp. 213–17; *Memoria de Gobernación*, 1900–1904, Document No. 8, pp. 317–21, and Document No. 9, pp. 350–52; *Memoria de Gobernación*, 1904–1906, Document No. 31, p. 75; *Decretos de Rurales*, pp. 185–86, 195, 209–10, 212–13; *El Hijo de Trabajo*, 16 March 1879, p. 3; *La Federación*, 12 September 1887, p. 1.

19. AGN, Leg. 490, Exp. Novedades; Leg. 582, Exp. Visitador; Leg. 690, Exp. 5° cuerpo, varios asuntos; Leg. 908, Exp. Juan J. Jiménez; *Decretos de Rurales*, p. 179. Other examples: AGN, Leg. 633, Exp. 1° Cuerpo Rural, destacamentos; Leg. 730, Exp. Moreno, Jesús; Leg. 700, Exp. Averiguación; Leg. 2192, Exp. Mercado, Jesús.

20. *El Monitor Republicano*, 6 March 1895, p. 3; AGN, Leg. 324, Exp. Historia reseña del 6° cuerpo; Leg. 582, Exps. Jefe político de Acámbaro, and Destacamento de Cantera; Leg. 587, Exp. Perdida; Leg. 668, Exp. 6° cuerpo; Leg. 690, Exp. 5° cuerpo; Leg. 825, Exp. Circulares de mil novecientos tres y cuatro; Leg. 908, Exp. Juan J. Jiménez; Leg. 1647, Exp. Pontones.

21. "Computer Study"; AGN, Leg. 443, Exps. Eduardo Martínez, Alberto Moreno, Alberto Domínguez, Antonio Rubio, Antonio Velázquez, and Espiridón Vera; Leg. 665, Exp. Manuel Rivera; Leg. 708, Exp. Anastasio Vela; Leg. 843, Exp. Aurelio Cruz; Leg. 895, Exp. Andrés Guerra; Leg. 928, Exps. Luis Elizando and Jesús Rodríguez.

22. AGN, Leg. 908, Exp. Juan J. Jiménez; *Decretos de Rurales*, pp. 107, 183–85.

23. AGN, Leg. 769, Exp. Comandancia del cuerpo; Leg. 1152, passim; Leg. 1672, Exp. Academias; Leg. 1777, Exp. Circulares (No. 63).

24. AGN, Leg. 679, Exp. [1st Corps] Conceptos [2nd Lt.] Francisco Alvarez.

25. *Memoria de Gobernación*, 1900–1904, Document No. 9, p. 349; *Decretos de Rurales*, pp. 107 and 183–85; AGN, Leg. 305, Exp. Díaz de León, Alberto; Leg. 512, Exp. Circular (No. 76); Leg. 1207, Exp. Informe; Leg. 2178, Exp. Circulares (No. 53).

26. AGN, Leg. 846, Exp. Correspondencia recibida; Leg. 888, Exp. Documentos varios mandados; Leg. 1207, Exp. Informe; Leg. 1647, Exp. Circular (No. 96); *Decretos de Rurales*, pp. 63 and 136; *Memoria de Gobernación*, 1885–1900, p. 36; *Memoria de Gobernación*, 1900–1904, Document No. 9, p. 350; *Memoria de Gobernación*, 1906–1908, Document No. 30, p. 51.

27. *Memoria de Gobernación*, 1906–1908, p. 10; AGN, Leg. 582, Exp. Juan C. Peña; Leg. 908, Exp. Juan J. Jiménez.

28. Bayley, "Police and Development," pp. 360–77.

29. Ben H. Procter, "The Texas Rangers"; R. C. MacLeod, "A Canadian Epoch: A Century of Mounted Police"; MacLeod, *Mounted Police*, p. 84.

30. *El Tiempo*, 24 August 1907, p. 3; *El Paladín*, 15 July 1906, p. 2; *El Monitor Republicano*, 13 May 1880, p. 3; 28 December 1892, p. 3; *La Federación*, 12 September 1887, p. 1; *El Hijo del Ahuizote*, 30 June 1889, p. 7; AGN, Leg. 305, Exp. 6° cuerpo; Leg. 312, Exp. Secretaría de Comunicaciones; Leg. 487, Exp. Miguel S. Macedo; Leg. 1207, Exp. Informe; Leg. 2079, Exp. 1° cuerpo, 1ª compañía.

10 / THE PRESIDENT'S POLICE

1. For regulations that governed duties of the Rural Police see *Memoria de Gobernación*, 1879–1880, Document No. 114, pp. 208–17; AGN, Leg. 623, Exp. Reglamento. For performance of duties see: Vanderwood, "Rural Police Force," pp. 175–202, 282–305.

2. The documents sections of the various *Memorias de Gobernación* list the location and size of the Rural Police detachments. Each corps also made monthly reports to constabulary headquarters on the disposition of its detachments. To analyze the patterns of geographical deployment of the units for this book, the detachments were located by different time

periods on a series of maps of the Republic of Mexico. I am greatly indebted to Major Francis A. Ritchey, a specialist in Mexican history now on active duty with the United States Marine Corps, who employed his military skills to plot the locations and movements of the Rural Police detachments between 1876 and 1910. (Hereafter noted as "Geographic Survey.") The constabulary's certificates of vigilance may be found in Mexico's National Archive. For an example see Leg. 985.

3. "Geographical Survey"; *El Monitor Republicano*, 10 March 1880, p. 3; 1 August 1894, p. 1; 1 March 1895, p. 3; *El Partido Liberal* (Mexico City) 31 July 1894, p. 2; *El Hijo del Ahuizote*, 3 June 1894, p. 7; 18 December 1898, p. 5; *El Diario del Hogar*, 11 February 1885, p. 1; *La Libertad*, 3 December 1878, p. 3; *La Nacional*, 22 August 1880, p. 3; *El Tiempo*, 12 June 1902, p. 3; 25 July 1908, p. 3; *El Mundo*, 5 May 1895, p. 7; *La Regeneración*, 23 January 1901, p. 6; 23 February 1901, pp. 8–9; 21 February 1901, pp. 12–13; 7 March 1901, pp. 9–10; 15 March 1901, pp. 9–10; 23 March 1901, p. 7; 30 March 1901, pp. 13–14; Valadés, *Porfirismo*, 1:70.

4. "Geographical Survey"; AGN, Leg. 487, Exp. Miguel Macedo; Leg. 824, Exp. Estados que manifiesten la fuerza.

5. "Geographical Survey"; AGN, Leg. 324, Exp. 5° cuerpo, relación histórica; Leg. 512, Exp. 9° cuerpo, auxilios; Leg. 653, Exp. 2° cuerpo, conducción de reemplazos; Leg. 714, Exp. Documentos del fin de mes; Leg. 827, Exp. Incendio; Leg. 908, Exp. Juan J. Jiménez.

6. AGN, Leg. 693, Exp. Sánchez Pérez, Alfredo.

7. AGN, Leg. 312, Exp. Secretaría de Comunicaciones; Leg. 393, Exp. Guadalupe Villanueva; Exp. 443, Exp. Francisco Morales; Leg. 573, Exp. Sotero, Montiel; Exp. 679, Conceptos; Leg. 693, Exps. Gómez, Manuel, and Zermeno, Casiano; Leg. 895, Exp. Castro, Carlos; Leg. 942, Exp. Madrigal, Jacinto; *El Paladín* (Mexico City), 15 July 1906, p. 2; *El Monitor Republicano*, 13 May 1880, p. 3; 28 December 1892, p. 3; *El Hijo del Ahuizote*, 30 June 1889, p. 7; *La Federación*, 12 September 1887, p. 1.

8. AGN, Leg. 582, Exp. Visitador; Leg. 824, Exp. José Sánchez; Leg. 854, Documentos; Leg. 908, Exp. Juan J. Jiménez.

9. AGN, Leg. 554, Exps. Querétaro and Destacamento de Otumba; Leg. 598, Sobre la aprensión; Leg. 714, Exp. Documentos del fin de mes; *Memoria de Gobernación*, 1879–1880, Document No. 23, p. 100.

10. *El Tiempo*, 24 August 1901, p. 2; 12 September 1903, p. 3; *El Monitor Republicano*, 8 January 1878, p. 3; 5 November 1896, p. 2; *La Libertad*, 13 November 1878, p. 3; 15 August 1879, p. 3; AGN, Leg. 700, Exp. Santa Lucrecia; Leg. 1338, Exps. del Ramo de Seguridad Pública; No. 73; No. 238.

11. AGN, Leg. 512, Exps. 1er cuerpo, auxilios; 1er cuerpo, fuerza ministrada para la conservación del orden; Leg. 582, Exp. Visitas; Leg. 824, Exps. Comandante del 5° cuerpo and Destacamentos queden a disposición; Leg. 852, Exp. Ayotla; Leg. 908, Exp. Juan J. Jiménez.

12. AGN, Leg. 700, Exp. Necaxa.

13. Ibid.

14. AGN, Leg. 487, Exp. Carátula . . . Nexaca; Leg. 908, Exp. Juan J. Jiménez.

15. *El Monitor Republicano,* 12 October 1880, p. 2; 30 November 1895, p. 2; AGN, Leg. 487, Exp. Homicidio; Leg. 7.8, Exp. Tacuba; Leg. 727, Exp. Rebelión en el Puebla de Tenancinga (Tlaxcala); Leg. 893, Exp. 5° Cuerpo Rural, historia; Leg. 1369, Exp. Indiferente.

16. AGN, Leg. 582, Exp. Disgusto; Leg. 824, Exp. Gobierno del Distrito; Leg. 1880, Exp. Jimulco; Leg. 2226, Exp. Moratillo.

17. AGN, Leg, 1338, Exp. No. 126; Leg. 2240, Exp. Gobernador de Tlaxcala.

18. *Engineering and Mining Journal* 75, no. 23 (June 6, 1903): 869.

19. Leg. 908, Exp. Juan J. Jiménez.

20. *El Tiempo,* 23 February 1905, p. 1. For accusations of the use of ley fuga—justified and not—against Rurales, see Vanderwood, "Rural Police," pp. 326–30; AGN, Leg. 1672, Pasa por las armas; *El Diario del Hogar,* 23 November 1892, p. 2; *La Regeneración,* 15 March 1901, p. 5.

22. AGN, Leg. 1292, Exp. Novedades.

23. AGN, Leg. 312, Exp. Cabo 2° Tranquilino Martínez: *El Monitor Republicano,* 22 December 1895, p. 3.

24. AGN, Leg. 582, Exp. Pueblo de Mexpam.

11 / It's the Image That Counts

1. Coffin, *Land without Chimneys,* p. 201.

2. Solomon B. Griffin, *Mexico of To-Day,* p. 103. Other examples abound: J. H. Bates, *Notes of a Tour in Mexico and California,* p. 44; [Elizabeth Cochrane], *Six Months in Mexico, by Nellie Bly* [pseud.], pp. 159–60, 198–99; Theo de Veer, *Mexico: Reis-Studies van een journalist door Theo de Veer,* pp. 186–87; Baron de Gustave Gostkowski, *De Paris a México par les Etats-Unis . . .* 1, p. 273; James A. Wilson, *Bits of Old Mexico,* p. 109; Maturin M. Ballou, *Aztec Land,* p. 281; Gadow, *Through Southern Mexico,* pp. 337–42; [Wise], *Land of the Aztecs,* p. 70; Knox, *Boy Travellers,* p. 70; Thomas U. Brockhurst, *Mexico To-Day: A Country with a Great Future and a Glance at the Prehistoric Remains and Antiquities of the Montezumas,* p. 32; Juan N. Navarro, "Mexico of Today," *National Geographic Magazine* 12, no. 4 (April 1901): 155; Vaquero [pseud.], *Adventures in Search of a Living in Spanish-America, by "Vaquero,"* pp. 56–57.

3. *El Tiempo,* 31 July 1901, p. 2.

4. *Buffalo Express,* 28 June 1901, p. 9.

5. *Illustrated Buffalo Express,* 2 June 1901, p. 8.

6. *El Imparcial,* 6 May 1897, p. 2.

7. Cosío Villegas, *Porfiriato: Vida política*, 2:170; *El Tiempo*, 3 November 1910, p. 7; 12 June 1912, p. 1; *El Imparcial*, 6 June 1911, p. 8; 9 June 1911, p. 5; 29 September 1912, p. 6; *El Diario*, 6 June 1911, p. 1. A sample of typical press comments that reenforce the myth of the Rurales includes *La Federación*, 10 November 1892, pp. 2–3; *El Pendón Liberal* (Mexico City), 21 November 1892, p. 1; *El Correo de Jalisco* (Guadalajara), 25 September 1903, p. 2; *México Nueva* (Mexico City), 17 September 1909, p. 7.

8. *Mexican Herald*, 25 June 1911, section 2, pp. 1, 8.

9. AGN, Leg. 729, Exp. Acuerdo del Sr. Ministro; Leg. 908, Exp. Juan J. Jiménez; Leg. 1672, Exp. Diversos órdenes.

10. *El Partido liberal* (Mexico City), 7 May 1889, p. 1; *El Imparcial*, 4 May 1899, p. 1; González Navarro, *Porfiriato: Vida social*, pp. 700–02; AGN, Leg. 718. Exp. Fiestas celebradas; Leg. 729, Exp. Acuerdo del Sr. Ministro. For Rurales on parade see *El Siglo XIX*, 17 September 1877, p. 3; *El Monitor Republicano*, 3 September 1877, p. 3; *El Mundo* (Mexico City) 5 May 1895, p. 7; *El Diario del Hogar*, 8 May 1908, p. 1; *El Tiempo*, 6 May 1908, p. 2. For Rurales at banquets see: Cosío Villegas, *Porfiriato: Vida política*, 2:169–70; *El Siglo XIX*, 21 January 1888, pp. 1–2; *El Partido liberal*, 7 May 1889, p. 1; 7 May 1890, p. 2; 5 May 1891, pp. 2, 5; *El Monitor Republicano*, 6 May 1890, p. 3; 14 April 1891, p. 3; 5 May 1891, p. 3; 4 May 1892, p. 3; 5 May 1894, p. 3.

11. Higinio Vásquez Santa Ana, *Canciones, cantares y corridos mexicanos*, pp. 194–95.

12. *El Tiempo*, 20 February 1900, p. 2.

13. *New York Times*, 23 July 1899, p. 8; *El Imparcial*, 30 May 1899, p. 1; *El Tiempo*, 7 June 1899, p. 2; 7 September 1899, p. 2; 22 February 1900, p. 2; *La Patria*, 31 May 1899, p. 3; *Two Republics* (Mexico City), 10 June 1899, p. 4; *La Nacional*, 29 May 1899, p. 3; *Mexican Herald*, 7 June 1899, p. 5; 14 June 1899, p. 14; *Evening Star* (Mexico City), 14 February 1900, p. 4. For rural police constabulary in Cuba see Herman Hagedorn, *Leonard Wood*, 1:213–14, 256; Eric Fisher Wood, *Leonard Wood, Conservator of Americanism*, pp. 132–34; Russell H. Fitzgibbon, *Cuba and the United States, 1900–1935*, pp. 57–58, 65, 110, 114–15, 124, 134; Charles E. Chapman, *A History of the Cuban Republic*, pp. 101–03; Rafael Martínez Ortiz, *Cuba: los primeros años de independencia*, 1:533. See also reports of various United States military and provisional governors: *Civil Report of Major-General John R. Brooke, US Army, Military Governor, Island of Cuba*, 3 vols. (Havana: [n.p.], 1899); *Civil Report of Major-General John R. Brooke, US Army, Military Governor, Island of Cuba* (Washington, D.C.: Government Printing Office, 1900); *Final Report of Major-General John R. Brooke, US Army, military governor on civil matters concerning the island of Cuba* (Havana: [n.p.], 1899); (Leonard Wood), *Civil Orders and Circulars, Headquarters, De-*

partment of Cuba, 1901 (Havana: [n.p.], 1901); (Military governor), _Civil Report, 1899–1900,_ 12 vols. (Havana: [n.p.], 1901); _Report of the Military Governor of Cuba on Civil Affairs December 20, 1899–December 31, 1900,_ 2 vols. (Washington, D.C.: Government Printing Office, 1901); _Civil Report of the Military Governor,_ 1901, 15 vols. (Havana: [n.p.], 1902.).

14. John Reed, _Insurgent Mexico,_ pp. 195–96.

15. Patrick A. O'Hea, _Reminiscences of the Mexican Revolution,_ p. 185.

16. Hugh B. C. Pollard, _A Busy Time in Mexico: An Unconventional Record of a Mexican Incident,_ p. 195.

12 / THE ROLLER COASTER CALLED CAPITALISM

1. López-Portillo y Rojas, _Elevación y caída,_ pp. 248–53.

2. Reynolds, _Mexican Economy,_ p. 25; Anderson, _Workers and Politics,_ pp. 21–22; Landes, _Unbound Prometheus,_ p. 78; Meyer, _Problemas campesinos,_ p. 223; W. Arthur Lewis, _The Evolution of the International Economic Order,_ pp. 47–52; Randall, _Comparative Economic,_ pp. 177–78.

3. D'Olwer, et al., _Porfiriato: Vida económica,_ 2:639–42, 658–60; Reynolds, _Mexican Economy,_ p. 137; Anderson, _Workers and Politics,_ 29–30; Meyer, _Problemas campesinos,_ pp. 222–25; Cumberland, _Genesis under Madero,_ pp. 14–15.

4. David M. Pletcher, "Fall of Silver," pp. 34–42; Delorme, "Political Basis," pp. 185 ff; Aston, "Limantour," pp. 119–30; Kemmerer, _Modern Currency;_ pp. 467, 475–77, 484–88; Valadés, _Porfirismo,_ 1:109–10; Andrew, "Mexican Dollar," p. 321; Ochoa Campos, _Revolución mexicana,_ 1:240; Randall, _Comparative Economic,_ p. 176.

5. Gaines, "Silver Standard," pp. 277–84; Delome, "Political Basis," pp. 191 ff; Pletcher, "Silver," pp. 50–52; Rosenzweig, _Porfiriato: Vida económica,_ 2:425, 699; Butt, "Where Silver Rules," pp. 3–9, 16; Kemmerer, _Modern Currency,_ pp. 497–501; Thompson, _People of Mexico,_ pp. 353–54; Ramón E. Ruiz, _Labor and the Ambivalent Revolutionaries, 1911–1913,_ p. 11. (All prices in this paragraph are in U.S. dollars and cents.)

6. Weyl, "Labor Conditions," p. 36; Butt, "Where Silver Rules," pp. 3–6; McCaleb, "Public Finances," p. 182; Kemmerer, _Modern Currency,_ p. 488; Pletcher, "Fall of Silver," pp. 40–47; Bernardo García Martínez, "La Comisión Geográfico-Exploradora," _Historia Mexicana_ 24, no. 4 (April–June 1975): 509; Gaines, "Silver Standard," pp. 280–86; Anderson, _Workers and Politics,_ p. 31; Michaels and Bernstein, "Modernization," p. 691; Cockroft, _Intellectual Precursors,_ p. 36.

7. Vernon, _Mexican Development,_ p. 54; Cumberland, _Genesis under Madero,_ pp. 12–13; González Navarro, "Braceros," p. 264; McCaleb, "Public Finances," pp. 187–88; Henderson, "Félix Díaz," pp.

43–45; Ruiz, *Ambivalent Revolutionaries*, pp. 8–9; Robert Sandels, "Antecedentes de la Revolución en Chihuahua," *Historia Mexicana* 24, no. 3 (January–March 1975): 398; Juan Felipe Leal, "El Estado y el bloque en el poder en México, 1867–1914," *Historia Mexicana* 23, no. 4 (April–June 1974): 720; Mark Wasserman, "Oligarquía e intereses extranjeros en Chihuahua durante el porfiriato," *Historia Mexicana* 22, no. 3 (January–March 1973): 314; Hu-DeHart, "Yaquis," p. 89; Friedrich Katz, "Peasants in the Mexican Revolution of 1910," in Joseph Spielberg and Scott Whiteford, eds., *Forging Nations: A Comparative View of Rural Ferment and Revolt*, p. 70; Mark Wasserman, "Oligarchy and Foreign Enterprise in Porfirian Chihuahua, 1876–1911," pp. 282–88.

8. Sandels, "Antecedentes," pp. 396–97.

9. For views of Díaz toward workers see Anderson, *Workers and Politics*, pp. 36, 122–24, 127–28, 142, 157–58; Martin, *Mexico of the XXth Century*, 2:215; Alexius, "Army," pp. 281–82.

10. Jean A. Meyer, *The Cristero Rebellion: The Mexican People between Church and State, 1926–1929*, pp. 9–10; Anderson, *Workers and Politics*, pp. 44–46, 50–55, 59, 88–89, 92–94, 183–88; Alberto Bremauntz, *Panorama social de las revoluciones de México*, pp. 137–38; David C. Bailey, *Viva Cristo Rey! The Cristero Rebellion and Church State Conflict in Mexico*, pp. 14–19; Ruiz, *Ambivalent Revolutionaries*, pp. 7–10.

11. Alexius, "Army," pp. 279–80; Anderson, *Workers and Politics*, pp. 95, 103–08, 127–28; Niblo, "Political Economy," pp. 100–01, 105–13, 135–45; Ochoa Campos, *Revolución mexicana*, 2:137–38, 271; Bremauntz, *Panorama*, pp. 137–38; Cosío Villegas, *Porfiriato: Vida política*, 2:720.

12. Coolidge, *Fighting Men*, pp. 213–16; Anderson, *Workers and Politics*, p. 110; Herbert O. Brayer, "The Cananea Incident," *New Mexico Historical Review* 13, no. 4 (October 1938): 390–92; *El Imparcial*, 26 June 1906, pp. 1, 3; Hermosillo, Sonora, Archivo General del Estado de Sonora, Ramo de Gobernación, Tomo 2184, Expediente Originales de la huelga. (Hereafter cited as Sonora Archive, Tomo, Exp.)

13. Anderson, *Workers and Politics*, pp. 110–11; Sonora Archive, Tomo 2184, Exps., Mensajes cambiados; Cartas y telegramas; Huelga de Cananea; Diversos listas y relaciones; Disturbios políticos relacionados con la huelga y posteriores de ella; Cartas, proclamas y discursos de los liberales; *El Heraldo de Cananea*, 9 June 1906, p. 1; Hart, *Mexican Working Class*, pp. 90–92; Mexico City, Patronato de la Historia de Sonora, Archivo Histórico, Vol. 22, Nos. 174–295, and Vol. 23, Nos. 1–299. (Hereafter cited as Patronato de Sonora, volume no. and document nos.)

14. *El Diario del Hogar*, 16 June 1909, pp. 1–2; Sonora Archive, Tomo 2184, Exp. Mensajes cambiados, and Exp. Pliego; Patronato de Sonora, Vol. 22, Nos. 174–295, and Vol. 23, Nos. 1–299. Quotations are

from Sonora Archive, Tomo 2184, Exp. Mensajes cambiados, Corral to
Izábal, 8 June 1906, and Patronato de Sonora, Vol. 22, Nos. 224–26,
Izábal to Corral, 2 June 1906.
  15. El Diario Oficial (Mexico City), 28 June 1906, p. 1; El Imparcial,
6 June 1906, p. 1; 29 June 1906, pp. 1, 3; Sonora Archive, Tomo 2184,
Exp. Mensajes cambiados; Patronato de Sonora, Vol. 22, Nos. 221, 228,
236–38; Vol. 23, No. 12. Quotation is from Patronato, Vol. 23, Nos.
51–53, Corral to Izábal, 6 June 1906.
  16. El Cosmopólita (Orizaba), 24 June 1906, quoted in Anderson,
Workers and Politics, p. 114.
  17. Cosío Villegas, Porfiriato: Vida política, 2:733; Anderson,
Workers and Politics, pp. 119–20, 202–04; Alexius, "Army," pp.
299–300; Ochoa Campos, Revolución mexicana, 2:250–52; Edward M.
Conley, "The Anti-Foreign Uprising in Mexico," The World Today (1906),
pp. 1059–62; Hart, Mexican Working Class, p. 93.
  18. APD, Leg. LXV, Nos. 002525, 1 October 1906; 002629, 3 October 1906; 00312–00316, and 000462 [January 1907]; El Imparcial, 3
October 1906, p. 1; La Nacional, 15 February 1959, pp. 3 and 9; 22
February 1959, pp. 3 and 8; Mexican Herald, 3 October 1906, pp. 1–2; 4
October 1906, p. 2; El País, 2 October 1906, p. 1; Alexius, "Army," pp.
291–94; Padua, Movimiento revolucionario, pp. 8–12; Jalapa, Veracruz,
Archivo General des Estado de Veracruz, Leg. 1906, Exps. passim; Trens,
Veracruz, 6: 378–85.
  19. APD, Leg. LXV, Nos. 002541, 2 October 1906; 002554, 2 Oc-
tober 1906; 002591, 2 October 1906; 002616, 2 October 1906; 002717, 6
October 1906; 003335, 25 October 1906; 003496, 31 October 1906; Leg.
LXVI, No. 000381, 3 January 1907; El Imparcial, 3 October 1906, p. 1;
Periódico Oficial (Veracruz), 6 October 1906, pp. 1–2; El Nacional, 15
February 1959, pp. 3, 9; 22 February 1959; pp. 3, 8; Mexican Herald, 3
October 1906, pp. 1–2; 4 October 1906, p. 2; La Patria, 7 October 1906,
p. 1; El País, 7 October 1906, p. 1; El Dictamen, 2 October 1906, p. 2; 8
October 1906, p. 2; 11 October 1906, p. 1; Alexius, "Army," pp. 291–94;
AGN, Leg. 1906, Exp. Partes.
  20. Anderson, Workers and Politics, pp. 138–46, 148, 155.
  21. Cosío Villegas, Porfiriato: Vida política, 2:718–19; Anderson,
Workers and Politics, pp. 138–46 and 150–55; Moisés González Navarro,
"Las huelgas textiles en el porfiriato," Historia Mexicana 6, no. 2 (October–December 1956), p. 85; AGN, Leg. 718, Exp. Huelga de las
fábricas; Exp. Huelgistas.
  22. Anderson, Workers and Politics, pp. 267–69; AGN, Leg. 718,
Exp. Huelga de las fábricas; Exp. Huelgistas.
  23. El Imparcial, 8 January 1907, p. 1; 9 January 1907, pp. 1–2; 10
January 1907, pp. 1–2; 11 January 1907, pp. 1–2; 12 January 1907, p. 2;
16 January 1907, p. 2; El Dictamen, 6–7 January 1907, p. 1; 8–9 January
1907, p. 1; 10–11 January 1907, p. 1; 14–15 January 1907, p. 2; 18

January 1907, p. 1; *El Tiempo*, 4 January 1907, p. 2; 5 January 1907, p. 2; 6 January 1907, p. 2; 9 January 1907, p. 2; 10 January 1907, p. 2; 15 January 1907, p. 2; 16 January 1907, pp. 2–3; 17 January 1907, p. 2; Anderson, *Workers and Politics*, pp. 163–64; Alexius, "Army," pp. 284–85; Daniel Gutiérrez Santos, *Historia militar de México, 1876–1914*, pp. 40–42; Florencio Barrera Fuentes, *Historia de la revolución mexicana: La etapa precursora*, pp. 213–22; Carlo de Fornaro, *México tal cual es: Comentarios por Carlo de Fornaro*, p. 57; Moisés González Navarro, "La huelga de Río Blanco," *Historia Mexicana* 6, no. 4 (April–June 1957): 510–32; AGN, Leg. 718, Exp. Huelga de las fábricas and Exp. Huelgistas; *El Clarín* (Orizaba), 9 July 1959, p. 2; Washington, D.C., National Archives, Records of the Department of State, Consular Reports for Mexico, Numerical Case Files, 1906–1910, Vol. 356, Case 3916, Report of William W. Canada, U.S. consul at Veracruz, 2 February 1907, correspondence relating to the Río Blanco strike in Orizaba, January 1907; Luis Araiza, *Historia del movimiento obrero mexicano*, pp. 11, 126; Hart, *Mexican Working Class*, pp. 96–98.

24. APD, Leg. LXVI, Nos. 000018, 000109–000113, and 000118, all 7 January 1907; 000159 and 000165–000174, 8 January 1907; 000255, 11 January 1907; Alexius, "Army," 284; González Navarro, "Huelgas," p. 88; Anderson, *Workers and Politics*, pp. 133, 146, 163–66, 176, 197; *El País*, 12 January 1907, p. 1; *El Imparcial*, 13 January 1907, p. 1; 16 January 1907, p. 2; *El Dictamen*, 14–15 January 1907, p. 2; 18–19 January 1907, p. 1; *El Tiempo*, 12 January 1907, p. 2; 16 January 1907, pp. 2–3; U.S. Department of State, Consular Reports for Mexico, Numerical Case Files, 1906–1910, Vol. 356, Case 3916, correspondence . . . Orizaba; for Herrera's statement, see Trens, *Veracruz*, 6:394–98; for federal and state politics in the aftermath of the repression see Trens, *Veracruz*, 6:398–404.

25. *La Evolución*, 18 May 1909, p. 1; 30 May 1909, p. 1; 9 June 1910, p. 4; 16 June 1909, p. 4; 25 August 1910, p. 4; *El Diario del Hogar*, 15 May 1909, p. 1; *México Nuevo*, 27 April 1909, p. 2; 30 April 1909, pp. 1–2; 10 May 1909, pp. 1 and 4; 21 May 1909, p. 2; 24 May 1909, pp. 1–2.

26. AGN. Leg. 711, Exp. Velardeña; *México Nuevo*, 20 May 1909, p. 1.

27. Patronato de Sonora, Vol. 52, Nos. 123–68, 292; AGN, Leg. 711, Velardeña; *La Evolución*, 9 June 1909, p. 1; 16 June 1909, p. 2; *El Correo de Jalisco*, 16 April 1909, pp. 1–3; 21 April 1909, p. 1; 1 May 1909, p. 1; *El Diario del Hogar*, 24 April 1909, p. 1; *México Nuevo*, 21 May 1909, p. 2; 9 July 1909, p. 1.

28. APD, Leg. LXVIII, No. 001543, 11 April 1909; No. 001554, 12 April 1909; AGN, Leg. 711, Exp. Valardeña; *El Tiempo*, 4 June 1909, p. 2; 5 June 1909, p. 2; 9 June 1909, p. 2; 12 June 1909, pp. 2–3; 13 June 1909, p. 2.

29. *La Evolución*, 30 May 1909, p. 1; 2 June 1909, p. 1; 6 June 1909,

p. 1; 11 June 1909, p. 1; 13 June 1909, p. 1; 13 June 1909, p. 2; 16 June 1909, p. 2; 20 June 1909, p. 2; 30 June 1909, p. 1; 25 July 1909, pp. 2–3; 29 October 1909, p. 3; Patronato de Sonora, Vol. 52, Nos. 123–68; *Memoria de Gobernación*, 1908–1911, p. 13, and Documents nos. 46–47, pp. 37–43; *El Diario del Hogar*, 14 May 1909, p. 2; *México Nuevo*, 10 June 1909, p. 1; 18 June 1909, p. 5; 4 July 1909, p. 4; 9 July 1909, pp. 1, 8; 6 August 1909, p. 7.

30. *La Evolución*, 6 August 1909, p. 2; *México Nuevo*, 6 August 1909, p. 7; "Jesus González Garza," *Diccionario Porrúa de historia, biografía y geografía de México*, 1:839.

31. Hu-DeHart, "Yaquis," pp. 84–89; APD, Leg. XXXIII, No. 000109, 26 January 1908; Patronato de Sonora, Vol. 19, No. 187, 18 February 1905; Beene, "Corral," pp. 122–24; Antonio Manero, *El antiguo régimen y la revolución*, pp. 188–89; Evelyn Hu-DeHart, "Resistance and Survival: A History of the Yaqui People's Struggle for Autonomy, 1533–1910," pp. 322–26, 368.

32. AGN, Leg. 980, Exp. Juan J. Jiménez; Alexius, "Army," pp. 294–99; APD, Leg. LXV, nos. 004455–00456 and 004504–004505, 28 December 1906; Leg. LXVI, nos. 000019, 000065–000069, and 000121–000122, 7 January 1907; RDS, 812.00/1032, Commander of USS Tacoma to Acting Secretary of Navy and Department of State, 20 March 1911.

33. Alfonso Taracena, *Porfirio Díaz*, pp. 152–53; Moses, *Railway Revolution*, p. 13.

13 / UNRAVELING THE OLD REGIME

1. Ochoa Campos, *Revolución mexicana*, 3:230. For the famous interview see James Creelman, "Porfirio Díaz, Hero of the Americas," *Pearson's Magazine* (March 1908), pp. 241–77. It appeared in translation in *El Imparcial* on 5 March 1908.

2. John Womack, *Zapata and the Mexican Revolution*, pp. 10–36.

3. *México Nuevo*, 12 June 1909, p. 1; 22 June 1909, p. 2; 6 July 1909, p. 1; 14 July 1909, p. 1; 8 August 1909, p. 1; 9 August 1909, p. 1; 10 August 1909, p. 1; Cosío Villegas, *Porfiriato: Vida política*, 2:833.

4. Stanley R. Ross, *Francisco Madero: Apostle of Mexican Democracy*, pp. 102–05; Cumberland, *Genesis under Madero*, p. 108.

5. Ross, *Madero*, pp. 105–12, 116; Cumberland, *Genesis under Madero*, pp. 110–18.

6. *Revista del Ejército y Marina* (July–December 1910), pp. 618–19; Vanderwood, "Counter-Guerrilla," pp. 557–59.

7. Vanderwood, "Counter-Guerrilla," p. 556.

8. Ibid., p. 557.

9. Arthur E. Stillwell and James R. Crowell, "I Had a Hunch," *Saturday Evening Post* 200, no. 32 (4 February 1928): 38, 46; Dr. Ira J.

Bush, *Gringo Doctor*, pp. 226–31; William H. Beezley, *Insurgent Governor: Abraham González and the Mexican Revolution in Chihuahua*, pp. 36–37; Vanderwood, "Counter-Guerrilla," pp. 560–61.
10. Manuel Calero, *Un decenio de la política mexicana*, pp. 37–38.
11. Vanderwood, "Counter-Guerrilla," pp. 561 ff.
12. Ibid., pp. 570–72.
13. *El Paso Morning Times*, 9 December 1910, p. 5; David Galula, *Counter-Insurgency Warfare: Theory and Practice*, p. 2.
14. AHDN, Leg. X1/481.5/331, Fs. 20–23.
15. Vanderwood, "Counter-Guerrilla," pp. 575–76.
16. Ibid., pp. 576–77.
17. APD, Leg. LXX, No. 009963, 26 April 1911.
18. Cumberland, *Genesis under Madero*, p. 151; Carlton Beals, *Porfirio Díaz, Dictator of Mexico*, pp. 453–54; Vanderwood, "Counter-Guerrilla," p. 579. For further details on and interpretation of the sudden collapse of the Porfirian regime see Vanderwood, "Counter-Guerrilla," pp. 551–79. For participation of the Rurales in defense of the government see Vanderwood, "Rural Police Force," pp. 335–70.

14 / Disorder in Search of Order

1. Antonio P. González (Kanta-Klaro) and J. Figueroa Domenech, *La Revolución y sus héroes: Crónica de los sucesos políticos occuridos en México desde octubre de 1910 a mayo de 1911*, pp. 185–86; Patronato de Sonora, Leg. 57, Nos. 64–65, 25 May 1911, and No. 216, 2 June 1911: O'Hea, *Reminiscences*, pp. 56–57.
2. Gregorio Ponce de León, *El interinato presidencial de 1911*, p. 66; *El Diario del Hogar*, 11 June 1911, p. 1; Patronato de Sonora, Vol. 57, Nos. 64–65, 25 May 1911, and 115, 29 May 1911; Vol. 59, No. 5, 1 July 1911; AHDN, XI/481.5/217, Fs. 354–56, 360–61, 364–65.
3. *El Imparcial*, 10 June 1911, p. 1; 15 July 1911, p. 1; 20 July 1911, p. 1; *Mexican Herald*, 23 May 1911, p. 1; 9 June 1911, p. 1, 10 June 1911, p. 1; Ponce de León, *Interinato*, pp. 32–33.
4. *El Tiempo*, 6 June 1911, p. 2; 10 June 1911, p. 1; *Mexican Herald*, 28 May 1911, p. 1; 31 May 1911, pp. 1–3; 3 June 1911, pp. 1–2; 7 June 1911, p. 3; 9 June 1911, p. 1; 18 June 1911, p. 1; 17 July 1911, p. 2; 11 August 1911, p. 6; *El País*, 28 May 1911, p. 2; *Memoria de Gobernación*, 1908–1911, p. 27, and Document No. 80, p. 80, and Document No. 87, p. 86; Ponce de León, *Interinato*, pp. 15, 178–79; Patronato de Sonora, Leg. 60, No. 42, Francisco Vásquez Gómez to Francisco Madero, 29 July 1911; Johanne Caroline Wehmeyer Bose, *Farewell to Durango: A German Lady's Diary in Mexico, 1910–1911*, p. 68.
5. General Juan Gualberto Amaya, *Madero y los auténticos revolucionarios de 1910 hasta la Decena Trágica y fin del General Pascual Orozco*, pp. 281–87; Patronato de Sonora, Vol. 58, Nos. 135, 21 June

1911, and 158, 22 June 1911; AHDN, XI/481.5/217, Fs. 393–404; XI/481.5/317, Fs. 413–35; *Mexican Herald*, 15 July 1911, p. 1; *El Tiempo*, 14 July 1911, p. 1; 15 July 1911, p. 1; Ponce de León, *Interinato*, pp. 83–84. For other examples of disorder and disobedience see: Patronato de Sonora, Vol. 57, Nos. 270, 23 June 1911, and 272, 29 June 1911; Vol. 59, Nos. 295–96, 17 July 1911; Vol. 60, No. 36, 27 July 1911; Vol. 62, No. 337, 27 October 1911; Vol. 63, No. 338, 28 October 1911; *El Imparcial*, 15 June 1912, pp. 1, 6; 23 June 1912, pp. 1, 6; *Mexican Herald*, 15 July 1911, p. 1; *El Tiempo*, 14 July 1911, p. 1; 15 July 1911, p. 1; AHDN, XI/481.5/317, Fs. 413–35; Ponce de León, *Interinato*, pp. 82–84; CEHM, León de la Barra informe to Congress, 6 November 1911, and General Jesús H. Salgado to León de la Barra, 24 July 1911; Bose, *Durango*, pp. 71–73.

6. *Mexican Herald*, 8 July 1911, p. 3; *El Imparcial*, 15 December 1911, p. 4; 6 July 1912, p. 5; *El Diario del Hogar*, 28 July 1911, p. 3; William H. Beezley, "Governor Carranza and the Revolution in Coahuila," *The Americas* 33, no. 1 (July 1976): 57; Ponce de León, *Interinato*, pp. 24–25, 67–68, 178; Patronato de Sonora, Vol. 60, Nos. 178–80, 1 August 1911 and 201, 2 August 1911; Vol. 61, No. 375, 24 September 1911; AGN, Leg. 929, Exp. Varios, Secretaría de Hacienda; Leg. 2205, Exp. Guardas dispersos; AHDN, XI/481.5/67. f. 59; Mexico City, Biblioteca del Instituto de Antropología e Historia (microfilm library), Archivo de Francisco I. Madero, roll 19, Nos. 0718–0719, Emilio Madero to Francisco Madero, 15 June 1911.

7. *Memoria de Gobernación*, 1911–1913, p. 58, and Annex No. 529, pp. 697–98; *El Tiempo*, 25 July 1911, p. 1; 27 July 1911, p. 6; 10 August 1911, p. 3; *Mexican Herald*, 30 July 1911, p. 5; *El País*, 23 July 1911, p. 1; *El Diario del Hogar*, 26 July 1911, p. 1; *El Imparcial*, 26 July 1911, p. 1; *El Demócrata*, 26 July 1911, p. 1; 27 July 1911, p. 1; *La Regeneración*, 9 September 1911, pp. 6–7; *La Actualidad* (Mexico City), 27 July 1911, p. 10; 30 July 1911, p. 6; Patronato de Sonora, Vol. 58, No. 273, 29 June 1911; Vol. 59, Nos. 385–88, 391–92, 22 July 1911, Vol. No, No. 42, 29 July 1911; CEHM, Madero to Vásquez Gómez, 26 July 1911; Madero to León de la Barra, 16 July and 23 July 1911.

8. Beezley, "Carranza," p. 57; Ponce de León, *Interinato*, pp. 24, 69, 176–80: *El País*, 27 June 1911, p. 3; *Mexican Herald*; 23 June 1911, p. 3; *El Imparcial*, 15 December 1911, p. 4; *El Demócrata*, 26 July 1911, p. 6; *El Diario del Hogar*, 28 July 1911, p. 1; AHDN, XI/481.5/67, fs. 352 and 358; XI/481.5/336, fs. 336–37; Beezley, *Gonzáles*, pp. 93, 107.

9. *El Imparcial*, 12 January 1912, p. 5; 19 January 1912, p. 1; 28 July 1912, p. 1; *El Tiempo*, 19 January 1912, p. 1; *Mexican Herald*, 19 January 1912, p. 1; *Memoria de Gobernación*, 1911–1913, p. 25; AHDN, XI/481.5/336, fs. 336–37; Ponce de León, *Interinato*, p. 69. For examples of wanton abuse of authority by the Rurales see: Patronato de Sonora, Vol. 63. Nos. 360–61, 30 November 1911; *El Imparcial*, 19 January 1912, p. 1;

28 July 1912, p. 1; *El Tiempo*, 1 December 1911, p. 1; 7 February 1912, p. 1; 14 February 1912, p. 1; 3 March 1912, p. 1; 19 March 1912, p. 1; 8 April 1912, p. 3; *Nueva Era*, 25 February 1912, p. 1; 9 September 1912, p. 1; 11 January 1913, pp. 1, 7.

10. Patronato de Sonora, Vol. 59, No. 119, 2 August 1911; Vol. 60, No. 202, 15 September 1911; Vol. 61, Nos. 83–91, 25 August 1911 and Nos. 389–90, 27 September 1911; CEHM, Madero to León de la Barra, 14 July 1911, and Madero to Emilio Vásquez Gómez, 26 July 1911.

11. Patronato de Sonora, Vol. 58, No. 273, 29 June 1911; González and Figueroa Domenech, *Revolución y héroes*, pp. 187–88.

12. Michael C. Meyer, *Huerta: A Political Portrait*, pp. 21–26; CEHM, Madero to León de la Barra, 15 August 1911; Huerta to León de la Barra, 26 August 1911; Huerta to Madero, 28 October 1911; Madero to Huerta, 31 October 1911; Madero to Gabriel Robles Domínguez, 12 November 1911; Womack, *Zapata*, pp. 97–128; Patronato de Sonora, Vol. 62, Nos. 353–54, 378–81, 28 October 1911; Vol. 63, No. 41, 4 November 1911.

13. Ponce de León, *Interinato*, p. 228; Gutiérrez Santos, *Historia militar*, pp. 95–96; *El Tiempo*, 22 September 1911, p. 1; 25 December 1911, p. 1; 30 December 1911, p. 6; 30 January 1912, pp. 1, 8; 2 February 1912, p. 1; 4 February 1912, p. 1; 5 June 1912, p. 4; 30 December 1912, p. 2; *Nueva Era* 16 December 1911, p. 1; 26 December 1911, p. 1; 14 March 1912, p. 6; 20 September 1912, p. 3; *El Imparcial*, 4 October 1911, p. 8; 31 January 1912, p. 8; 1 February 1912, p. 1; 2 February 1912, p. 7; 20 September 1912, p. 3; AGN, Leg. 898, Exp. Varios; Leg. 929, Exp. 50°, Cuerpo Rural, asuntos diversos; Michael C. Meyer, *Mexican Rebel: Pascual Orozco and the Mexican Revolution, 1910–1915*, pp. 44–48, 50–52, 97–98; *Memoria de Gobernación*, 1911–1913, p. 9, Doc. No. 58, p. 95; Doc. No. 60, p. 96; Doc. No. 61, p. 96; Doc. No. 63, pp. 96–97; Doc. No. 64, p. 97; *El Correo* (Chihuahua), 3 October 1911, p. 1; 4 October 1911, p. 1; 20 October 1911, p. 1; 22 November 1911, p. 1; 30 January 1912, p. 1; 1–2 February 1912, p. 1; 3–4 February 1912, p. 1.

14. *Memoria de Gobernación*, 1911–1913, p. 59; AGN, Leg. 898, Exp. Varios; Leg. 925, Exp. Cuerpos; Leg. 929, Exp. Comandante de Cuerpo Rural; Exp. Asuntos pagadores [53° cuerpo]; Exp. 58° Cuerpo Rural, asuntos diversos; Exp. Guerrilla de Chignahuapán: Leg. 1771, Exp. Oficina de hacienda; Exp. Estudio de fuerza; *El Diario Oficial* (Mexico City), 16 September 1912, p. 3; *El Tiempo*, 2 April 1912, pp. 1–2; 28 June 1912, p. 7; 30 December 1912, p. 2; *El Imparcial*, 24 November 1912, p. 9; *Nueva Era*, 21 September 1911, p. 6; 8 April 1912, p. 6; 6 August 1912, p. 1; 17 September 1912, p. 2; 20 September 1912, p. 3.

15. *Mexican Herald*, 4 January 1913, p. 1; 18 January 1913, p. 1; *El Imparcial*, 3 February 1912, p. 1; 12 March 1912, p. 1; 25 March 1912, p. 4; 28 March 1912, p. 5; 18 June 1912, p. 1; *El Tiempo*, 17 March 1912, p. 7; 3 May 1912, p. 7; 24 June 1912, p. 4; *Nueva Era*, 14 November 1911, p.

6; 5 March 1912, p. 4; 21 July 1912, p. 4; 23 August 1912, p. 4; AGN, Leg.
929, Exp. Telegrama: jefe de las armas; Leg. 2196, Exp. Carpeta de acuer-
dos; Leg. 2226, Exp. Quejas; Leg. 2234, Exp. Quejas; Leg. 2246, Exp.
Comisiones.
    16. *El Imparcial*, 5 April 1912, p. 5; 14 July 1912, p. 6; 13 August
1912, p. 2; 6 October 1912, pp. 1 and 9; 12 November 1912, p. 1; AHDN,
XI/481.5/217, fs. 663–64; *Mexican Herald*, 11 April 1912, p. 1; *El
Tiempo*, 27 December 1911, p. 6; AGN, Leg. 645, Exp. 8° Rural Cuerpo
tuvo un tiroteo.
    17. *El Imparcial*, 9 February 1912, p. 1.
    18. *Nueva Era*, 23 December 1911, p. 6.
    19. *Mexican Herald*, 10 February 1913, p. 1; Gutiérrez Santos,
Historia militar, pp. 135–36; *El Diario* (Mexico City), 11 February 1913,
p. 4; Guillermo Cota Soto, *Historia militar de México*, pp. 105–06; *El Imparcial*, 11 February 1913, p. 1; Guillermo Canales Montejano, *Historia
militar de México: 10 casos concretos*, pp. 142–46; Meyer, *Huerta*, pp.
45–48.
    20. Juan Barragán Rodríguez, *Historia del ejército y de la revolución
constitucionalista*, 1:119–22; Gutiérrez Santos, *Historia militar*, p. 138; *El
Imparcial*, 11 February 1913, p. 1; *El Diario*, 23 February 1913, p. 4;
Canales Montejano, *Historia militar de México*, pp. 146–48; Victoriano
Huerta, *Memorias de Victoriano Huerta*, pp. 23–24; Gonzalo N. Espinosa,
Joaquín Piña, and Carlos Ortiz B., *La decena roja: La revolución felixista;
caída del gobierno maderista; elevación al poder del General Victoriano
Huerta*, p. 62; *Mexican Herald*, 11 February 1913, p. 1; 12 February
1913, pp. 1–2; Meyer, *Huerta*, pp. 45–63; Fernández Rojas, *De Porfirio
Díaz*, pp. 327–28; Emigdio S. Paniagua, *El combate de la Ciudadela narrado por un extranjero*, p. 57.
    21. Meyer, *Huerta*, pp. 83–87; Ross, *Madero*, pp. 326–29; Huerta,
Memorias, pp. 36–37; Austin, Texas, University of Texas at Austin, Nettie
Lee Benson Latin American Collection, Pablo González Archive
(microfilm), Roll 47, contains substantial documentation on the official investigation into Madero's death, including the trial of the accused
(hereafter cited as González Archive); *Mexican Herald*, 24 February 1913,
p. 1; Gutiérrez Santos, *Historia militar*, pp. 147–48.
    22. Meyer, *Huerta*, pp. 83–87.
    23. Bayley, "Police and Political Change," pp. 104–05.
    24. *El Imparcial*, 21 February 1913, p. 4; 1 May 1913, p. 8; 30 May
1913, pp. 1, 8; 11 June 1913, p. 5; *La Tribuna*, 2 April 1913, p. 1; 3 April
1913, p. 1; 7 April 1913, p. 1; 5 May 1913, p. 2; 16 July 1913, pp. 1–2; 30
August 1913, pp. 1, 4; *El País*, 30 September 1913, pp. 1, 4; AGN, Leg.
2196, Exp. Novedades; Leg. 2205, Exp. Secretaría de Gobernación [letter
to Secretary of the Treasury dated 24 July 1913]; Exp. Secretaría de
Guerra [letter to Internal Affairs Secretary dated 3 July 1913]; González
Archive, Roll 47, Francisco Cárdenas to Félix Díaz, 15 April 1913.

25. Edward I. Bell, *The Political Shame of Mexico*, p. 352.
26. John Womack, Jr., "The Mexican Economy during the Revolution, 1910–1920: Historiography & Analysis," *Marxist Perspectives* 1, no. 4 (Winter 1978): 83–90; Bernstein, *Mining*, p. 100; David M. Pletcher, "An American Mining Company in the Mexican Revolution of 1911–1920," *Journal of Modern History* 20, no. 1 (March 1948): 19–26.
27. Meyer, *Huerta*, pp. 88, 98–99.
28. AGN, Leg. 663, Exps., passim; Leg. 682, Exp. Situación de fuerza; Leg. 690, Exp. 5° cuerpo; Leg. 1771, Exp. Estado de fuerza; Leg. 2226, Exp. Secretaría de Guerra y Marina; Exp. Acuerdo de Gobernación; *El Imparcial*, 8 July 1913, p. 5; 30 August 1913, p. 7; 21 January 1914, p. 3; 28 January 1914, p. 4; 8 February 1914, p. 8; 9 February 1914, p. 7; *La Tribuna*, 6 August 1913, p. 2; 22 January 1914, p. 1; *El país*, 31 July 1913, pp. 2, 4; 17 September 1913, pp. 4, 7, 8; *El Diario*, 31 July 1913, p. 2.
29. AGN, Leg. 636, Exp. Revistas, 1ᵉʳ Cuerpo; Exp. 2° Cuerpo Rural . . . ; Exp. 15° Cuerpo Rural . . . ; Exp. 20° Cuerpo Rural . . . ; Leg. 645, Exp. Orquesta típica rural, Leg. 682, Exp. . . . Novedades;Leg. 908, Exp. Circulars [23 February 1914 and 21 April 1914]; Leg. 1771, Exp. 6° Cuerpo . . . ; Exp. Estado de fuerza . . . ; Leg. 2191, Exp. Rincón, Ricardo; Leg. 2234, Exp. Hojas de servicios de los jefes; *El Imparcial*, 5 December 1913, p. 4; 26 December 1913, p. 7; 21 January 1914, p. 3; 8 February 1914, p. 8; 11 March 1914, p. 7; 12 April 1914, p. 2; 25 April 1914, p. 6; *La Tribuna*, 22 January 1914, p. 1.
30. Meyer, *Huerta*, pp. 156–77, 188.
31 Robert E. Quirk, *An Affair of Honor: Woodrow Wilson and the Occupation of Veracruz*, passim; Meyer, *Huerta*, pp. 111, 197–207.
32. Manuel González Ramírez, *La capitulación del ejército de la dictadora ante Carranza y Obregón*, pp. 27–30; Barragán Rodríguez, *Historia del ejército*, 1:600–03; Robert E. Quirk, *The Mexican Revolution, 1914–1915: The Convention of Aguascalientes*, pp. 47–49; Edwin Lieuwen, *Mexican Militarism, 1910–1940: The Political Rise and Fall of the Revolutionary Army*, p. 24; Meyer, *Huerta*, pp. 89, 191–92, 197–208; Alfredo Aragón, *Le Désarmement de l'armée fédérale par la Révolution de 1913*, p. 15; *El Imparcial*, 12 August 1914, p. 1; 13 August 1914, p. 1; 14 August 1914, p. 6; 16 August 1914, p. 9; *El País*, 14 August 1914, pp. 1, 3; *La Liberal*, 29 August 1914, p. 5; *El Independiente*, 26 July 1914, p. 3; 2 August 1914, p. 1; *El Demócrata*, 6 November 1914, p. 2.
33. For examples of officers in Rurales who later joined the Carranza army see: Mexico City, Secretaría de la Defensa Nacional, Departamento de Archivo de Correspondencia e Historia, Archivo de Cancelados, Exps. Aduna, Ignacio; Barreras, Elías; Codero, Salvador; Gálvez, Aurelio; Gómez, Luis G.; Lagarde, Carlos; Ramos, Liberio; Mireles, Francisco; Rangel, Desiderio; Sánchez, Pedro; Trejo, Luis. Also Lieuwen, *Militarism*, p. 22.

34. José Valdovinos Garza, *Tres capítulos de la política Michoacana*, pp. 12–27; Ernest Otto Schuster, *Pancho Villa's Shadow: The True Story of Mexico's Robin Hood As Told by His Interpreter*, pp. 246, 264; Casasola, *Historia gráfica*, 2:1297.

35. Roger D. Hansen, *The Politics of Mexican Development*, pp. 176–77, 207.

36. Valdovinos Garza, *Tres capítulos*, pp. 15–20; J. W. F. Dulles, *Yesterday in Mexico: A Chronicle of the Revolution, 1919–1936*, pp. 66–70, 178–80; Womack, *Zapata*, pp. 325–27; Casasola, *Historia gráfica*. 2:1297.

37. Emily S. Rosenberg, "Economic Pressures in Anglo-American Diplomacy in Mexico, 1917–1918," *Journal of Inter-American Studies and World Affairs* 17, no. 2 (May 1975): 123–52; Douglas W. Richmond, "El nacionalismo de Carranza y los cambios socioeconómicos—1915–1920," *Historia Mexicana* 26, no. 1 (July–September 1976): 107–31; Lawrence A. Cardoso, "Labor Emigration to the Southwest, 1916–1920; Mexican Attitudes and Policy," *Southwestern Historical Quarterly* 79, no. 4 (April 1976): 400–16; Womack, "Mexican Economy," pp. 85, 100.

38. For strong presentations of this thesis see Adolfo Gilly, *La revolución interrumpida: México, 1910–1920: Una guerra campesina por la tierra y el poder*, and Hart, *Mexican Working Class*. Friedrich Katz considers the question regionally in "Agrarian Changes in Northern Mexico in the Period of Villista Rule, 1913–1915," in Wilkie, Meyer, and Monzón de Wilkie, *Contemporary Mexico*.

Bibliography

I. Archives

A. Mexico

Cholula, Puebla. University of the Americas. Archivo de Porfirio Díaz.

Hermosillo, Sonora. Archivo General del Estado de Sonora. Ramo de Gobernación.

Jalapa, Veracruz. Archivo General del Estado de Veracruz, Ramo de Gobernación.

Mexico City. Archivo General de la Nación. Ramo de Gobernación.

_____. Biblioteca del Instituto de Antropología e Historia and Archivo de Francisco I. Madero.

_____. Biblioteca Nacional. Archivo de Benito Juárez and Archivo de José María Lafragua.

_____. Centro de Estudios de Historia de México, Condumex, S.A. Archivo de Jenaro Amezcua, Archivo de Venustiano Carranza, and Archivo de Francisco León de la Barra.

_____. Patronato de la Historia de Sonora.

_____. Secretaría de la Defensa Nacional. Departamento de Archivo de Correspondencia e Historia. Archivo Histíco and Archivo de Cancelados.

B. United States

Austin, Texas. University of Texas at Austin. Nettie Lee Benson Latin American Collection. Correspondencia de Achille François Bazaine, 1862–1867.

_____. _____. _____. Genaro García Collection. Mariano Riva Palacio Papers.

_____. _____. _____. Mexico, Ministerio de Guerra y Marina. Memoria leída en la Cámara de Diputados por el ministro del ramo, general Ignacio Zaragoza, el día 9 de mayo de 1861, e informe sobre facciosos en el valle de México dado por él mismo el 11 del propio mes. (Ms. copy signed by I. Zaragoza on 11 May 1861 in Mexico City.)

————. ————. ————. Pablo González Papers (microfilm).
Berkeley, California. University of California, Berkeley, H. H. Bancroft Library Silvestre Terrazas Papers.
San Marino, California. Huntington Library. Doheny Collection.
Washington, D.C. National Archives. Records of the Department of State. Consular Reports for Mexico. Numerical Case Files, 1906–1910.
————. ————. Records of the Department of State Relating to the Internal Affairs of Mexico, 1910–1929. Record Group 59. National Archives Microfilm Publication (Microcopy No. 274), 1910–1911.

II. Printed Documents

Archivo mexicano: Collección de leyes, decretos, circulares y otros documentos. 6 vols. Mexico City: Imprenta de V. G. Torres, 1856–1862.

Arrillaga, José Basilio, ed. *Recopilación de leyes, decretos, bandos, reglamentos, circulares y providencias de los supremos poderes y otras autoridades de la república mexicana formada de orden del supremo gobierno por el licenciado José Basilio Arrillaga.* 9 vols. Mexico City: Imprenta de A. Boliz, a cargo de M. Zornoza, 1858–1864.

Buenrostro, Felipe. *Historia del primero y segundo congresos constitucionales de la república mexicana.* 9 vols. Mexico City: Tipografía de F. Mata, 1874.

Carreño, Alberto María. *Archivo de General Porfirio Díaz, memorias y documentos.* . . . 30 vols. in 15. Mexico City: Editorial "Elede," 1947–1961.

Clark, Victor S. "Mexican Labor in the United States." *Bulletin of the Bureau of Labor 17 (1908) (Department of Commerce and Labor).* Washington, D.C.: Government Printing Office, 1909.

Código de La Reforma o colección de leyes, decretos y supremas órdenes, expedidas desde 1856 hasta 1861. Mexico City: Imprenta Literaria, 1861.

Collección de decretos, reglamentos y circulares referentes a los Cuerpos Rurales de la Federación desde su fundación hasta la fecha. Mexico City: Tipografía "El Lápiz del Aguila," 1900.

Colección e leyes, decretos, circulares y demás resoluciones del gobierno general con notas y concordancias. 10 vols. Mexico City: Imprenta de Jens y Zapiain, 1877–1881.

Colección de leyes, decretos y órdenes expedidas por el congreso nacional y por el supremo gobierno. . . . 7 vols. Mexico City: Imprenta de J. M. Lara, 1850–1855.

Colección de leyes, decretos y circulares expedidas por el supremo gobierno de la república. Comprende desde su salida de la capital el 31 de mayo de 1863 hasta su regreso a la misma en 15 de julio de 1867. . . . 3 vols. Mexico City: Imprenta del gobierno, en palacio, 1867.

Colección de leyes, decretos y reglamentos que interinamente forman el sistema político, administrativo y judicial del imperio: Ministerio de Guerra. 8 vols. Mexico City: Imprenta de Andrade y Escalante, 1865–1866.

Constitución federal de los Estados Unidos Mexicanos sancionada y jurada por el congreso general constituyente el día 5 de febrero de 1857. Mexico City: Imprenta de la Reforma, 1861.

Cuba. Military Governor, 1899 (John R. Brooke). *Civil Report of Major-General John R. Brooke, US Army, Military Governor, Island of Cuba.* 3 vols. Havana, 1899. Also consulted were reports of other military and provisional governors to Cuba until 1909.

Datos biográficos de General de División C. Porfirio Díaz, con acopio de documentos históricos. Mexico City: Imprenta de Ireneo Paz, 1884.

Dublán, Manuel, and Lozano, José María, eds. *Legislación mexicana, o colección completa de las disposiciones legislativas expedidas desde la independencia de la República.* 34 vols. Mexico City: Imprenta de Comercio, a cargo de Dublán y Lozano, hijos [etc.], 1876–1904.

Fabela, Isidro, ed. *Documentos históricos de la revolución mexicana.* 26 vols. Mexico City: Fondo de Cultura Económica and Editorial Jus, 1960–.

Flores Magón, Ricardo. *Epistolario y textos de Ricardo Flores Magón.* Mexico City: Fondo de Cultura Económica, 1964.

———. *Semilla libertaria.* 2 vols. Mexico City: Grupo Cultural "Ricardo Flores Magón," 1923.

Fuentes para la historia de la revolución mexicana. 5 vols. Mexico City: Fondo de Cultura Económica, 1954–1959.

Great Britain. Foreign Office, 1893. Miscellaneous Series No. 302. *Reports on Subjects of General and Commercial Interest, Mexico: Report on the Effect of Depreciation of Silver in Mexico.* London. Her Majesty's Stationery Office, 1893.

González Ramírez, Manuel, ed. *Manifiestos políticos, 1892–1912.* Mexico City: Fondo de Cultura Económico, 1957.

Juárez, Benito Pablo. *Archivos privados de D. Benito Juárez y D. Pedro Santacilia.* Mexico City: Publicaciones de la Secretaría de Educación, 1928.

———. *Documentos, discursos y correspondencia.* 2 vols. Mexico City: Secretaría del Patrimonio Nacional, 1964.

———. *Exposiciones (como se gobierna).* 5 vols. Mexico City: Secretaría del Patrimonio Nacional, 1964.

Legislación mejicana, o sea collección completa de las leyes, decretos y circulares que se han expendido desde la consumación de la independencia . . . comprende de enero de 1848 a diciembre de 1856. 13 vols. Mexico City: Imprenta de J. R. Navarro, 1853–1856.

Lerdo de Tejada, Sebastián. *Memorias de Sebastián Lerdo de Tejada: Estudio preliminar de Leonardo Pasquel.* Mexico City: Citlaltépetl, 1959.

———. *Memorias inéditas de don Sebastián Lerdo de Tejada.* Brownsville, Texas: Imprenta de "El Porvenir," 1889.

Leyes, decretos, circulares y providencias de la intervención, el supremo poder ejecutivo provisional, la regencia y el imperio. 3 vols. Oaxaca: Impreso por Manuel Rincón, 1865.

Mexico. Congreso. Cámara de Diputados. *Diario de los debates de la Cámara de Diputados, 1871–1910.* 24 vols. Mexico City: Tipografía Literaria de Filomeno Mata, 1871–1910.

———. Ministerio de Guerra y Marina. *Memoria del Secretario de Estado y del Despacho de Guerra y Marina, leída a las cámaras del Congreso Nacional de la República Mexicana (1844–1908).* 28 vols. Mexico City: Impresa por Ignacio Cumplido, 1844.

———. Ministro de Hacienda y Crédito Público. *Exposición de la Secretaría de Hacienda de los Estados-Unidos Mexicanos del 5 de 1879 sobre la condición actual de México, y el aumento del comercio con los Estados-Unidos rectificando el informe dirigido por el honorable John W. Foster, enviado extraordinario y ministro plenipotenciario de los Estados Unidos en México el 9 de octubre de 1878 al Sr. Carlisle Mason, presidente de la Asociación de Manufactureros de la Ciudad de Chicago en el estado de Illinois de los Estados-Unidos de América.* Mexico City: Imprenta del gobierno, en palacio, 1879.

———. *Memoria de la Secretaría de Hacienda y Crédito Público: 25 de mayo de 1911–22 de febrero de 1913.* Mexico City: Secretaría de Hacienda y Crédito Público Publicaciones Históricas, 1949.

———. Presidente. *Informes y manifestos de los poderes ejecutivo y legislativo de 1821 a 1904.* 3 vols. Mexico City: Imprenta del Gobierno Federal, 1905.

———. *Reglamento para el servicio de la Policía Rural de la Federación.* Mexico City: Imprenta del Gobierno Federal, 1912.

———. Secretaría de Agricultura y Fomento, Dirección de Estadística. *Tercer censo de población de los Estados Unidos Mexicanos, verificado el 27 de octubre de 1910.* 3 vols. Mexico City: Oficina Impresora de la Secretaría de Hacienda, Departamento de Fomento, 1918.

———. Secretaría de Gobernación. *Memoria que el Secretario de Estado y del Despacho de Gobernación presenta . . . (1871–1916).* 17 vols. Mexico City: Imprenta del gobierno, en palacio, 1871.

———. Secretaría de Relaciones Exteriores. *Memoria del Secretario de Estado y del Despacho de Relaciones Exteriores y Gobernación de la República Mexicana . . . (1841–1847).* 2 vols. Mexico City: Imprenta de Vicente G. Torres, 1844.

México (state). Archivo de la cámara de Diputados del Estado de Mexico. MSS. "Actas de la Diputación Provincial de Mexico, 1822–1823." V. Sesión 49 (13 November 1823).

———. Gobernador. *Memoria presentada a la H. Legislatura del Estado de Mexico, por el gobernador constitucional del mismo. . . .*

Toluca: Tipografía del Instituto Literario, 1871. (Governors of the various states issued *Memorias* periodically. More than 50 such *Memorias* from various states, covering the period 1870–1910, were consulted for this book.)

Mondragón, Manuel. *Proyecto de organización del ejército.* . . . Mexico City: Tipografía Mercantil, 1911.

Recopilación de leyes, decretos y providencias de los poderes legislativo y ejectutivo de la unión desde que se estableció en la ciudad de México el supremo gobierno, en 15 de julio de 1867. . . . 85 vols. Mexico City: Imprenta del gobierno, en palacio, 1870–1909.

La Reforma, leyes y circulares espedidas por el supremo gobierno constitucional de la república, desde su manifiesto de 7 de julio de 1859. Mexico City: Tipografía de Navor Chávez, 1861.

Tovar, Panaleón, ed. *Historia parlamentario del cuarto congreso constitucional.* 4 vols. Mexico City: Imprenta de I. Cumplido, 1872–1874.

Los Tratados de Teoloyucan. Mexico City: Bloque de Obreros Intelectuales, 1964.

U.S. House of Representatives. *Papers Relating to the Foreign Relations of the United States: Transmitted to Congress with the Annual Message of the President, December 3, 1889.* Washington, D.C.: Government Printing Office, 1890.

U.S. Senate. Committee on Foreign Relations. *Investigation of Mexican Affairs, Preliminary Report and Hearings of the Committee on Foreign Relations, United States Senate pursuant to S. Res. 106 directing the Committee on Foreign Relations to Investigate the Matter of Outrages on Citizens of the United States in Mexico.* 2 vols. (66th Congress, 2d Sess., Doc. No. 285.) Washington, D.C.: Government Printing Office, 1920.

U.S. War Department. *Annual Reports of the War Department for the Fiscal Year ended June 30, 1899.* Washington, D.C.: Government Printing Office, 1900.

Verdugo, Agustín, ed. *Colección legislativa completa de la república mexicana con todas las disposiciones territoriales (continuación de la Legislación Mexicana de Dublán y Lozano).* 12 vols. Mexico City: Talleres Tipográficos de "El Correo Español," 1902–1912.

Weyl, Walter E. "Labor Conditions in Mexico." *Bulletin of the [U.S.] Department of Labor* 38 (January 1902). Washington, D.C.: Government Printing Office, 1902.

III. CONTEMPORARY ACCOUNTS

Alamán, Lucas. *Historia de Méjico.* 5 vols. Mexico City: Editorial Jus, 1968.

Andrew, A. Piatt. "The End of the Mexican Dollar." *Quarterly Journal of Economics* 18 (May 1904): 321–353.

Aragón, Alfredo. *Le Désarmement de l'armée fédérale par la Révolution de 1913*. Paris: [n.p.], 1915.

Arias, Juan de Dios. *Reseña histórica de la formación y operaciones del cuerpo de ejército del norte durante la intervención francesa*. Mexico City: Imprenta de M. Chávez, 1867.

Baerlein, Henry. *Mexico, the Land of Unrest*. . . . Philadelphia: J. B. Lippincott Company, 1913.

Ballou, Maturin M. *Aztec Land*. Boston: Houghton, Mifflin and Company, 1890.

Bancroft, Hubert Howe. *History of Mexico*. 6 vols. San Francisco: The History Company, 1833–1888.

———. *Vida de Porfirio Díaz. Renseña histórica y social del pasado y presente de México*. San Francisco: The History Company, 1887.

Bates, J. H. *Notes of a Tour in Mexico and California*. New York: Burr Printing House, 1887.

Becher, Henry C. *A Trip to Mexico, Being Notes of a Journey from Lake Erie to Lake Tezcuco and Back*. . . . Toronto: Willing and Williamson, 1880.

Bell, Edward I. *The Political Shame of Mexico*. New York: McBride, Nest and Company, 1914.

Berge, Dennis E., tr. and ed. *Considerations on the Political and Social Situation of the Mexican Republic, 1847*. El Paso: Texas Western Press, 1975.

Bigelow, John. "The Railway Invasion of Mexico." *Harper's New Monthly Magazine* 65, no. 389 (October 1882): 745–751.

Bonaparte, Roland Napoléon, et al. *Le Mexique au debut du XXᵉ siécle*. 2 vols. Paris: Librairie C. Delagrave, 1904.

Bose, Johanne Caroline Wehmeyer. *Farewell to Durango: A German Lady's Diary in Mexico, 1910–1911*. Bose, John Carlos, tr. Blew, Robert W., ed. Lake Oswego, Oregon: Smith, Smith and Smith Publishing Company, 1978.

Brockhurst, Thomas Unett. *Mexico To-Day: A Country with a Great Future and a Glance at the Prehistoric Remains and Antiquities of the Montezumas*. London: John Murray, 1883.

Bullock. W. *Six Months' Residence and Travels in Mexico: Containing Remarks on the Present State of New Spain, Its Natural Productions, State of Society, Manufactures, Trade, Agriculture and Antiquities, etc*. London: John Murray, 1824.

Bulnes, Francisco. *El verdadero Díaz y la Revolución*. Mexico City: Editora Nacional, 1967.

———. *The Whole Truth about Mexico: President Wilson's Responsibility*. Scott, Dora, tr. New York: M. Bulnes Book Company, 1916.

Butt, Archibald Willingham. "Where Silver Rules: Wages, Prices and Conditions in the Most Prosperous Silver Using Country of the World." In *Pamphlets on Money*, vol. 6. Mexico City: n.p.], 1896.

Cabrera, Francisco de A. *Bandolerismo y Guardia Civil.* 5 vols. Havana: Imprenta Mercantil, de los Sucesores de S. S. Spencer, 1889–1892.

Calderón de la Barca, Frances E. *Life in Mexico during a Residence of Two Years in That Country.* New York: E. P. Dutton and Company, [1913?].

Calero, Manuel. *Un decenio de política mexicana.* New York: L. Middleditch Company, 1920.

Campaña de 1910 a 1911: Estudio en general de las operaciones del 18 de noviembre de 1910 al 25 de mayo de 1911, en la parte que corresponde a la 2° zona militar. Mexico City: Secretaría de Guerra y Marina, Talleres del Departamento de Estado Mayor, 1913.

Campbell, Reau. *Campbell's New Revised Complete Guide and Descriptive Book of Mexico.* Chicago: [n.p.], 1909.

Castillo, José R. del. *Historia de la revolución social de México, primera etapa: La caída de General Díaz. Apuntes y observaciones para formar la historia política de México de 1908 a 1915.* Mexico City: [n.p.], 1915.

Castillo Negrete, Emilio del. *Mexico en el siglo XIX o sea su historia desde 1800 hasta la época presente.* Mexico City: Imprenta del Editor, 1890.

Castillo Velasco, José María. "Adiciones de el Diputado José María Castillo Velasco al projecto de Constitución federal, sobre municipalidades." In González de Cossio, Francisco, *Historia de la tenencia y explotación del campo desde la época precortesiana hasta las leyes del 6 de enero de 1915.* 2 vols. Mexico City: Talleres Gráficos de la Nación, 1957.

Castro, Lorenzo. *The Republic of Mexico in 1882.* New York: Thompson and Moreau, 1882.

Ceballos, Ciro B. *Aurora y ocaso: (Por los "cuistres"): (Ensayo histórico de política contemporánea, 1867–1906).* 2 vols. Mexico City: Imprenta Central, 1907–1912.

Chabrand, Emile. *De Barcelonnette au Mexique, Inde-Birmanie-Chine-Japon-Etats-Unis.* Paris: Librairie E. Plon, Nourrit et Cⁱᵉ, 1892.

Cochrane, Elizabeth. *Six Months in Mexico,* by Nellie Bly [pseud.]. New York: Norman L. Nunro, 1888.

Coffin, Alfred O. *Land without Chimneys, or, The Byways of Mexico.* Cincinnati: Editor Publishing Company, 1898.

Conley, Edward M. "The Anti-Foreign Uprising in Mexico." *The World Today* (1906): 1059–1062.

Conrotte, Manuel. *Notas mejicanas.* Madrid: Romo y Füssel, 1899.

Creelman, James. *Díaz: Master of Mexico.* New York: D. Appleton and Company, 1912.

Los Cuerpos Rurales y su fiesta del 2 de mayo. Mexico City: Tipografía de "El Partido Liberal," 1889.

Cusi, Ezio. *Memorias de un colono.* Mexico City: Editorial Jus, 1969.

Didapp, Juan Pedro. *Gobiernos militares de México: Los ataques al ejército y las maquinaciones políticas del partido científico para regir los destinos nacionales.* Mexico City: Tipografía de J. I. Guerrero y Compañía, 1904.

Duclós Salinas, Adolfo. *Méjico pacificado: El progreso de Méjico y los hombres que gobiernan, Porfirio Díaz–Bernado Reyes.* St. Louis: Hughes and Company, 1904.

Dunbar, Edward. *The Mexican Papers.* . . . New York: J. A. H. Hasbrouck and Company, 1860–1861.

Emerson, Edwin, "The Rurales of Mexico." *The Century Illustrated Monthly Magazine* 82, no. 2 (June 1911): 271–278.

Enríquez, Vidal. *Apuntes de organización del ejército.* Mexico City: Secretaría de Guerra y Marina, 1910.

Espinosa, Gonzalo N.; Piña, Joaquín; and Ortiz B., Carlos. *La decena roja; la revolución felixista; caída del gobierno maderista; elevación al poder del general Victoriano Huerta.* Mexico City: [n.p.], 1913.

Estrada, Roque. *La Revolución y Francisco Madero: Primera segunda y tercera etapas.* Guadalajara: Imprenta Americana, 1912.

Ethics in Action: Porfirio Díaz and His Work by a Soldier of the Old Guard. Mexico City: Imprenta de Hull, 1907.

Evans, Albert S. *Our Sister Republic: A Gala Trip through Tropical Mexico in 1869–70.* . . . Hartford: Columbian Book Company, 1870.

Fernández Rojas, José. *De Porfirio Díaz a Victoriano Huerta, 1910–1913.* Guadalajara: Tipografía de la Escuel a de Artes y Oficios del Estado, 1913.

Flandrau, Charles M. *Viva Mexico.* New York: Harper and Brothers, 1951.

Folsom, Charles J. *Mexico in 1842: a Description of the Country, its Natural and Political Features: with a Sketch of its History, Brought down to the Present Year, to which is Added an Account of Texas and Yucatan: and of the Santa Fe Expedition.* New York: Wiley and Putnam; Robinson, Pratt and Company, 1842.

Fornaro, Carlo de. *México tal cual es: Comentarios por Carlo de Fornaro.* Philadelphia: International Publishing Company, 1909.

Foster, John W. *Diplomatic Memoirs.* 2 vols. New York: Houghton Mifflin Company, 1910.

"The French and English Police Systems." *The Cornhill Magazine* 44, no. 262 (October 1881): 421–435.

Gadow, Hans F. *Through Southern Mexico: Being an Account of the Travels of a Naturalist.* London: Witherby and Company, 1908.

Gaines, Morrill W. "Effects of the Silver Standard in Mexico." *Yale Review* 12 (May 1903–February 1904): 276–289.

García Cubas, Antonio. *El libro de mis recuerdos.* Mexico City: Editorial Patria, 1945.

García Granados, Ricardo. *Historia de México desde la restauración de la república en 1867, hasta la caída de Huerta.* 2 vols. Mexico City: Editorial Jus, 1956.

————. *Por qué y como cayó Porfirio Díaz.* Mexico City: A. Botas e Hijo, 1928.

Gastelum, Ignacio M. *Apuntes biográficos de Heraclio Bernal.* Culiacán: Tipografía de Retes y Díaz, 1888.

Geiger, John Lewis. *A Peep at Mexico: Narrative of a Journey across the Republic from the Pacific to the Gulf in December 1873 and January 1874.* London: Trubner and Company, 1874.

Gillpatrick, Wallace. *The Man Who Likes Mexico.* New York: The Century Company, 1911.

————. *Wanderings in Mexico: The Spirited Chronicle of Adventure in Mexican Highways and By-Ways, by Wallace Gillpatrick. . . .* London: E. Nash, 1912.

Glantz, Margo, ed. *Viajes en México: Crónicas extranjeras.* Mexico City: Secretaría de Obras Públicas, 1964.

Gómez, Manuel Z. *Biografía del Gral. de División C. Ignacio Zaragosa.* Mexico City: Imprenta de Vicente García Torres, 1862.

González (Kanta-Klaro), Antonio P., y Figueroa Domenech, J. *La Revolución y sus héroes: Crónica de los sucesos políticos ocurridos en México desde octubre de 1910 a mayo de 1911.* Mexico City: Herrero Hermanos, Sucesores, 1911.

González-Blanco, Pedro. *De Porfirio Díaz a Carranza.* Madrid: Imprenta Helénica, 1916.

Goodhue, Bertram G. *Mexican Memories: The Record of a Slight Sojourn below the Yellow Rio Grande, by Bertram Grosvenor Goodhue. . . .* New York: G. M. Allen Company, 1892.

Gostkowski, Gustave, baron de. *De Paris à Mexico par les Etats-Unis. . . .* Paris: P. V. Stock, 1899.

Graham, A. A. *Mexico with Comparisons and Conclusions.* Topeka: Crane and Company, 1907.

Green, Frank W. *Notes on New York, San Francisco and Old Mexico,* by Frank W. Green. Wakefield: E. Carr, "Herald" Offices, Westgate, 1886.

Griffin, Solomon B. *Mexico of To-Day.* New York: Harper and Brothers, 1886.

La guerra de los indios en Méjico. New York: Tipografía de la Crónica, 1849.

Guerrero, Julio. *La génesis del crimen en México, estudio de psiquiatría social.* Mexico City: Librería de la V^{da} de Ch. Bouret, 1901.

Gutiérrez de Lara, Lázaro, and Pinchon, Edgcumb. *The Mexican People: Their Struggle for Freedom.* New York: Arno Press, 1970.

Hall, Captain Basil. *Extracts from a Journal Written on the Coasts of Chile, Peru, and Mexico in the Years 1820, 1821, 1822.* 2 vols. Edinburgh: Archibald Constable and Company, 1824.

Hardie, F. H. "The Mexican Army." *Journal of Military Service Institution of the United States* (November 1894): 1203–1208.

Hardy, Lieut. R. W. H. *Travels in the Interior of Mexico in 1825, 1826, 1827, and 1828.* London: Henry Colburn and Richard Bentley, 1829.

Hill, S. S. *Travels in Peru and Mexico.* 2 vols. London: Longman, Green, Longman and Roberts, 1860.

Huerta, Victoriano. *Memorias de Victoriano Huerta.* Mexico City: Ediciones "Vértice," 1957.

Humboldt, Alexander von. *Political Essay on the Kingdom of New Spain.* John Black, tr. New York: Ains Press, Inc., 1966.

Javier, Thomas A. "The Mexican Army." *Harpers New Monthly Magazine* 79, no. 474 (November 1889): 813–827.

Kemmerer, Edwin Walter. *Modern Currency Reforms: A History of Recent Currency Reforms in India, Porto Rico, Philippine Islands, Straits Settlements and Mexico.* New York: Macmillan Company, 1916.

Knox, Thomas W. *The Boy Travellers in Mexico: Adventures of Two Youths in a Journey to Northern and Central Mexico, Campeachey, and Yucatan, with a Description of the Republics of Central America and the Nicaragua Canal.* New York: Harper and Brothers Publishers, 1902.

LaFragua, José María. *Miscelánea de política.* 2 vols. Mexico City: Aldina, Robredo and Rosell, 1943.

Lara y pardo, Luis. *De Porfirio Díaz a Francisco Madero: La sucesión dictatorial de 1911.* New York: Polyglot Publishing and Commercial Company, 1912.

Lempriere, Charles. *Notes in Mexico in 1861 and 1862: Politically and Socially Considered.* London: Longman, Green, Longman, Roberts and Green, 1862.

Limantour, José Yves. *Apuntes sobre mi vida pública.* Mexico City: Editorial Porrúa, 1965.

List, A. J. *A Practical Treatise on Rural Police.* Edinburgh: Fraser and Crawford, 1841.

López Albújar, Enrique. *Los caballeros del delito: Estudio criminológico del bandolerismo en algunos departamentos del Perú.* Lima: Compañía de Impresiones y Publicidad, 1936.

Lyon, Capt. G. F. *Journal of a Residence and Tour in the Republic of Mexico in the year 1826, with some Account of the Mines in that Country.* 2 vols. London: John Murray, 1828.

McCaleb, Walter Flavius. *The Public Finances of Mexico.* New York: Harper and Brothers, 1921.

McCarty, Joseph H. *Two Thousand Miles through the Heart of Mexico.* New York: Phillips and Hunt, 1886.

Macedo, Miguel S. *La criminalidad en México: Medios de combatirla.* Mexico City: Oficina Tipografía de la Secretaría de Fomento, 1897.

Manero, Antonio. *El antiguo régimen y la revolución.* Mexico City: Tipografía y Litografía "La Europea," 1911.

Martin, Percy F. *Mexico of the XXth Century.* 2 vols. New York: Dodd, Mead and Company, 1907.

_____. *Mexico's Treasure House (Guanajuato): An Illustrated and Descriptive Account of the Mines and Their Operations in 1906.* New York: Cheltenham Press, 1906.

Mayer, Brantz. *Mexico as It Was and as It Is.* New York: J. Winchester, New World Press, 1844.

_____. *Mexico; Aztec, Spanish and Republican: A Historical, Geographical, Political, Statistical and Social Account of that Country. . . .* 2 vols. Hartford: S. Drake and Company, 1850.

Millard, Bailey. "The Shame of Our Army; Why Fifty Thousand Enlisted American Soldiers Have Deserted." *Cosmopolitan Magazine* 49, no. 4 (September 1910): 411–420.

Mills, A. L., 1st Lt., U.S. Cavalry. "The Military Geography of Mexico." *Military Geography* 15, no. 72 (1894).

Mora, José María Luís. *El clero, la milicia y las revoluciones.* Mexico City: Empresas Editoriales, 1951.

Moses, Bernard. *The Railway Revolution in Mexico.* San Francisco: Berkeley Press, 1895.

Navarro, Juan N. "Mexico of Today." *National Geographic Magazine* 12, no. 4 (April 1901): 152–157.

O'Hea, Patrick A. *Reminiscences of the Mexican Revolution.* Mexico City: Editorial Fournier, 1966.

Orozco, Wistano Luis, *Los ejidos de los pueblos.* Mexico City: Ediciones "El Caballito," 1975.

_____. *Legislación y jurisprudencia sobre terrenos baldíos.* Mexico City: [n.p.], 1895.

Otero, Mariano. "Ensayo sobre el verdadero estado de la cuestión social y política que se agita en la república mexicana." Mexico City: Ignacio Cumplido, 1842. In Reyes Heroles, Jesús, ed., *Mariano Otero, Obras: Recopilación, selección, comentarios y estudio preliminar.* 2 vols. Mexico City: Editorial Porrúa, 1967.

Padua, C. D. *Movimento revolucionario—1906 en Veracruz. Relación cronológica de las actividades del P.L.M. en los ex-cantones de Acayucan, Minatitlán, San Andrés Tuxtla y centro del país.* Cuernavaca: [n.p.], 1936.

Paniagua, Emigdio S. *El combate de la Ciudadela narrado por un extranjero.* Mexico City: Tipografía Artística, 1913.

Paz, Ireneo. *Algunas campañas, 1863–1876.* Mexico City: Ediciones de la Secretaría de Educación Pública, 1944.

Pérez, Juan C. *Almanaque estadístico de las oficinas y guía de forasteros para 1874.* Mexico City: Imprenta de Gobierno, 1873.

Ponce de León, Gregorio. *El interinato presidencial de 1911*. Mexico City: Imprenta y Fototipía de la Secretaría de Fomento, 1912.

Popoca y Palacios, Lambert. *Historia del bandalismo en el estado de Morelos, ¡ayer como ahora! 1860 (Plateados) 1911 (Zapatistas)*. Puebla: Tiplografía Guadalupana, 1912.

Portilla, Anselmo de la. *Méjico en 1856 y 1857: Gobierno del General Comonfort*. New York: Imprenta de S. Hallet, 1858.

Price, Thomas W. *Brief Notes Taken on a Trip to the City of Mexico in 1878, by Thomas W. Price*. . . . [n.p.], 1878.

Prida, Ramón. *¡De la dictadura a la anarquía!: Apuntes para la historia política de México durante los últimos cuarenta y tres años, por Ramón Prida*. 2 vols. El Paso: "El Paso del Norte," 1914.

Reclus, [Michel] Elie. *Primitive Folk: Studies in Comparative Ethnology*. New York: Charles Scribner's Sons, 1899.

Revista de Ejército y Marina (Mexico City). (1910–1911).

Rickard, Thomas A. *Journeys of Observation*. San Francisco: Dewey Publishing Company, 1907.

Ribot, Héctor. *La Revolución de 1912*. Mexico City: Imprenta la Calle de Humboldt Número 5, 1913.

Riva Palacio, Vicente. *Historia de la administración de don Sebastián Lerdo de Tejada*. Mexico City: Imprenta y Litografía del Padre Cobos, 1875.

———. *México a través de los siglos*. 5 vols. Barcelona: Espasa y Compañía, 1888–1889.

Rodríguez, Ricardo. *Historia auténtica de la administración del sr. Gral. Porfirio Díaz*. 2 vols. Mexico City: Oficina Tipografía de la Secretaría de Fomento, 1904.

Roumagnac, Carlos. *Los criminales en México*. Mexico City: Tipografía "El Fénix," 1904.

"The Rurales of Mexico." *The Travel Magazine* 12, no. 9 (June 1907): 380–381.

Rynning, Captain Thomas H. *Gun Notches: The Life Story of a Cowboy-Soldier*. New York: A. L. Burt Company, 1931.

Santos Coy, José María. *La nación nueva*. Mexico City: Tipografía de la viuda de Francisco Díaz de León, 1906.

Sherman, Mrs. Bell M. "The Personal Recollections of Porfirio Díaz, President of Mexico." *Cosmopolitan* 49, nos. 1–6 (June-November 1910): 207–216 (July); 343–350 (August); 497–505 (September); 633–639 (October); 791–798 (November).

Sidro y Surga, José, and Quevedo y Donís, Antonio de. *La Guardia Civil: Historia de esta institución y de todas las que se han conocido en España con destino a la perseucución de malhechores*. . . . Madrid: Imprenta y Litografía Militar del Atlas, a cargo de D. Antonio Pérez Dubrull, 1858.

Sierra, Justo. *The Political Evolution of the Mexican People.* Ramsdell, Charles, tr. Austin: University of Texas Press, 1969.

Stephens, C.A. *The Knockabout Club in the Tropics. The Adventures of a Party of Young Men in New Mexico, Mexico, and Central America.* Boston: Estes and Lauriat, 1884.

Tayloe, Edward Thornton. *Mexico, 1825–1827: The Journal and Correspondence of Edward Thornton Tayloe.* Gardiner, C. Harvey, ed. Chapel Hill: University of North Carolina Press, 1959.

Tays, E. A. H. "Present Labor Conditions in Mexico." *The Engineering and Mining Journal* 84, no. 14 (5 October 1907): 621–624.

Thompson, J. Eric S., ed. *Thomas Gage's Travels in the New World.* Norman: University of Oklahoma Press, 1958.

Thompson, Wallace. *The People of Mexico: Who They Are and How They Live, by Wallace Thompson.* New York: Harper and Brothers, 1921.

Turner, John Kenneth. *Barbarous Mexico.* Chicago: Charles H. Kerr and Company, 1911.

Tweedie, Ethel Brilliana. *The Maker of Modern Mexico.* New York: John Lane Company, 1906.

———. *Mexico As I Saw It.* London: Hurst and Blackett, Limited, 1901.

Vaquero [pseud.]. *Adventures in Search of a Living in Spanish-America, by "Vaquero."* London: John Bale, Sons, and Danielsson, Limited, 1911.

Veer, Theo de. *Mexico: Reis-Studies van een journalist door Theo de Veer.* Amsterdam: Scheltema and Holkema's Boekhandel, 1910.

Vera Estañol, Jorge. *Historia de la revolución mexicana: Orígenes y resultados.* Mexico City: Editorial Porrúa, 1967.

Wallace, Dillon. *Beyond the Mexican Sierras.* Chicago: A. C. McClurg, 1910.

Ward, H. G. *Mexico.* 2 vols. London: Henry Colburn, 1829.

Wells, David A. *A Study of Mexico.* New York: D. Appleton and Company, 1897.

Wilson, James A. *Bits of Old Mexico.* San Francisco: [n.p.], 1910.

Wilson, Robert A. *Mexico: Its Peasants and Its Priests; or, Adventures and Historical Researches in Mexico and Its Silver Mines during Parts of the Years 1851–52–53–54. . . .* New York: Harper and Brothers, 1856.

Winter, Nevin O. *Mexico and Her People To-Day. An Account of the Customs, Amusements, History and Advancement of the Mexicans, and the Development and Resources of Their Country.* Boston: L. C. Page and Company, 1923.

[Wise, Henry Augustus]. *Through the Land of the Aztecs, or, Life and Travel in Mexico by a Gringo.* London: Sampson Low, Marston and Company, 1892.

Woodbridge, Dwight E. "Travelling on the West Coast of Mexico. What

the Traveller Needs and What He Will Find. Some Business and Min-
ing Conditions." *The Engineering and Mining Journal* 84, no 14 (5
October 1907): 627–630.
Zamacois, Niceto de. *Historia de Méjico, desde sus tiempos más remotos
hasta nuestros días*. . . . 22 vols. in 25. Mexico City: J. F. Parres y
Compª, 1880.
Zayas Enríquez, Rafael de. *Los Estados Unidos Mexicanos. Sus progresos
en veinte años de paz, 1877–1897. Estudio histórico y estadístico,
fundado en los datos oficiales más recientes y completos*. New York:
H. A. Rost, Compañía y Publicista, [n.d.].
————. *Porfirio Díaz*. New York: D. Appleton and Company, 1908.

IV. Newspapers

La Actualidad (Mexico City). 1911.
El Ahuizote (Mexico City). 1911–1912.
Boletín de la Policía Rural (Mexico City). 1875.
El Cable Transatlántico (Mexico City). 1881.
El Clarín (Río Blanco, Veracruz). 1958–1959.
El Combate (Mexico City). 1880.
El Constitucional (Mexico City). 1861, 1869, and 1874.
El Correo (Chihuahua, Chihuahua). 1909–1912.
El Correo de Lunes (Mexico City). 1884.
El Cosmopólita (Orizaba, Veracruz). 1899.
El Demócrata (Mexico City). 1914 and 1920.
El Diario (Mexico City). 1911 and 1913.
El Diario del Hogar (Mexico City). 1899–1911.
El Diario Oficial del Gobierno Supremo de la República (Mexico City).
1867–1877, 1910–1911 and 1914.
El Dictamen (Veracruz, Veracruz). 1907, 1910 and 1920.
El Eco de Ambos Mundos (Mexico City). 1873.
El Eco de Tabasco (San Juan de Bautista, Tabasco). 1908–1910.
El Excelsior (Mexico City). 1920.
The Evening Star (Mexico City). 1900.
El Foro. (Mexico City). 1878.
El Heraldo (Pachuca, Hidalgo). 1905–1911.
El Heraldo (Zamora, Michoacán). 1908–1910.
El Heraldo de Chiapas (Tuxtla Gutiérrez, Chiapas). 1908–1911.
El Heraldo Ilustrado (Mexico City). 1920.
El Heraldo de México (Mexico City). 1920.
El Hijo del Ahuizote (Mexico City). 1885–1903.
El Hijo del Trabajo (Mexico City). 1876–1884.
El Imparcial (Mexico City). 1897–1914.
El Independencia (Mexico City). 1861.
El Independiente (Mexico City). 1914.
La Liberal (Mexico City). 1914.

Libertad (Mexico City). 1878–1884.
La Mañana (Mexico City). 1911–1913.
The Mexican Herald (Mexico City). 1899, 1910–1914.
El Monitor Republicano (Mexico City). 1861–1896 and 1920.
El Movimiento (Mexico City).
El Mundo (Mexico City). 1899.
El Mundo Ilustrado (Mexico City). 1895 and 1911.
El Nacional (Mexico City). 1880–1881.
New York Times. 1899.
Nueva Era (Mexico City). 1911–1913.
El Obrero Internacional (Mexico City). 1874.
El Obrero Mexicano (Mexico City). 1910–1911.
El Observador (Zacatecas, Zacatecas). 1899.
El Observador (Guanajuato, Guanajuato). 1887–1890, 1905–1908, and
    1910–1912.
La Opiniíon Federal (Mexico City). 1861.
El País (Mexico City). 1907 and 1910–1914.
El Pájaro Verde (Mexico City). 1906–1907.
El Partido Liberal (Mexico City). 1885–1896.
La Patria (Mexico City). 1880, 1899, 1910–1911, and 1914.
El Popular (Mexico City). 1899.
La Prensa (Guanajuato, Guanajuato). 1909–1910.
La Regeneración (Mexico City). 1900–1901 and 1911.
El Reproductor (Orizaba, Veracruz). 1911.
La República (Mexico City). 1880.
La Restauración (Guadalajara, Jalisco). 1920.
El Siglo XIX (Mexico City). 1856–1858 and 1861–1890.
La Socialista (Mexico City). 1878–1886.
El Tiempo (Mexico City). 1883–1912.
Trait d'Union (Mexico City). 1880.
La Tribuna (Mexico City). 1880 and 1914.
El Tulteca (Tula de Tamaulipas, Tamaulipas). 1905–1910.
Two Republics (Mexico City). 1899.
La Unión Federal (Mexico City). 1861.
El Universal (Mexico City). 1899 and 1920.
El Univeral Ilustrado (Mexico City). 1920.
La Victoria (Oaxaca, Oaxaca). 1860–1864.
La Vigilante (Mexico City). 1879–1880.
La Voz de México (Mexico City). 1880 and 1899.

V. Secondary Sources

Aguirre Anaya, Carlos. "The Geographic Displacement of Population, 1895–1910: Perspectives in the Study of Urban Systems." *Latin American Research Review* 10, no. 2 (Summer 1975): 123–124.

240   *Bibliography*

Alexius, Robert M. "The Army and Politics in Porfirian Mexico." Ph.D. dissertation, University of Texas at Austin, 1976.

Almada, Francisco R. *La revolución en el estado de Chihuahua.* 2 vols. Mexico City: Impreso de los Talleres Gráficos de la Nación, 1964.

Altman, Ida, and Lockhart, James, eds. *Provinces of Early Mexico: Variants of Spanish American Regional Evolution.* Los Angeles: University of California, Los Angeles, Latin American Center Publications, 1976.

Amaya, General Juan Gualberto. *Madero y los auténticos revolucionarios de 1910 hasta la Decena Trágica y fin del General Pascual Orozco: Primera etapa, 1900–1913.* Mexico City: [n.p.], 1946.

Anderson, Rodney D. *Outcasts in their Own Land: Mexican Industrial Workers, 1906–1911.* DeKalb: Northern Illinois University Press, 1976.

———. "Mexican Workers and the Politics of Revolution, 1906–1911." *Hispanic American Historical Review* 54, no. 1 (February 1974): 94–113.

Andreski, Stanislav. *Military Organization and Society.* Berkeley: University of California Press, 1968.

———. *Parasitism and Subversion: The Case of Latin America.* New York: Pantheon Books, 1966.

Aragón, Agustín. *Porfirio Díaz, estudio histórico-filosófico.* Mexico City: Editorial Literaria. 1964.

Araiza, Luis. *Historia del movimiento obrero mexicano.* Mexico City: Talleres de Editorial "Cuauhtemoc," 1964–1965.

Archer, Christon I. *The Army in Bourbon Mexico, 1760–1810.* Albuquerque: University of New Mexico Press, 1977.

Arrangoiz, Francisco de Paula de. *México desde 1808 hasta 1867.* Mexico City: Editorial Porrúa, 1968.

Aston, B. W. "The Public Career of Don José Ives Limantour." Ph.D. dissertation, Texas Tech University, 1972.

Bailey, David C. *¡Viva Cristo Rey! The Cristero Rebellion and Church-State Conflict in Mexico.* Austin: University of Texas Press, 1974.

Bakewell, P. J. *Silver Mining and Society in Colonial Mexico: Zacatecas, 1546–1700.* Cambridge: The University Press, 1971.

Barragán Rodríguez, Juan. *Historia del ejército y de la revolución constitucionalista.* 2 vols. Mexico City: Talleres Gráficos del Editorial Stylo, 1945.

Barrera Fuentes, Florencio. *Historia de la Revolución Mexicana: La etapa precursora.* Mexico City: Biblioteca del Instituto Nacional de Estudios Históricos de la Revolución Mexicana, 1955.

Bayley, David H. "The Police and Political Change in Comparative Perspective." *Law and Society Review* 6, no. 1 (August 1971): 91–112.

———. "The Police and Political Development in Europe." In Tilly,

Charles, ed., *The Formation of National States in Western Europe.* Princeton: Princeton University Press, 1975.

Bazán Alarcón, Alicia. "El Real Tribunal de la Acordada y la delincuencia de la Nueva España." *Historia Mexicana* 6, no. 1 (January 1964): 317–345.

Bazant, Jan. "The Division of Some Mexican Haciendas during the Liberal Revolution, 1856–1862." *Journal of Latin American Studies* 3, no. 1 (May 1971): 25–37.

――――. "Peones, arrendatarios y aparceros, 1868–1904." *Historia Mexicana* 24, no. 1 (July-September 1974): 94–121.

Beals, Carlton. *Porfirio Díaz, Dictator of Mexico.* Philadelphia: J. B. Lippincott Company, 1933.

Beene, Delmar Leon. "Sonora in the Age of Ramón Corral." Ph.D. dissertation, University of Arizona, 1972.

Beezeley, William H. "Governor Carranza and the Revolution in Coahuila." *The Americas* 33, no. 1 (July 1976): 50–61.

――――. *Insurgent Governor: Abraham González and the Mexican Revolution in Chihuahua.* Lincoln: University of Nebraska Press, 1973.

Berbusse, Edward J. *The United States in Puerto Rico, 1898–1900.* Chapel Hill: University of North Carolina Press, 1966.

Bernstein, Marvin D. *The Mexican Mining Industry, 1890–1950: A Study of the Interaction of Politics, Economics, and Technology.* New York: State University of New York Press, 1964.

Black, C. E. *The Dynamics of Modernization: A Study in Comparative History.* New York: Harper and Row, 1966.

Blaisdell, Lowell L. *The Desert Revolution: Baja California, 1911.* Madison: University of Wisconsin Press, 1962.

Blasier, Cole. "Studies of Social Revolution: Origins in Mexico, Bolivia, and Cuba." *Latin American Research Review* 2, no. 3 (Summer 1967): 28–64.

Blok, Anton. "The Peasant and the Brigand: Social Banditry Reconsidered." *Comparative Studies in Society and History* 14, no. 4 (September 1972): 494–503.

Boyer, Richard. "Mexico in the Seventeenth Century: Transition of a Colonial Society." *Hispanic American Historical Review* 57, no. 3 (August 1977): 455–478.

Brading, Donald. "A Creole Nationalism and Mexican Liberalism." *Journal of Inter-American Studies and World Affairs* 15, no. 2 (May 1973): 139–190.

――――. "Estructura de la producción agrícola en el Bajío, 1700–1850." In Florescano, Enrique, ed., *Haciendas, latifundios, y plantaciones en América Latina.* Mexico City: Siglo XXI Editores, 1975.

――――. *Miners and Merchants in Bourbon Mexico, 1763–1810.* Cambridge: The University Press, 1971.

_____, and Wu, Celia. "Population Growth and Crisis: León, 1720–1860." *Journal of Latin American Studies* 5, no. 1 (May 1973): 1–36.

Bravo Ugarte, José. *Historia de México*. 3 vols. Mexico City: Editorial Jus, 1953.

_____. *Historia sucinta de Michoacán*. 3 vols. Mexico City: Editorial Jus, 1964.

Brayer, Herbert O. "The Cananea Incident." *New Mexico Historical Review* 13, no. 4 (October 1938): 387–415

Bremauntz, Alberto. *Panorama social de las revoluciones de México*. Mexico City: Ediciones Jurídico Sociales, 1960.

Brenan, Gerald. *The Spanish Labyrinth*. Cambridge: The University Press, 1964.

Brenner, Anita. *The Wind That Swept Mexico*. 2nd ed. Austin: University of Texas Press, 1971.

Breymann, Walter N. "The *Científicos:* Critics of the Díaz Regime, 1892–1903." *Proceedings of the Arkansas Academy of Science* 7 (1954): 91–97.

Brungardt, Maurice. "The Civic Militia in Mexico: 1820–1835." Unpublished paper, University of Texas at Austin, Benson Latin American Collection, 1970.

Bryan, Anthony T. "The Career of General Bernardo Reyes: Continuity and Change in Mexican Politics, 1885–1913." M.A. thesis, University of Nebraska, 1967.

Bulnes, Francisco. *La Guerra de Independencia: Hidalgo–Iturbide*. Mexico City: Editora Nacional, 1969.

Bush, Dr. Ira J. *Gringo Doctor*. Caldwell, Idaho: Caxton Printers, 1939.

Cadenhead, Ivie E. *Jesús González Ortega and Mexican National Politics*. Fort Worth: Texas Christian University Press, 1972.

Calderón, Francisco. *Historia moderna de México: La república restaurada: La vida económica*. Mexico City: Editorial Hermes, 1955.

Canales Montejano, Guillermo. *Historia militar de México: 10 casos concretos*. Mexico City: Ediciones Ateneo, 1940.

Cardoso, Lawrence A. "Labor Emigration to the Southwest, 1916–1920: Mexican Attitudes and Policy." *Southwestern Historical Quarterly* 79, no. 4 (April 1976): 400–416.

Carr, Barry. "Las peculiaridades del norte mexicano, 1880–1927: Ensayo de interpretación." *Historia Mexicana* 22, no. 3 (January-March 1973): 320–346.

Carr, Raymond. *Spain, 1808–1939*. Oxford: Clarendon Press, 1966.

Casasola, Gustavo. *Historia gráfica de la revolución mexicana*. 5 vols. Mexico City: Editorial F. Trillas, 1960.

Case, Robert. "Resurgimento de los conservadores en México, 1876–1877." *Historia Mexicana* 25, no. 1 (July-September 1975): 204–231.

Chandler, Billy Joe. *The Bandit King, Lampião of Brazil.* College Station: Texas A&M Press, 1978.

Chapman, Charles E. *A History of the Cuban Republic.* New York: Macmillan Company, 1927.

Chapman, John G. "Steam, Enterprise and Politics. The Building of the Veracruz-Mexico City Railway, 1837–1880." Ph.D. dissertation, University of Texas at Austin, 1972.

Chevalier, François. "The North Mexican Hacienda: Eighteenth and Nineteenth Centuries." In Lewis, Archibald R., and McGann, Thomas F., eds., *The New World Looks at Its History.* Austin: University of Texas Press, 1963.

_____. " 'Caudillos' et 'caciques' en amérique: Contribution a l'étude des liens personnels." *Bulletin Hispanique*, no. 1-2 (January-June 1962): 30–47.

Chucho el Roto o la nobleza de un bandido mexicano. Mexico City: Ediciones Argos, [n.d.].

Coatsworth, John H. "Anotaciones sobre la producción de alimentos durante el porfiriato." *Historia Mexicana* 26, no. 2 (October-December 1976): 167–187.

_____. "The Impact of Railroads on the Economic Development of Mexico, 1877–1910." Ph.D. dissertation, University of Wisconsin, 1972.

_____. "The Mobility of Labor in Nineteenth-Century Mexican Agriculture." Paper presented at the annual meeting of the American Historical Association, San Francisco, December 1978.

_____. "Obstacles to Economic Growth in Nineteenth-Century Mexico." *American Historical Review* 83, no. 1 (February 1978): 80–100.

_____. "Los orígenes del autoritarismo moderno en México." *Foro Internacional* 16, no. 2 (October-December 1975): 205–232.

_____. "Railroads, Landholding, and Agrarian Protest in the Early Porfiriato." *Hispanic American Historical Review* (February 1974): 48–71.

Cobb, R. C. *The People and the Police: French Popular Protest, 1789–1820.* Oxford: Clarendon Press, 1970.

Cockcroft, James D. *Intellectual Precursors of the Mexican Revolution, 1900–1913.* Austin: University of Texas Press, 1968.

Coerver, Don M. "Federal-State Relations during the Porfiriato: The Case of Sonora, 1879–1884." *The Americas* 33, no. 4 (April 1977): 567–584.

_____. *The Porfirian Interregnum: The Presidency of Manuel González of Mexico, 1880–1884.* Fort Worth: Texas Christian University Press, 1979.

Coolidge, Dane. *Fighting Men of the West.* New York: E. P. Dutton, 1968.

Cordero y Torres, Enríque. *Primera obra completa sobre la historia general del Estado de Puebla (1531–1963) con el rubro de historia compendiada del Estado de Puebla.* 3 vols. Puebla: Grupo Literario "Bohemia Poblana," 1965–1966.

Cortés Conde, Roberto. *The First Stages of Modernization in Latin America.* New York: Harper and Row, 1974.

Cosío Villegas, Daniel. *Historia moderna de Mexico: La república restaurada: La vida política.* Mexico City: Editorial Hermes, 1955.

———. *Historia moderna de México: El porfiriato: La vida política interior.* 2 vols. Mexico City: Editorial Hermes, 1970.

———. "El Porfiriato: Era de consolidación." *Historia Mexicana* 13, no. 1 (July-September 1963): 76–87.

———. *The United States versus Porfirio Díaz.* Benson, Nettie Lee, tr. Lincoln: University of Nebraska Press, 1963.

Cota Soto, Guillermo. *Historia militar de México.* 2 vols. Mexico City: [n.p.]. 1947.

Couturier, Edith B. "Hacienda de Hueyapan: The History of a Mexican Social and Economic Institution, 1550–1940." Ph.D. dissertation, Columbia University, 1965.

———. "Modernización y tradición en una hacienda (San Juan Hueyapan, 1902–1911)." *Historia Mexicana* 18, no. 1 (July-September 1968): 35–55.

Cross, Harry E. "The Mining Economy of Zacatecas, Mexico in the Nineteenth Century." Ph.D. dissertation, University of California, Berkeley, 1976.

Cumberland, Charles C. *Mexican Revolution: Genesis under Madero.* Austin: University of Texas Press, 1952.

Dabbs, Jack A. *The French Army in Mexico, 1861–1867.* The Hague: Mouton and Company, 1963.

Davies, Keith A. "Tendencias demográficas urbanas durante el siglo XIX en México." *Historia Mexicana* 21, no. 3 (January-March 1972): 481–524.

DeHart, Evelyn Hu. "Development and Rural Rebellion: Pacification of the Yaquis in the Late Porfiriato." *Hispanic American Historical Review* 54, no. 1 (February 1974): 72–93.

———. "Resistance and Survival: A History of the Yaqui Peoples' Struggle for Autonomy, 1533–1910." Ph.D. dissertation, University of Texas at Austin, 1976.

Delorme, Robert L. "The Political Basis of Economic Development: Mexico, 1884–1911, a Case Study," Ph.D. dissertation, University of Minnesota, 1968.

Díaz, Lilia. "El liberalismo militante." In vol. 3 of *Historia general de México.* 4 vols. Mexico City: El Colegio de México, 1976.

Díaz Díaz, Fernando, *Santa Anna y Juan Alvarez frente a frente.* Mexico City: Sep/Setentas, 1972.

Diccionario Porrúa de historia, biografía y geografía de México. 2 vols. Mexico City: Editorial Porrúa, 1970.

DiTella, Torcuato S. "The Dangerous Classes of Early Nineteenth Century Mexico." *Journal of Latin American Studies* 5, no. 1 (May 1973): 79–105.

Dulles, J. W. F. *Yesterday in Mexico: A Chronicle of the Revolution 1919–1936.* Austin: University of Texas Press, 1972.

Dye, Alexander. "Railways and Revolution in Mexico." *Foreign Affairs* 5, no. 2 (January 1927): 321–323.

Eeckaute, Enise. "Les Brigands en Russie du VIIᵉ siécle: Mythe et realité." *Revue d'Histoire Moderne et Contemporaine* 12 (July-September 1965): 162–202.

Fernández-Mensasque, Fernando Casado. "El Tribunal de la Acordada de Nueva España." *Anuario de Estudios Americanos* (1950): 279–323.

Fitzgibbon, Russell H. *Cuba and the United States, 1900–1935.* New York: Russell and Russell Inc., 1964.

Flores, Ma. Guadalupe, and Peregrina, Angelica. "Historiografía: Las gavillas en Jalisco de 1856 a 1863." *Boletín del Archivo Histórico de Jalisco* 2, no. 2 (May-August 1978): 2–8.

Florescano, Enrique. "Mexico: Ensayo de interpretación." In Cortés Conde, Roberto, and Stein, Stanley J., eds., *Latin America: a Guide to Economic Study, 1830–1930.* Berkeley: University of California Press, 1977.

———, and Lanzagorta, María del Rosario. "Política económica, antecedentes y consequencias." In González, Luis; Florescano, Enrique; et al., *La economía mexicana en la época de Juárez.* Mexico City: Secretaría de Industria y Comercio, 1972.

———, and Gil Sánchez, Isabel. *Descripciones económicas generales de Nueva España, 1784–1817.* Mexico City: Instituto Nacional de Antropología e Historia, 1973.

———, and Gil Sánchez, Isabel. *Descripciones económicas regionales de Nueva España. Provincias del centro, sureste y sur, 1766–1827.* Mexico City: Instituto Nacional de Antropología e Historia, 1976.

———, and Gil Sánchez, Isabel. *Descripciones económicas regionales de Nueva España. Provincias del norte, 1790–1814.* Mexico City: Instituto Nacional de Antropología e Historia, 1976.

Flores Caballero, Romeo. "Comercio interior." In González, Luis; Florescano, Enrique; et al., *La economía en la época de Juárez.* Mexico City: Secretaría de Industria y Comercio, 1972.

Forrest, Jack L. "United States Recognition of the Porfirio Díaz Government, 1876–1878." Ph.D. dissertation, University of Oklahoma, 1967.

Fraser, Donald J. "La política de desamortización en las comunidades indígenas." *Historia Mexicana* 21, no 4 (April-June 1972): 615–652.

Friedrich, Paul. *Agrarian Revolt in a Mexican Village.* Englewood Cliffs: Prentice-Hall, 1970.

Galaviz de Capdevielle, Elena. "Descripción y pacificación de la Sierra Gorda." *Estudios de Historia Novohispana* 4 (1971): 113–149.

Galula, David. *Counter-Insurgency Warfare: Theory and Practice.* New York: Praeger, 1964.

García Martínez, Bernardo. "La Comisión Geográfico-Exploradora." *Historia Mexicana* 24, no. 4 (April-June 1975): 485–555.

Gerhard, Peter. "La evolución del pueblo rural mexicano, 1519–1975." *Historia Mexicana* 24, no. 4 (April-June 1975): 566–578.

Gilderhus, Mark. "Carranza and the Decision to Revolt, 1913: A Problem in Historical Interpretation." *The Americas* 33, no. 2 (October 1976): 298–310.

Gill, Mario. "Heraclio Bernal, caudillo frustrado." *Historia Mexicana* 4, no. 1 (July-September 1954): 138–158.

Gilly, Adolfo. *La revolución interrumpida: México, 1910–1920: Una guerra campesina por la tierra y el poder.* Mexico City: Ediciones "El Caballito," 1971.

Giron, Nicole. *Heraclio Bernal: ¿Bandolero, cacique o precursor de la Revolución?* Mexico City: Instituto Nacional de Antropología e Historia, 1976.

Goldfrank, Walter L. "The Ambiguity of Infrastructure: Railroads in Prerevolutionary Mexico." *Studies in Comparative International Development* 11, no. 3 (Fall 1976): 3–24.

González y González, Luis. "El liberalismo triunfante." In vol. 3 of *Historia general de México.* 4 vols. Mexico City: El Colegio de México, 1976.

_____. "The Period of Formation." In Cosío Villegas, Daniel, et al., *A Compact History of Mexico.* Mexico City: El Colegio de México, 1973.

_____. *San José de Gracia: Mexican Village in Transition.* Upton, John, tr. Austin: University of Texas Press, 1972.

_____; Cosío Villegas, Emma; and Montroy, Guadalupe. *Historia moderna de México: La República restaurada: La vida social.* Mexico City: Editorial Hermes, 1956.

González Monroy, Jesús. "El lapso más tormentoso de la dictadura porfirista: El porfirismo y la oposición." (Los Angeles, 1950.) Microfilmed typescript at Museum of Anthropology and History, Mexico City.

González Navarro, Moisés. "Los braceros en el porfiriato." *Estudios Sociologicas* 5 (1954): 261–280.

_____. "Las guerras de castas." *Historia Mexicana* 26, no. 1 (July-September 1976): 70–106.

_____. *Historia Moderna de México: El porfiriato: La vida social.* Mexico City: Editorial Hermes, 1957.

_____. "La huelga de Río Blanco." *Historia Mexicana* 6, no. 4 (April-June 1957): 510–533.

_____. *Las huelgas textiles en el porfiriato.* Puebla: Editorial José M. Cajica, Jr., 1970.

_____. "Las huelgas textiles en el porfiriato." *Historia Mexicana* 6, no. 2 (October-December 1956): 201–216.

_____. "Tenencia de la tierra y población agrícola." *Historia Mexicana* 19, no. 1 (July-September 1969): 62–86.

_____. "La venganza del sur." *Historia Mexicana* 21, no. 4 (April-June 1972): 677–692.

González Ramírez, Manuel. *La capitulación del ejército del dictador ante Carranza y Obregón.* Mexico City: Ediciones del Patronato de la Historia de Sonora, 1964.

_____. *La huelga de Cananea.* In *Fuentes para la historia de la Revolución.* 5 vols. Mexico City: Fondo de Cultura Ecónomica, 1954–1959.

Gutiérrez Santos, Daniel. *Historia militar de México, 1876–1914.* Mexico City: Ediciones Atena, 1955.

Gwynn, Major General Charles W. *Imperial Policing.* London: Macmillan and Company, 1936.

Hagedorn, Hermann. *Leonard Wood.* 2 vols. New York: Harper and Brothers, 1931.

Hale, Charles A. *Mexican Liberalism in the Age of Mora, 1821–1853.* New Haven: Yale University Press, 1968.

_____. " 'Scientific Politics' and the Continuity of Liberalism in Mexico, 1867–1910." In *Dos revoluciones: México y los Estados Unidos.* Mexico City: Editorial Jus, 1976.

Hansen, Roger D. *The Politics of Mexican Development.* Baltimore: Johns Hopkins University Press, 1971.

Harris, Charles H. *A Mexican Family Empire: The Latifundio of the Sánchez Navarros, 1765–1867.* Austin: University of Texas Press, 1975.

Hart, John M. *Anarchism and the Mexican Working Class, 1860–1931.* Austin: University of Texas Press, 1978.

_____. "Anarchist Thought in Nineteenth-Century Mexico." Ph.D. dissertation, University of California, Los Angeles, 1970.

_____, "Miguel Negrete: La epopeya de un revolucionario." *Historia Mexicana* 24, no. 1 (July-September 1974): 70–93.

_____. "Nineteenth Century Urban Labor Precursors of the Mexican Revolution: The Development of an Ideology." *The Americas* 30, no. 3 (January 1974): 297–318.

Henderson, Peter V. "Counterrevolution in Mexico: Félix Díaz and the Struggle for National Supremacy, 1910–1920." Ph.D. dissertation, University of Nebraska, 1973.

Hobsbawm, Eric J. *Bandits.* New York: Delacorte Press, 1969.

_____. "Economic Fluctuations and Some Social Movements." *Economic Historical Review* 5, no. 1 (1952): 1–25.

248   *Bibliography*

_____. "Social Bandits: Reply." *Comparative Studies in Society and History* 14, no. 4 (September 1972): 503–505.

Holden, William Curry. *Teresita.* Owings Mills, Md.: Stemmer House Publishers, Inc., 1978.

Hollon, W. Eugene. *Frontier Violence: Another Look.* Oxford: Oxford University Press, 1974.

Holt, J. C. "The Origins and Audience of the Ballads of Robin Hood." *Past and Present* no. 18 (November 1960): 89–110.

Horan, James D. *The Authentic West: The Gunfighters.* New York: Crown Publishers, 1976.

_____. *Desperate Men: Revelations from the Sealed Pinkerton Files.* New York: G. P. Putnam's Sons, 1949.

Huntington, Samuel P. *The Soldier and the State: The Theory and Politics of Civil-Military Relations.* Cambridge: Harvard University Press, 1957.

Iturribarría Jorge Fernando. *Porfirio Díaz ante la historia.* Mexico City: Unión Gráfica, 1967.

Janowitz, Morris. *The Military in the Political Development of New Nations: An Essay in Comparative Analysis.* Chicago: University of Chicago Press, 1964.

Katz, Friedrich. "Agrarian Changes in Northern Mexico in the Period of Villista Rule, 1913–1915." In Wilkie, James W.; Meyer, C.; and Monzón de Wilkie, Edna, eds., *Contemporary Mexico: Papers of the IV International Congress of Mexican History.* Berkeley: University of California Press, 1976.

_____. "Labor Conditions on Haciendas in Porfirian Mexico: Some Trends and Tendencies." *Hispanic American Historical Review* 54, no. 1 (February 1974): 1–47.

_____. "Peasants in the Mexican Revolution of 1910." In Speilberg, Joseph, and Whiteford, Scott, eds., *Forging Nations: A Comparative View of Rural Ferment and Revolt.* East Lansing: Michigan State University Press, 1976.

Keesing, Donald B. "Structural Change Early in Development: Mexico's Changing Industrial and Occupational Structure from 1895–1950." *Journal of Economic History* 29, no. 4 (December 1969): 716–737.

Kelley, James R. "Professionalism in the Porfirian Army Officer Corps." Ph.D. dissertation, Tulane University, 1970.

Kitchens, John W. "Some Considerations on the Rurales of Porfirian Mexico." *Journal of Inter-American Studies and World Affairs* 9, no. 3 (July 1967): 441–445.

Knapp, Frank A. *The Life of Sebastián Lerdo de Tejada, 1823–1889.* Austin: University of Texas Press, 1951.

Knowlton, Robert J. *Church Property and the Mexican Reform, 1856–1910.* DeKalb: Northern Illinois University Press, 1976.

Kroeber, Clifton B. "La cuestión del Nazas hasta 1913." *Historia Mexicana* 20, no. 3 (January-March 1971): 428–456.

Landes, David S. *The Unbound Prometheus: Technological Change and Industrial Development in Western Europe from 1750 to the Present.* Cambridge: The University Press, 1969.

Leal, Juan Felipe. "El estado y el bloque en el poder en México, 1867–1914." *Historia Mexicana* 23, no. 4 (April-June 1974): 700–721.

Lee, Everett S. "The Turner Thesis Reexamined." *American Quarterly* 13, no. 1 (Spring 1961): 77–83.

Levett, Allan Edward. "Centralization of City Police in the Nineteenth Century United States." Ph.D. dissertation, University of Michigan, 1975.

Lewis, W. Arthur. *Economic Survey, 1919–1939.* London: Allen and Unwin Ltd., 1940.

———. *The Evolution of the International Economic Order.* Princeton: Princeton University Press, 1978.

Lieuwen, Edwin. *Mexican Militarism: The Political Rise and Fall of the Revolutionary Army, 1910–1940.* Albuquerque: University of New Mexico Press, 1968.

López Cámara, Francisco. *La estructura económica y social de México en la época de la Reforma.* Mexico City: Siglo XXI Editores, 1967.

López-Portillo y Rojas, José. *Elevación y caída de Porfirio Díaz.* Mexico City: Libería Español, 1921.

Lozoya, Jorge Alberto. "Un guión para el estudio de los ejércitos mexicanos del siglo diecinueve." *Historia Mexicana* 27, no. 1 (April-June 1968): 553–568.

Lunenfeld, Marvin. "The Council of the Santa Hermandad of Ferdinand and Isabella (1476–1498). A Study in Castilian Centralization and Urban Independence." Ph.D. dissertation, New York University, 1968.

———. *The Council of the Santa Hermandad: A Study of the Pacification Forces of Ferdinand and Isabella.* Coral Gables: University of Miami Press, 1970.

Macaulay, Neill. *The Prestes Column: A Revolution in Brazil.* New York: New Viewpoints, 1974.

Machado, Manuel A. "The Mexican Revolution and the Destruction of the Mexican Cattle Industry." *Southwestern Historical Quarterly* 79, no. 1 (July 1975): 1–20.

MacLachlan, Colin M. *Criminal Justice in Eighteenth-Century Mexico: A Study of the Tribunal of the Acordada.* Berkeley: University of California Press, 1974.

MacLeod, R. C. "A Canadian Epic: A Century of the Mounted Police." Unpublished manuscript at the Amon Carter Museum of Western Art, Fort Worth, Texas, 1972.

_____. *The North-West Mounted Police and Law Enforcement, 1873–1905*. Toronto: University of Toronto Press, 1976.

Marcosson, Isaac F. *Metal Magic: The Story of the American Smelting and Refining Company*. New York: Farrar, Straus, 1949.

María y Campos, Armando. *La vida del General Lucio Blanco*. Mexico City: Talleres Gráficos de la Nación, 1953.

Marín, Fausto Antonio. *La rebelión de la sierra (vida de Heraclio Bernal)*. Mexico City: Ediciones "América," 1950.

Marín-Tamayo, Fausto. *¡Aquí está Heraclio Bernal! . . . "El Rayo de Sinaloa."* Mexico City: Poulibros "La Prensa," 1957.

Martin, Percy F. *Maximilian in Mexico: The Story of the French Intervention*. New York: C. Scribner's Sons, 1914.

Martínez, John. *Mexican Emigration to the United States, 1910–1930*. San Francisco: R. and E. Research Associates, 1971.

Martínez Ortiz, Rafael. *Cuba: Los primeros años de independencia*. 2 vols. Paris: Imprimerie Artistique "Lux," 1921.

Martínez Ruíz, Enrique. *Creación de la Guardia Civil*. Madrid: Editora Nacional, 1976.

_____. "La Crisis del orden público en España y la creación de la Guardia Civil." *Revista de Estudios Históricos de la Guardia Civil* 5 (1970): 49–70.

Mecham, J. Lloyd. "The Jefe Político in Mexico." *Southwestern Social Science Quarterly* 13, no. 4 (March 1933): 333–352.

Mercer, A. S. *The Banditti of the Plains or the Cattleman's Invasion of Wyoming in 1892*. Norman: University of Oklahoma Press, 1976.

Meyer, Jean A. *The Cristero Rebellion: The Mexican People between Church and State, 1926–1929*. Southern, Richard, tr. Cambridge: Cambridge University Press, 1976.

_____. "El Ocaso de Manuel Lozada." *Historia Mexicana* 18, no. 4 (April-June 1969): 535–568.

_____. *Problemas campesinos y revueltas agrarias (1821–1910)*. Mexico City: Secretaría de Educación Pública, 1973.

Meyer, Michael C. *Huerta: A Political Portrait*. Lincoln: University of Nebraska Press, 1972.

_____. *Mexican Rebel: Pascual Orozco and the Mexican Revolution, 1910–1915*. Lincoln: University of Nebraska Press, 1967.

Meyers, William K. "Politics, Vested Rights, and Economic Growth in Porfirian Mexico: The Company Tlahualilo in the Comarca Lagunera, 1855–1911." *Hispanic American Historical Review* 57, no. 3 (August 1977): 425–454.

Michaels, Albert L., and Bernstein, Marvin. "The Modernization of the Old Order: Organization and Periodization in Twentieth-Century Mexico." In Wilkie, James W.; Meyer, Michael C.; and Monzón de Wilkie, Edna, eds., *Contemporary Mexico: Papers of the IV International Congress of Mexican History*. Berkeley: University of California Press, 1976.

Miller, David Lynn. "The Creelman Interview and the Reaction of the Metropolitan Press of Mexico." M.A. special topics paper, Mexico City College, 1948.

_____. "Porfirio Díaz and the Army of the East." Ph.D. dissertation, University of Michigan, 1960.

Miranda, José. "La propiedad comunal de la tierra y la cohesión social de los pueblos indígenas mexicanos." *Cuadernos Americanos* 149, no. 6 (November-December 1966): 168–181.

Moody, Ralph. *Stagecoach West.* New York: Thomas Y. Crowell Company, 1967.

Moore, Wilbert E. *Industrialization and Labor: Social Aspects of Economic Development.* New York: Russell and Russell, 1965.

Moreno Toscano, Alejandra. "Cambios en los patrones de urbanización en México, 1810–1910." *Historia Mexicana* 22, no. 2 (October-December 1972): 160–187.

_____, and Florescano, Enrique. "El sector externo y la organización espacial y regional de México (1521–1910)." In Wilkie, James W.; Meyer, Michael C.; and Monzón de Wilkie, Edna, eds., *Contemporary Mexico: Papers of the IV International Congress of Mexican History.* Berkeley: University of California Press, 1976.

Mosse, George. *Police Forces in History.* Beverly Hills: Sage International Institute for Strategic Studies, 1975.

Muñoz y Pérez, Daniel. *General Don Ignacio Zaragoza.* Mexico City: Academia Nacional de Historia y Geografía, 1961.

Murray, Alice Mary. "Díaz and the Church: The Conciliation Policy, 1876–1900." M.A. thesis, Mexico City College, 1959.

Nakayama A., Antonio. *Sinaloa: El drama y sus actores.* Mexico City: Colección Científica No. 20, Instituto Nacional de Antropología e Historia, 1975.

Nava Rodríguez, Luís. *Transcendencia histórica de Tlaxcala.* Mexico City: Editorial Progreso, 1969.

Niblo, Stephen R. "The Political Economy of the Early Porfiriato: Politics and Economics in Mexico, 1876 to 1880." Ph.D. dissertation, Northern Illinois University, 1971.

Ochoa Campos, Moisés. *La revolución mexicana.* 4 vols. Mexico City: Talleres Gráficos de la Nación, 1966.

d'Olwer, Luis Nicolau, et al. *Historia moderna de México: El porfiriato: La vida económica.* 2 vols. Mexico City: Editorial Hermes, 1965.

Orozco y Berra, Manuel. *Apéndice al diccionario universal de historia y geografía.* 3 vols. Mexico City: Imprenta de J. M. Andrade y F. Escalante, 1855–1856.

Ortíz Vidales, Salvador. *La arriería en México: Estudio folklórico, costumbrista, e histórico.* Mexico City: Ediciones Botas, 1941.

_____. *Los bandidos en la literatura mexicana.* Mexico City: Editorial Porrúa, 1949.

Pang, Eul-Soo. "Agrarian Crisis, Social Banditry, and Messianism in Brazil, 1870–1940." Unpublished paper presented at meeting of Pacific Coast Council of Latin American Studies, Fullerton, California, 20 October 1978.

Pani, Alberto. *Hygiene in Mexico: A Study of Sanitation and Educational Problems.* Gogorza, Ernest L. de, tr. New York: G. P. Putnam and Sons, 1917.

Pasqual, Leonardo. *Memorias de Sebastián Lerdo de Tejada.* Mexico City: Editorial Citlaltépetl, 1959.

Peregrina, Angelica. "Documentos: Antonio Rojas, un bandido jalisciense." *Boletin del Archivo Histórico de Jalisco* 2, no. 2 (May-August 1978): 9–12.

Pérez Verdía, Luis. *Compendio de la historia de México desde sus primeros tiempos hasta los últimos años.* Guadalajara: Librería Font, 1951.

Perry, Laurens B. "The Dynamics of the Insurrection of Tuxtepec: Mexico in 1876." Ph.D. dissertation, University of Michigan, 1970.

———. "El modelo liberal y la política práctica en la república restaurada, 1867–1876." *Historia Mexicana* 23, no. 4 (April-June 1974): 646–699.

Phelan, John Leddy. *The People and the King: The Comunero Revolution in Colombia, 1781.* Madison: University of Wisconsin Press, 1978.

Pletcher, David M. "An American Mining Company in the Mexican Revolution of 1911–1920." *Journal of Modern History* 20, no. 1 (March 1948): 19–26.

———. "The Building of the Mexican Railway." *Hispanic American Historical Review* 30, no. 1 (February 1950): 26–52.

———. "Development of Railroads in Sonora." *Inter-American Economic Affairs* 1, no. 4 (March 1948): 3–44.

———. "The Fall of Silver in Mexico, 1870–1910 and Its Effect on American Investments." *Journal of Economic History* 18, no. 1 (March 1958): 33–55.

———. "Inter-American Trade in the Early 1870s—A State Department Survey." *The Americas* 33, no. 4 (April 1977): 593–612.

Podán, Mateo. *Porfirio Díaz, debe y haber; estado del activo y passivo históricos del famoso estadista y caudillo mexicano.* Mexico City: Ediciones Botas, 1944.

Pollard, Hugh B.C. *A Busy Time in Mexico: An Unconventional Record of a Mexican Incident.* New York: Duffield and Co., 1913.

Powell, Philip Wayne. "The Chichimecas: Scourge of the Silver Frontier in Sixteenth-Century Mexico." *Hispanic American Historical Review* 25, no. 3 (August 1945): 315–338.

Powell, T. G. "Los liberales, el campesinado indígena y los problemas agrarios durante la Reforma." *Historia Mexicana* 21, no. 4 (April-June 1972): 653–675.

———. "Priests and Peasants in Central Mexico: Social Conflict during

'La Reforma.'" *Hispanic American Historical Review* 57, no. 2 (May 1972): 653–675.

Prassel, Frank Richard. *The Western Peace Officer*. Norman: University of Oklahoma Press, 1972.

Procter, Ben H. "The Texas Rangers." Unpublished manuscript at Amon Carter Museum of Western Art, Fort Worth, Texas, 1972.

Quevedo y Zubieta, Salvador. *Manuel González y su gobierno en México, anticipo a la historia típica de un presidente mexicano*. Mexico City: Editorial Nacional, 1956.

Quintana, José Miguel. *Lafragua, político y romántico*. Mexico City: Editorial Academia Literaria, 1958.

Quirk, Robert E. *An Affair of Honor: Woodrow Wilson and the Occupation of Veracruz*. New York: W. W. Norton and Company, 1967.

_____. *The Mexican Revolution, 1914–1915: The Convention of Aguascalientes*. Bloomington: Indiana University Press, 1960.

Quirós, Constancio Bernaldo de. *El bandolerismo en España y México*. Mexico City: Editorial Jurídica Mexicana, 1959.

Raat, William D. "The Antipositivist Movement in Prerevolutionary Mexico, 1892–1911." *Journal of Interamerican Studies and World Affairs* 19, no. 1 (February 1977): 83–98.

_____. "Ideas and Society in Don Porfirio's Mexico." *The Americas* 30, no. 1 (July 1973): 32–53.

_____. "Los intelectuales, el positivismo y la cuestión indígena." *Historia Mexicana* 20, no. 3 (January-March 1971): 412–427.

_____. "Positivism in Díaz Mexico, 1876–1910: An Essay in Intellectual History." Ph.D. dissertation, University of Utah, 1967.

Rabasa, Emilio. *La evolución histórica de México*. Mexico City: Editorial Porrúa, 1956.

Ramírez Fentanes, Luis. *Zaragosa*. Mexico City: Secretaría de la Defensa Nacional, 1962.

Randall, Laura. *A Comparative Economic History of Latin America, 1500–1914: Volume 1: Mexico*. New York: Institute of Latin American Studies, Columbia University, 1977.

Rees, Peter. *Transportes y comercio entre México y Veracruz, 1519–1910*. Zúñiga, Ana Elena, tr. Mexico City: Secretaría de Educación Pública 1976.

Reith, Charles. *A New Study of Police History*. London: Oliver and Boyd, 1956.

Reyes, J. Ascensión. *Heraclio Bernal (El Rayo de Sinaloa)*. San Antonio: Casa Editorial Lozano, 1920.

Reynolds, Clark W. *The Mexican Economy, Twentieth-Century Structure and Growth*. New Haven: Yale University Press, 1970.

Richmond, Douglas W. "El nacionalismo de Carranza y los cambios socioeconómicos—1915–1920." *Historia Mexicana* 26, no. 1 (July-September 1976): 107–131.

Rincón Gallardo, Carlos. *El libro de charro mexicano.* Mexico City: Editorial Porrúa, 1960.

Ríos, Enrique M. de los, et al. *Liberales ilustres mexicanos de la Reforma y la Intervención.* Mexico City: Imprenta de "Hijo del Ahuizote," 1890.

Rodríguez O., Jaime E. *The Emergence of Spanish America: Vicente Rocafuerte and Spanish Americanism.* Berkeley: University of California Press, 1975.

Roeder, Ralph. *Juárez and His Mexico.* 2 vols. New York: Viking Press, 1947.

Romney, Joseph B. "American Interests in Mexico: Development and Impact during the Rule of Porfirio Díaz." Ph.D. dissertation, University of Utah, 1969.

Rosenberg, Emily S. "Economic Pressures in Anglo-American Diplomacy in Mexico, 1917-1918." *Journal of Inter-American Studies and World Affairs* 17, no. 2 (May 1975): 123-152.

Rosenzweig, Fernando. "El desarrollo económico de México de 1877 a 1911." *El Trimestre Económico* 32 (3), no. 127 (July-September 1965): 405-454.

———. "El proceso político y el desarrollo económico de México." *El Trimestre Económico* 29 (4), no. 16 (October-December 1962): 513-530.

Ross, Stanley R. *Francisco I. Madero: Apostle of Mexican Democracy.* New York: Columbia University Press, 1955.

Rude, George. *The Crowd in History: A Study of Popular Disturbances in France and England, 1730-1848.* New York: John Wiley and Sons, 1964.

Ruiz, Eduardo. *Historia de la Guerra de Intervención en Michoacán.* Morelia: Balsal Editores, 1969.

Ruiz, Ramón E. *Labor and the Ambivalent Revolutionaries, 1911-1923.* Baltimore: Johns Hopkins University Press, 1976.

Samponaro, Frank. "The Political Role of the Army in Mexico, 1821-1848." Ph.D. dissertation, University of New York at Stony Brook, 1974.

Sánchez Lamego, Miguel A. "Agustín Díaz, ilustre cartógrafo mexicano." *Historia Mexicana* 24, no. 4 (April-June 1975): 556-565.

———. *Historia militar de la revolución constitucionalista.* 5 vols. Mexico City: Talleres Gráficos de la Nación, 1956-.

Sandels, Robert. "Antecedents de la Revolución en Chihuahua." *Historia Mexicana* 24, no. 3 (January-March 1975): 390-402.

Schiff, Warren. "German Military Penetration into Mexico during the Late Díaz Period." *Hispanic American Historical Review* 39, no. 4 (November 1959): 568-579.

Schmidt, Arthur P. "The Social and Economic Effect of the Railroad in Puebla and Veracruz, Mexico, 1867-1911." Ph.D. dissertation, Indiana University, 1973.

Schmitt, Karl Michael. "Evolution of Mexican Thought on Church-State Relations, 1876–1911." Ph.D. dissertation, University of Pennsylvania, 1954.

Scholes, Walter V. *Mexican Politics during the Juárez Regime, 1855–1872.* Columbia, Mo.: University of Missouri Studies, no. 30, 1957.

_____. "Mexico in 1896 as Viewed by an American Consul." *Hispanic American Historical Review* 30, no. 2 (May 1950): 250–257.

Schuster, Ernest Otto. *Pancho Villa's Shadow: The True Story of Mexico's Robin Hood as Told by his Interpreter.* New York: Exposition Press, 1947.

Sherman, William L., and Greenleaf, Richard E. *Victoriano Huerta: A Reappraisal.* Mexico City: Imprenta Aldina, 1960.

Silva Herzog, Jesús. *El agrarismo mexicano y la reforma agraria; exposición y crítica.* Mexico City: Fondo de Cultura Económico, 1959.

_____. *El pensamiento económico en México.* Mexico City: Fondo de Cultura Económico, 1947

Sims, Harold D. "Espejo de Caciques: Las Terrazas de Chihuahua." *Historia Mexicana* 18, no. 3 (January-March 1969): 379–399.

Singelmann, Peter. "Political Structure and Social Banditry in Northeast Brazil." *Journal of Latin American Studies* 7, no. 1 (May 1975): 59–83.

Sinkin, Richard N. "Modernization and Reform in Mexico, 1858–1876." Ph.D. dissertation, University of Michigan, 1972.

_____. "The Mexican Constitutional Congress, 1856–1857: A Statistical Analysis." *Hispanic American Historical Review* 53, no. 1 (February 1973): 1–26.

Smart, Charles A. *¡Viva Juárez! A Biography.* Philadelphia: Lippincott, 1963.

Smith, Bruce. *Rural Crime Control.* New York: Institute of Public Administration, Columbia University, 1933.

_____. "Rural Police Protection." In *Illinois Crime Survey.* Chicago: Illinois Association for Criminal Justice, 1929.

Smith, Cornelius. *Emilio Kosterlitzky, The Eagle of Sonora.* Glendale, Cal.: A. H. Clark, 1970.

Solís, Leopoldo. *La realidad económica mexicana: Retrovisión y perspectivas.* Mexico City: Siglo XXI Editores, 1970.

Spicer, Edward H. "El problema Yaqui." *America Indígena* 5, no. 4 (October 1945): 273–286.

Stagg, Albert. *The Almadas and Alamos, 1783–1867.* Tucson: University of Arizona Press, 1978.

Stein, Stanley J., and Stein, Barbara H. *The Colonial Heritage of Latin America: Essays on Economic Dependence in Perspective.* New York: Oxford University Press, 1970.

Stillwell, Arthur E., and Crowell, James R. "I Had a Hunch." *Saturday Evening Post* 200, no. 32 (4 February 1928): 38 ff.

Stokes, William S. "Violence as a Power Factor in Latin American Politics." *Western Political Quarterly* 5, no. 3 (September 1952): 445–468.

Strode, Hudson. *Timeless Mexico.* New York: Harcourt, Brace and Company, 1944.

Sullivan, James Harold. "The Indian Policy of Porfirio Díaz." M. A. thesis, University of the Americas, 1965.

Tannenbaum, Frank. *The Mexican Agrarian Revolution.* New York: Macmillan Company, 1929.

_____. *Peace by Revolution, an Interpretation of Mexico.* New York: Columbia University Press, 1933.

Taracena, Alfonso. *Porfirio Díaz.* Mexico City: Editorial Jus, 1960.

_____. *La verdadera revolución mexicana: La primera etapa: 1901 a 1911.* Mexico City: Editorial Jus, 1965.

Taylor, William B. *Drinking, Homicide and Rebellion in Colonial Mexican Villages.* Stanford: Stanford University Press, 1979.

_____. *Landlord and Peasant in Colonial Oaxaca.* Palo Alto: Stanford University Press, 1972.

_____. "Town and Country in the Valley of Oaxaca, 1750–1812." In Altman, Ida, and Lockhart, James, eds. *Provinces of Early Mexico: Variants of Spanish American Regional Evolution.* Los Angeles: UCLA Latin American Center, 1976.

Thompson, Wallace. *The Mexican Mind: A Study of National Psychology, by Wallace Thompson.* Boston: Little, Brown and Company, 1922.

Tilly, Charles. "Rural Collective Action in Modern Europe." In Spielberg, Joseph, and Whiteford, Scott, eds., *Forging Nations: A Comparative View of Rural Ferment and Revolt.* East Lansing: Michigan State University Press, 1976.

Tischendorf, Alfred Paul. *Great Britain and Mexico in the Era of Porfirio Díaz.* Durham, N.C.: Duke University Press, 1961.

Traylor, Samuel W. *Out of the Southwest.* Allentown, Pa.: G. P. Schlicer and Son, 1936.

Trens, Manuel B. *Historia de Veracruz.* 6 vols. Jalapa: Enríquez, 1947.

Valadés, José C. *Historia general de la revolución mexicana.* 10 vols. Mexico City: M. Quesada Brandi, 1963–1967.

_____. *El Porfirmismo, historia de un régimen.* 2 vols. Mexico City: Antigua Librería Robredo de J. Porrúa e hijos, 1941.

Valdovinos Garza, José. *Tres capítulos de la política michoacana.* Mexico City: Ediciones "Casa de Michoacán," 1960.

Vanderwood, Paul J. "The Counter-Guerrilla Strategy of Porfirio Díaz." *Hispanic American Historical Review* 56, no. 4 (November 1976): 551–579.

_____. "Genesis of the Rurales: Mexico's Early Struggle for Domestic Security." *Hispanic American Historical Review* 50, no. 2 (May 1970): 323–344.

_____. "Mexico's Rurales: Reputation versus Reality." *The Americas* 34, no. 1 (July 1977): 102–112.

_____. "The Rurales: Mexico's Rural Police Force, 1861–1914." Ph.D. dissertation, University of Texas, 1970.

_____. "Los Rurales: Producto de una necesidad social." *Historia Mexicana* 22, no. 1 (July-September 1972): 34–51.

Vázquez Santa Ana, Higinio. *Canciones, cantares y corridos mexicanos.* Mexico City: Imprenta M. Leon Sánchez, [n.d.].

Vernon, Raymond. *The Dilemma of Mexico's Development: The Roles of the Private and Public Sectors.* Cambridge: Harvard University Press, 1963.

Villarello Vélez, Ildefonso. *Historia de la revolución mexicana en Coahuila.* Mexico City: Talleres Gráficos de la Nación, 1970.

Villoro, Luís. "La Revolución de Independencia." In vol. 2 of *Historia general de México.* 4 vols. Mexico City: El Colegio de México, 1976.

Wasserman, Mark. "Oligarchy and Foreign Enterprise in Porfirian Chihuahua, 1876–1911." Ph.D. dissertation, University of Chicago, 1975.

_____. "Oligarquía e intereses extranjeros en Chihuahua durante el Porfiriato." *Historia Mexicana* 22, no. 3 (January-March 1973): 279–319.

Wasserstrom, Robert. "A Caste War That Never Was: The Tzeltal Conspiracy of 1848." *Peasant Studies* 7, no. 2 (Spring 1978): 73–85.

West, Robert C. *The Mining Community in Northern New Spain: The Parral Mining District.* Berkeley: University of California Press, 1949.

Wheat, Raymond C. *Francisco Zarco: El portavoz liberal de "La Reforma."* Mexico City: Editorial Porrúa, 1957.

Wilkie, James W.; Meyer, Michael C.; and Monzón de Wilkie, Edna, eds. *Contemporary Mexico: Papers of the IV International Congress of Mexican History.* Berkeley: University of California Press, 1976.

Williman, John B. "Church and State in Veracruz, 1840–1940: The Concord and Conflicts of a Century." Ph.D. dissertation, St. Louis University, 1970.

Wolf, Eric R. *The Mexican Bajío in the Eighteenth Century: An Analysis of Cultural Integration.* New Orleans: Tulane University, Middle American Research Institute Series No. 17, 1955.

_____. *Peasant Wars of the Twentieth Century.* New York: Harper and Row, 1969.

_____, and Hansen, Edward C. "Caudillo Politics: A Structural Analysis." *Comparative Studies in Society and History* 9, no. 1 (January 1967): 168–179.

Womack, Jr., John. "The Mexican Economy during the Revolution, 1910–1920: Historiography & Analysis." *Marxist Perspectives* 1, no. 4 (Winter 1978): 80–123.

_____. *Zapata and the Mexican Revolution.* New York: Alfred A. Knopf, 1969.

Wood, Eric Fisher. *Leonard Wood, Conservator of Americanism.* New York: George H. Doran Company, 1920.

Yeager, Gene. "Porfirian Commercial Propaganda: Mexico in the World of Industrial Expositions." *The Americas* 34, no. 2 (October 1977): 230–243.

Zoraida Vázquez, Josefina. "Los primeros tropiezos." In *Historia general de México.* 4 vols. Mexico City: El Colegio de México, 1976.

Index

Acayucan (Veracruz): Indians from, raid Soteapa, 149–50; mentioned, 15, 145
Acordada, 21–22, 24
Agrarian reform. *See* Land redistribution
Agrarian unrest. *See* Native disorder
Aguirre, José M., 34
Alvarez, Juan, 27, 33, 39, 46, 47
Americans: deserters pillage in Hidalgo, 37; at Cananea, 147, 148, 149; mercenaries at Casa Grandes, 161. *See also* United States
Army, colonial, 18, 19, 22, 23, 24
Army, federal: from Independence to Reform, 29, 30, 31–34; under Liberals, 40, 41, 42, 48; Díaz manipulates, 71–72, 83–84, 112, 157; González professionalizes, 72; force for repression, 89–90, 145; at Tomóchic, 92–93; kills Santanón, 102; at Soteapa, 150; at Río Blanco, 151; at Velardeña, 153–54; in 1910–11, 158, 160, 161–63; Madero retains Porfirian, 167; under Huerta, 176–77; dissolved, 178; mentioned, 103, 109, 116, 179
Arriaga, Jesús ("Chucho el Roto"), 95, 96–98
Arriero, Ballo, 34
Arroyo, Gabriel, 151, 152

Arteaga, Prisciliano, 70
Artisans: displaced by development, 81, 108; join Rurales, 107; percentage of Rural recruits, 109
Asians, 82, 167

Bajío, the, 108, 109
Bandits: seen as agents of order and disorder, xi–xii, 30, 63; precedents and motives for converting to police, xii, 51–52, 58, 71; recruited as Rurales by Juárez, xiv; sources of information on and definition of, xv; characterized, xvi; as guerrillas, xviii, 4, 6–7, 56–57; after Independence, 5, 26, 30; during French Intervention, 6–8, 11; motives for becoming, 12–15; during colonial era, 16–17, 23; under Juárez, 46–48, 54–56; under Díaz, 67–68; and development, 94–95, 166; former rebels become, under Madero, 169; under Carranza, 179. *See also names of individual bandits and bandit groups*: Banditry, types of; Social banditry
Banditry, types of: mid-nineteenth-century Mexican, xv–xvi, 14–15; Hobsbawm's, xvi–xvii, 14–15; Peruvian, 11–12; Brazilian, 12, 13, 14. *See also* Social banditry
Bayley, David, xiii, 45, 116–17